THE KEY
TO THE BULGE

The Stackpole Military History Series

THE AMERICAN CIVIL WAR
Cavalry Raids of the Civil War
Ghost, Thunderbolt, and Wizard
Pickett's Charge
Witness to Gettysburg

WORLD WAR I
Doughboy War

WORLD WAR II
After D-Day
Armor Battles of the Waffen-SS, 1943–45
Armoured Guardsmen
Army of the West
Australian Commandos
The B-24 in China
Backwater War
The Battle of Sicily
Battle of the Bulge, Vol. 1
Battle of the Bulge, Vol. 2
Beyond the Beachhead
Beyond Stalingrad
The Brandenburger Commandos
The Brigade
Bringing the Thunder
The Canadian Army and the Normandy Campaign
Coast Watching in World War II
Colossal Cracks
A Dangerous Assignment
D-Day Deception
D-Day to Berlin
Destination Normandy
Dive Bomber!
A Drop Too Many
Eagles of the Third Reich
Eastern Front Combat
Exit Rommel
Fist from the Sky
Flying American Combat Aircraft of World War II
Forging the Thunderbolt
Fortress France
The German Defeat in the East, 1944–45

German Order of Battle, Vol. 1
German Order of Battle, Vol. 2
German Order of Battle, Vol. 3
The Germans in Normandy
Germany's Panzer Arm in World War II
GI Ingenuity
Goodwood
The Great Ships
Grenadiers
Hitler's Nemesis
Infantry Aces
Iron Arm
Iron Knights
Kampfgruppe Peiper at the Battle of the Bulge
The Key to the Bulge
Kursk
Luftwaffe Aces
Luftwaffe Fighter Ace
Massacre at Tobruk
Mechanized Juggernaut or Military Anachronism?
Messerschmitts over Sicily
Michael Wittmann, Vol. 1
Michael Wittmann, Vol. 2
Mountain Warriors
The Nazi Rocketeers
No Holding Back
On the Canal
Operation Mercury
Packs On!
Panzer Aces
Panzer Aces II
Panzer Commanders of the Western Front
Panzer Gunner
The Panzer Legions
Panzers in Normandy
Panzers in Winter
The Path to Blitzkrieg
Penalty Strike
Red Road from Stalingrad
Red Star under the Baltic
Retreat to the Reich
Rommel's Desert Commanders
Rommel's Desert War
Rommel's Lieutenants
The Savage Sky
The Siegfried Line

A Soldier in the Cockpit
Soviet Blitzkrieg
Stalin's Keys to Victory
Surviving Bataan and Beyond
T-34 in Action
Tank Tactics
Tigers in the Mud
Triumphant Fox
The 12th SS, Vol. 1
The 12th SS, Vol. 2
Twilight of the Gods
The War against Rommel's Supply Lines
War in the Aegean
Wolfpack Warriors
Zhukov at the Oder

THE COLD WAR / VIETNAM
Cyclops in the Jungle
Expendable Warriors
Flying American Combat Aircraft: The Cold War
Here There Are Tigers
Land with No Sun
Phantom Reflections
Street without Joy
Through the Valley

WARS OF THE MIDDLE EAST
Never-Ending Conflict

GENERAL MILITARY HISTORY
Carriers in Combat
Cavalry from Hoof to Track
Desert Battles
Guerrilla Warfare
Ranger Dawn
Sieges

THE KEY TO THE BULGE

The Battle for Losheimergraben

Stephen M. Rusiecki

STACKPOLE BOOKS

Copyright © 1996 by Stephen M. Rusiecki

Published in paperback in 2009 by
STACKPOLE BOOKS
5067 Ritter Road
Mechanicsburg, PA 17055
www.stackpolebooks.com

THE KEY TO THE BULGE: THE BATTLE FOR LOSHEIMERGRABEN, by Stephen M. Rusiecki, was originally published in hard cover by Praeger, an imprint of Greenwood Publishing Group, Inc., Westport, CT. Copyright © 1996 by Stephen M. Rusiecki. Paperback edition by arrangement with Greenwood Publishing Group, Inc. All rights reserved.

No part of this book may be reproduced or transmitted in any form or by any means electronic or mechanical including photocopying, reprinting, or on any information storage or retrieval system, without permission in writing from Greenwood Publishing Group.

Cover design by Tracy Patterson

Printed in the United States of America

10 9 8 7 6 5 4 3 2 1

ISBN 978-0-8117-3591-9 (Stackpole paperback)

The Library of Congress has cataloged the hardcover edition as follows:

Rusiecki, Stephen M.
    The key to the bulge : the battle for Losheimergraben / Stephen M. Rusiecki ; foreword by Lyle J. Bouck, Jr.
       p.   cm.
    Includes bibliographical references and index.
    ISBN 0-275-95302-5 (alk. paper)
    1. Ardennes, Battle of the, 1944–1945. 2. Losheimergraben (Hellenthal, Germany)—History, Military. I. Title.
D756.5.A7R87   1996
940.54'21431—dc20   96-21317

For Angie and JB…

Contents

Maps	ix
Foreword	xi
Preface	xiii
1. The Great Gamble	1
2. The "Checkerboard" Men	7
3. Germany's Last Warriors	13
4. Seize the Crossroads!	25
5. Fusiliers in the Flank	45
6. Buchholz Station	63
7. Defense of the Weisser Stein	75
8. Lanzerath: "Hold at All Costs!"	83
9. Desperate Stand	107
10. The Final Push	121
11. The Customs Houses	139
12. Completing the Record	147
Appendix A - Table of Comparative Ranks	161

Appendix B - Awards and Decorations	163
Appendix C - Select Order of Battle	169
Appendix D - Glossary of Terms and Equipment	173
Notes	177
Selected Bibliography	187
Index	191

Photographic essay follows page 106.

Maps

1. Hitler's Plan	3
2. Planned Routes of Advance for the I SS Panzer Corps	15
3. Losheimergraben	27
4. 1st Battalion, 394th Infantry Regiment's Situation Overlay	47
5. Buchholz Station	71
6. The I&R Platoon's Positions at Lanzerath	95

Foreword

As a fortunate surviving participant of the historic battle around Lanzerath and Losheimergraben, vivid reflections often flash through my mind. I secretly hurt for those wounded and killed as a result of my actions. For the sake of sanity, I choose not to dwell on these painful thoughts. Other general memories relate to the discomforts faced by the infantry on the front line, who lived in frozen foxholes minus a bed, electricity, and plumbing, not to mention the ever-present armed enemy who stalked the area in an attempt to kill you and your comrades. A constant case of jitters and an extended state of fear existed. Your imagination tried to run away with your eyes as you would stare at the form of a tree against the snow during the night. Every once in a while this tree would seem to move and suddenly "attack you." You needed to be constantly alert to avoid booby traps, mines, artillery, and raiding patrols. Buzz bombs traveled at low altitudes overhead. One had to care for the wounded, usually in scenes mixed with screaming, crying, moaning, cursing, and yelling. The most difficult part to cope with was the sickening sight of close friends being killed. You learned to expect the unexpected.

In the wind-swept and snow-covered hills of the Ardennes forest, nights and days ran together. Only a new replacement could tell you the date or that it was Tuesday or Sunday. Surprising challenges came in bunches and soon occupied a major part of your waking hours.

When German paratroopers charged our platoon position in Lanzerath and our withering fire caused them to fall back, a surge of adrenaline created a lift in the confidence level. We knew they couldn't penetrate our fortified defensive position. We were certain we could fulfill our orders to "hold." However, as the day lengthened and the firefight intensified, doubt crept into my mind about the integrity of what we were doing. An aura of modified shock surrounded me; the training gears meshed and instinct guided reaction.

Artillery and, later, small-arms fire destroyed our communications link with Regimental Headquarters. Ammunition was desperately low and casualties mounted. The promised help did not arrive. My thoughts were torn between remaining in place as ordered and pulling back without permission. In my opinion, the position was untenable. Fleeting visions of a court-martial swirled about me as word was disseminated "to break contact with the enemy and prepare to withdraw under the cover of darkness." On my signal, we would move out, take the wounded, and link up at a rendezvous point at the end of the trail on Buchholz Station Road. As dusk faded, we were about to implement our plan. Just then the strongest German attack of the day came from the right flank. A second wave overpowered our position. Trapped and helpless, we felt like we were in a vacuum. The Germans captured us at gun and bayonet point.

As a wounded POW, my disgust and disappointment soon turned to hostile anger; we had failed. As reality set in, taking care of each other became more important than ever; the walking wounded had to look out for the seriously wounded. When we collected our thoughts, escape was our next consideration, and the sooner the better, while we were still in the front lines. But our chances never materialized. Next, we had to fight off gloom and depression.

That experience convinced me that a determined and positive attitude is an important asset in life. Daily concerns offer various disappointments, setbacks, and even defeats. We must realize recovery is always possible; we must persist.

In 1991, a group of us returned to visit our old battlefield. I walked up the hill near Lanzerath, entered the remains of my old crumbling foxhole, and looked out over the field to the front. I closed my eyes and in a flash relived December 16, 1944. For the first time, I realized a part of me was still in that hole. Goose bumps rose on my skin and chilled me. I walked down the hill to join others in the group. We then dedicated a beautiful monument that honored the 99th Infantry Division. We found the compassion and expressions of gratitude offered by the proud and loving people of rural Belgium, especially the children, exhilarating and heart warming. This testimony allowed us to believe that our hardships and sacrifices of five decades ago were worth the effort.

Dr. Lyle J. Bouck, Jr.

Preface

The Ardennes Offensive. "Wacht am Rhein." The Battle of the Bulge. Bastogne. St. Vith. Hitler's Great Offensive. All of these names evoke images of war-weary American and German soldiers trudging into battle through knee-deep snow in the freezing, painful winter of December 1944. For many veterans, the memories of this winter struggle are bitter. For historians, they are fascinating. Whatever the great battle of 16 December 1944 is called, no one will forget the sheer intensity, scope, and power of the struggle. Some have called it Hitler's last true stroke of genius. The Fuehrer rallied a supposedly weakened, defeated German military and formed three great armies to strike at the Allied defenses sitting on Germany's very border. After penetrating these defenses, Hitler could seize the real prize: the port of Antwerp. Capture of this vital port would cripple the Allied supply lines. The Allies would be split in two, with the British isolated in the north. A German victory of this magnitude could tear the very fabric of the Allied coalition. But this was not to be. Even though three great German armies, two of them panzer, sat poised to attack along a front that extended north to central Belgium and south to Luxembourg, success for Hitler would remain out of reach. The 101st Airborne Division delayed the Germans at Bastogne in the very center of their drive to the west. St. Vith became another stumbling block, thanks to the 7th Armored Division among others. However, these places were in the center of the "bulge" the Germans created in the Allied lines. Yet these locations weren't even where Hitler had focused his main effort, his concentrated push to Antwerp. The focus of the German plan rested on the north shoulder, just above a wide series of valleys called the Losheim Gap. It was in the Losheim Gap that Hitler wanted early success. A small border crossing at Losheimergraben would open the gate to the west. But young American GIs frustrated Hitler's plan by defending this northern shoulder of the "bulge." The Germans experienced similar frustration in the center and the south. Winston Churchill later referred to the GIs' stand during the Ardennes Offensive as one of the great American victories of all time. And it was. But the "victory" was not without pain and suffering.

My fascination with the Battle of the Bulge began in 1986. As a young infantry lieutenant stationed in Germany, I was responsible for organizing what the Army calls a "Staff Ride." Normally reserved for officers, these Staff Rides provide a guided tour of a battlefield, the tactical lessons to be learned, and the mistakes and successes of the armies involved. A British "Bulge" enthusiast, Will Cavanagh, gave the officers and men of my battalion a tour of the northern shoulder of this particular battle. His personal research was extraordinary. He was a walking encyclopedia of events and anecdotes relating to the battle.

Because I was an avid World War II enthusiast myself, I listened intently to every story he told and studied every piece of ground where our tour bus stopped. He even had us walk through parts of the forest in knee-deep snow to get a feel for the conditions the Germans and the Americans endured during the actual battle. Then the bus stopped at a small road intersection at a place called Losheimergraben on the German–Belgian border. I listened as Will related the tale of a young German regimental commander who, instead of senselessly killing some isolated Americans defending the position, chose to offer them the option of surrender. The Americans were the remainder of an infantry battalion forced to withdraw under pressure by the Germans. These young GIs took refuge in the few customs houses located at the intersection. It would have been an easy matter for the German officer to save crucial time by blowing the buildings and their occupants sky-high. But he chose to talk them into surrendering. He even entered one of the cellars alone to help the American soldiers look for the pins to put back into their grenades.

The story fascinated me, especially since we had already visited the site of the infamous Malmedy Massacre earlier that day. The German officer's actions were an uncharacteristic act of chivalry in a war marked by extreme brutality and suffering. The human element in combat always interested me. I had to find out more about this German officer who offered these Americans a chance at life. After some digging, I found his name: Wilhelm Osterhold. I contacted him by mail, and he invited me to spend a weekend at his home near Hamburg. He told me fascinating tales about Losheimergraben. Moreover, he put me in touch with other German participants. I was hooked.

I wrote letters in search of information about the battle. I contacted members of the American 99th Infantry Division who opposed Osterhold's men in the battle. While studying the books and official sources on the subject, I learned of other significant actions, such as the I&R Platoon's valiant stand at Lanzerath, which occurred during the battle. Eventually, I realized that the German plan for the entire Ardennes Offensive of 16 December 1944 rested on the successful seizure of the Losheimergraben Crossroads.

My correspondence continued. I became custodian of primary source information about the battle unknown to previous historians. While attending the Infantry Officer's Advanced Course at Fort Benning, Georgia, in 1987 and

1988, I chose to write my required Battle Analysis on Losheimergraben. A mere 30 pages, I realized, did not do the battle justice. There was too much to tell. I knew too much. So I decided to write this book.

The pages ahead are the product of my research, correspondence, and interviews. I learned about the battle from its participants in such detail that I have managed to recreate actual dialogue and off-hand remarks made by the men at the time, albeit with some authorial license. This is a tale of the human will and spirit in a life-and-death struggle. A knowledge of such struggles is crucial to my preparation as a professional soldier, for, God forbid, the next war. But my tale is a tale told without regard to political beliefs or affiliations. No one in this book is a "bad guy." These men are soldiers from another time doing what, at the moment, they believed to be right and just. Their odyssey is a lesson for both the human heart and the mind. The lessons they leave us are not simply facts or tactics, but of the ever-present ability of man to overcome great odds and, in some cases, to display an exceptional penchant for gallantry, for chivalry. We cannot forget their legacy; they paid too high a price. If I ever find myself on a battlefield, under conditions similar to those during the great Battle of the Bulge, I hope I perform as well as these men. German or American, they're my heroes.

There are far too many people who helped contribute to this book for me to thank individually. However, there are those who did go "above and beyond the call of duty," and I would like to thank them by name. First there is Oberst Wilhelm Osterhold, the man whose act of chivalry inspired my research. He is a remarkable man and a gallant soldier. He helped me learn what I could about the battle. I would also like to thank Will Cavanagh for introducing me to the battle. Dick Byers, of the 99th Division Association's Archives Committee, always managed to find what I asked for and never once claimed he couldn't do it; he's an incredible man. Colonel Jerry Simmons was most gracious in his interest in the project; he helped clear up several "gray" areas in the battle. My good friend Jeff Thompson helped me reproduce the numerous photos I acquired for use in the book. I must also thank my energetic and supportive editor, Dan Eades, who helped me polish the manuscript. Finally, I would like to thank the remarkable and energetic Lyle Bouck, the platoon leader of the Intelligence and Reconnaissance Platoon at Lanzerath. For his dedication to the memory of the battle and his assistance in my preparation of this book, I will always be thankful. Lastly, I must thank my wonderful wife, Angie, and my son, J.B., for their tireless support of both this work and my military career. Without them, neither means a thing.

I alone am responsible for all mistakes, misprints, and factual misinterpretations.

CHAPTER 1

The Great Gamble

In the summer of 1944, Adolf Hitler's back was against the wall. As of 6 June, he now fought a war on two separate fronts—the Allies in the West and the Russians in the East. To date, Hitler had lost several million men in casualties and the figures continued to rise. With the losses of North Africa and Stalingrad the year before, things looked grim for the Third Reich. Allied successes on the Mediterranean front, specifically in Italy, were draining precious resources and manpower on a daily basis. On 20 July, a conspiracy among the ranks of his own senior officers was quickly put down after their abortive attempt on his life at the Wolfschanze in East Prussia. To Hitler, their rebellion confirmed his already skeptical view of the Wehrmacht's generalship. He no longer trusted anyone except the few privileged members of his inner circle. If Germany was to win the war, it was up to him to find a solution. The Fuehrer of Nazi Germany had to turn the tide.[1]

By August of 1944, Hitler was certain that the rapid advance of the Allies in the West would cause them to outrun their supply system—the original invasion beaches in Normandy. He also felt that the coalition forces, specifically the Americans and the British, had a separate agenda and vastly different aims, making their alliance a fragile one. He was intuitively correct about the impending supply problem; the Allies soon lost their logistical steam. The supply situation forced them into an active defense after chasing much of the German Army back over the Siegfried Line. But before the Allies ran out of gas, Hitler began to plan a counteroffensive. He knew his best chance lay in exploiting his suspicion that the coalition in the West would crumble if placed under pressure. He saw Allied unity as fragile, and he had a low regard for the American fighting man.

His plans for a counteroffensive grew. To stand beleaguered on the defense would assure him eventual defeat.[2] An all-out attack was his only hope. An offensive would accomplish little in the East or in Italy; the opportunity for success lay in the West. On 1 September, Hitler reinstated Generalfeldmarschall Gerd von Rundstedt as Oberbefehlshaber (commander-in-chief, or OB) West. But von Rundstedt was a puppet; Hitler would pull the strings.

On 16 September, at a routine operations conference, Hitler dropped a bombshell on the senior leaders of the Wehrmacht. Hitler spoke of a great counteroffensive using three great armies. These armies would drive west to the Meuse River and, from there, to the ultimate prize, Antwerp. The attack, he insisted, would split the British and American armies in two, isolating Montgomery's forces in the north. The Allies of the West—Great Britain and the United States—would be forced to sue for a separate peace. Hitler's strategy was similar to one employed by his idol, Frederick the Great, many years before. With the Western front subdued, Hitler could concentrate his forces against the Red Army in the East. He shouted his hope for a second Dunkirk, for the need for secrecy, for deception, rantings that fell on the skeptical ears of the Wehrmacht. He outlined his plan, saying he would rebuild three armies quickly, two of them panzer, and they would be moved to the front opposite the Ardennes forest. The use of a special brigade of Germans dressed as Americans and an elaborate deception plan would confuse the enemy. The main effort would fall to the northern panzer army, which would drive to Antwerp and seize its strategic port. Hitler planned his attack for November, when the weather would be terrible. The fog and mist characteristic of that time of year would shield his forces from superior Allied air support. If the panzers could exploit the Losheim Gap unmolested, Hitler believed their success would be certain.

Despite Hitler's assurances of victory, the senior military leadership left the meeting befuddled and skeptical. Generalfeldmarschall Walter Model, Hitler's "fireman," commander of Army Group B and next in command to von Rundstedt, was uncertain of success. Even SS-Oberstgruppenfuehrer Sepp Dietrich, one of Hitler's most trusted officers, viewed the plan with suspicion. They had many reasons for their doubts. First, where would Hitler scrounge the resources necessary to launch an attack? Where would the men and materiel come from? Hitler had already begun combing rear-echelon units for replacements. And he did find some—but they were men of less ability and experience than the norm. Panzers were a fixed quantity; a large shortage of panzers remained. Many panzers would have to be shifted from elsewhere to the West, depriving their units of combat power.

The planning also raised doubts. Hitler insisted that anyone who knew of the plan early must sign a pledge of secrecy upon penalty of death. Regimental and battalion commanders were not to be briefed until one or two days prior to the attack. All movement forward to the assembly areas and attack positions would occur at night, with armored vehicles moving on straw-covered roads to muffle their sounds. In addition, the entire three-army front was to employ a two-hour artillery preparation prior to the actual movement of ground forces. To assist the infantry and panzers in navigation, and to intimidate the Allies,

The Great Gamble

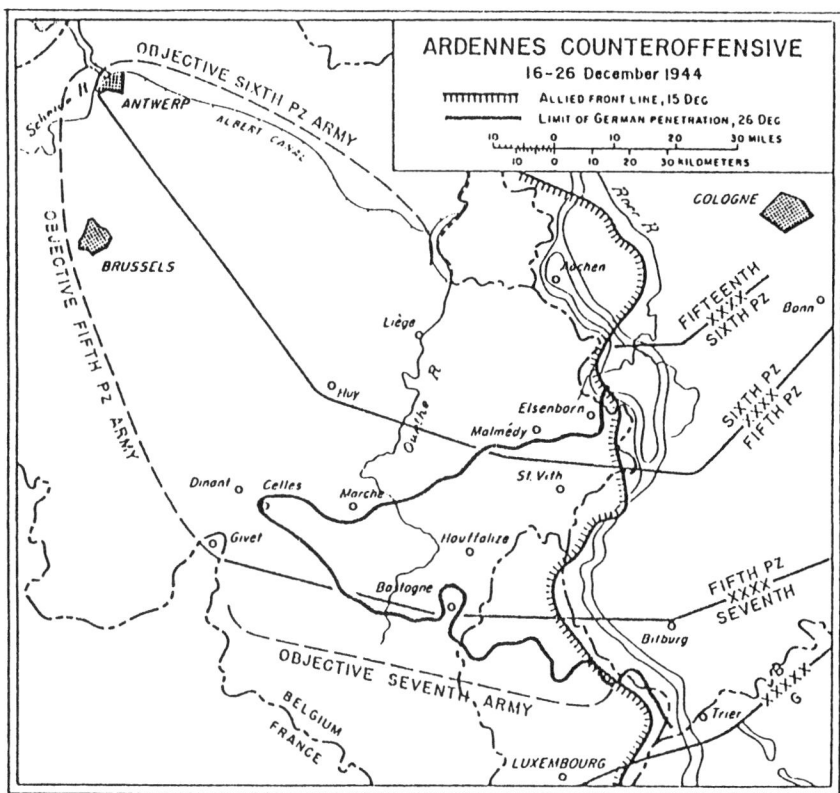

Hitler's Plan: The goal versus reality. Courtesy U.S. Army.

thirty to forty flak searchlights would illuminate the early morning skies. The searchlights were intended to bounce off the anticipated cloud cover and then onto the ground, "lighting a path to victory." Even more astonishing to his generals, Hitler wanted to attack through the Losheim Gap in the Ardennes forest.

The Ardennes forest is a beautiful, serene, and magnificent region of Europe. Heavily forested in some areas, sparse in others, the Ardennes was and is a great tourist attraction, with beautiful scenery, spring-water health spas, gently rolling hills, and a wondrous mountain range that is, quite literally, breathtaking. The Ardennes forms a large triangle, extending north to Eupen, Belgium, south to northern Luxembourg, and west to the Meuse River valley. The area itself is nearly impassable save for an eight- or nine-kilometer gap, the Losheim Gap, in the northern part of the Ardennes. The gap was named for the town that marked its northern limit, Losheim, Germany, a small hamlet just across from the Belgian border. The gap was famous for two previous German military successes (which is probably why Hitler wanted to use it again). The first was in 1914, when the Kaiser's army rode through the pass and straight to the Meuse. The next came in 1940, when a division commander named Generalmajor Erwin Rommel (later field marshal and commander of the German Afrikakorps) drove his 7th Panzer Division through the pass to the Meuse on the third day of hostilities in France. Now, Hitler again wanted to reach the Meuse quickly, using this difficult route to catch his enemies off guard.

The generals planning the offensive could see no hope for success. They prepared alternate plans for a "smaller solution," one with the main objective as the Meuse and not Antwerp. Hitler rejected these lesser proposals out of hand, determined to go ahead with his original concept. By mid-October, he was already successfully rebuilding the three armies necessary for the offensive, all of which belonged to Model's Army Group B. The main effort would be in the north where the newly formed 6th SS Panzer Army, commanded by SS-Oberstgruppenfuehrer Sepp Dietrich, would drive along five preplanned routes to Antwerp. These routes began at Monschau in the north and from Losheim in the south. To Dietrich's south, General der Panzertruppen Hasso von Manteuffel would command the 5th Panzer Army. Manteuffel's sector extended from the center of the Losheim Gap to Bastogne in the south. Just below him was General der Panzertruppen Erich Brandenberger's 7th Army, which would attack to hold the southern shoulder of the penetration from Bastogne down to Diekirch and Echternach, Luxembourg.

Hitler planned to employ these armies against the Allies sometime in November. His generals made the plans but remained skeptical. Von Rundstedt even said that if they were to succeed in just getting to the Meuse, everyone should get down on his knees and thank God! Despite their attitude, enormous effort went into planning and refitting the counteroffensive. Some of Hitler's generals believed a partial success would help the German effort, even if the overall plan failed.

The operation was to begin on schedule. As part of his deception plan, Hitler prohibited the use of radios, which further compounded Allied intelligence-gathering problems. The code name of the operation, "Wacht am Rhein," literally meant "Watch on the Rhine." This name appealed to Hitler because it sounded like a defensive operation. If the Allies learned of it, the name might confuse them, all part of the deception plan.

November came and went without providing the needed weather conditions. The start date was postponed until mid-December, when German meteorologists predicted a long period of fog and haze. This brief respite gave the German forces more time to move forward to their assembly areas and to prepare for the coming offensive. Allied intelligence identified the buildup, but most Western military leaders believed the Germans incapable of launching a significant attack on the Allied line.

The German deception worked perfectly. Many senior Allied officers were away on temporary passes or leaves. Others dismissed the data out of hand. The bickering and jealousies of several senior intelligence officers led some to fail to believe the information available to them.[3]

When Hitler set the final date for 16 December, he could not have known how successful he had been in duping the enemy in the West. His coming offensive was a complete tactical and strategic surprise. Hitler's bold move took advantage of the doubts and prejudices of the Allied command structure. It was indeed his own special brand of bizarre genius, a genuine masterstroke!

CHAPTER 2

The "Checkerboard" Men

Lieutenant General Courtney Hodges' First Army occupied the Allied defensive sector from Aachen to the southern fringes of Luxembourg. Like the rest of the Allies, the First Army fell victim to an overextended supply line. The "Red Ball Express," a series of continuous truck convoys originating in the Normandy ports, brought supplies forward to rebuild the Army's offensive capability. In the meantime, Hodges' divisions conducted small, limited actions along the Siegfried Line. Allied units were stripped of their truck resources to support the "Red Ball Express," which delivered supplies all the way to the First Army's defensive positions on the German border.[1]

The First Army was a strong and capable fighting force. Many of its divisions were seasoned in combat, and this defensive lull on the "ghost front," named for the area's inactivity, allowed less experienced units to take over. The philosophy was to "blood" these green units by active patrolling on the front lines, preparing new troops for the sights and sounds of the battlefield. Senior commanders believed this experience would prove invaluable when the Allied push to take Germany resumed.

One such unit was the 99th Infantry Division, which replaced the 9th Infantry Division in the V Corps sector. Commanded by MG (Major General) Leonard T. Gerow, the V Corps defended from Eupen to Losheimergraben. MG J. Lawton Collins's VII Corps bordered the V Corps on the north; MG Troy Middleton's VIII Corps was to the south. The 99th Division, commanded by the capable MG Walter Lauer, was one of these "green" units that needed front-line experience. Although stripped for replacements while in the United States, the division was a well-trained organization, "green" only in combat experience.

Activated at Camp Van Dorn, Mississippi, on 15 November 1942, the division participated in the Third Army Number 4 Louisiana Maneuvers on 16

September 1943. In November, the division moved to Camp Maxey, Texas, where it trained before deploying overseas.[2] The division had men from a wide variety of backgrounds, but most came from the Midwest. The average soldier in the ranks was of extraordinarily high quality. Many came from the Army Specialized Training Program (ASTP), which trained and educated men with a high academic aptitude. The young recruits chosen for the program would attend some form of civilian education, such as college, and then proceed to Officer Candidate School (OCS). However, because of the immense manpower shortage caused by the reality of war, the program failed. These young ASTP men became replacements in the combat units fighting overseas, most going as basic infantrymen. Other replacements included men from Army Air Force ground units and antiaircraft units.

The 99th Division supplied many overseas units with replacements from its ranks as well. However, by the time the division staged for movement to the theater of operations in Europe, it was nearly at full strength. The only drawback was many of the newer recruits lacked the earlier, more cohesive training conducted by the division.

On 13 September 1944, the division staged at Camp Myles Standish, Massachusetts, in preparation for movement overseas. The 99th left the Boston Port of Embarkation on 30 September and arrived in England on 10 October.[3] In a matter of weeks, the division was offloading men and equipment in Le Havre, France, and moving east to the German border, the Siegfried Line. Because the division had the dubious distinction of being "green," LTG Hodges slated it for employment in the defensive front line. On 14 November, the division moved from Wirtzfeld, Belgium, and occupied defensive positions just inside Germany, relieving elements of the 9th Infantry Division.[4]

The 99th Division had three infantry regiments. All three went into the defense, deployed on line from north to south. In the north was the 395th Regiment, followed by the 393rd in the center and the 394th in the south. In addition, the 394th provided one battalion for the division reserve, located on the southern flank. The 99th's actual sector ran from Monschau in the north to Losheimergraben in the south, just above the VIII Corps boundary. This sector, a 35-kilometer front, was greatly overextended. For this reason, MG Lauer placed much of his combat power forward, leaving himself only a modest reserve.

MG Lauer had one concern, however, and that lay on his southern flank. Below the 99th was the V and VIII Corps boundary, running straight through the famed Losheim Gap, notorious for its use by the German panzer forces in 1940 during the invasion of France. This nine-mile gap had few forces covering it. Only Task Force X of the 14th Cavalry Group occupied the gap and, because the cavalrymen were not geared or equipped for a full-scale defense, could only cover the area with outposts from their reconnaissance squadrons and tank destroyer units. One such unit, Company A of the 820th Tank Destroyer Battalion, occupied an outpost in the small hamlet of Lanzerath, a village just outside the corps boundary south of the 99th Division. This obvious weak spot in the

Allied lines bothered Lauer so much that he chose to locate his reserve there, just behind the 394th Infantry at Buchholz Station. As an added precaution, he instructed the commander of the 394th, COL Don Riley, to place an outpost north of Lanzerath to watch the gap in case anything happened. Lauer doubted the tank destroyer men's ability to provide reliable and timely information.

The southern flank of the division held another concern for Lauer as well. The most improved and direct road through the division's sector ran straight into the 394th Regiment's positions. The road originated in Losheim, Germany, and intersected the north-south international highway behind the regiment's defenses. It was a valuable and high-speed avenue of approach for any attacking force. Lauer, despite a personality conflict with COL Riley, gave the regimental commander the key tasks of defending not only these vital crossroads, but also the southern flank of the division and, for that matter, the corps.

COL Riley's 394th Infantry moved into position on 14 November, relieving the 60th Infantry Regiment, 9th Infantry Division.[5] The 60th Regiment's troops seemed ecstatic over their new rest opportunity. They welcomed the men of the 394th with open arms. In fact, when the 394th's soldiers arrived in sector, the near-festive mood displayed by the veteran infantrymen astounded them. PFC Howard Bowers, a machine gun ammunition bearer in Company D, 1st Battalion, was amazed to see bonfires roaring in full view of German outposts, located no more than one kilometer away. The 60th's GIs were shouting, yelling, and having a good time. Yet, when the men of the 394th arrived, many of the veterans left quickly and unceremoniously. Within minutes, the 394th's officers made certain the fires were out and the area was quiet.[6]

The relief went smoothly. The veterans of the 60th Regiment explained the enemy situation and the disposition of the pre-dug defensive positions. Some soldiers even told SSG George Ballinger, a machine gun section leader in Company B, that the regiment's left flank was called "Creepy Corner" because of the constant German patrolling there.[7] This tale and other local combat facts and folklore found their way into the ears and imaginations of the 394th's new soldiers. The senior soldiers and officers dismissed much of the lore, but the younger, impressionable troops took the stories to heart.

COL Riley's mission in his new sector, like that of the rest of the division, was to conduct an active defense accented by aggressive patrolling forward and to the flanks.[8] COL Riley, already short by one battalion, defended with his two remaining battalions abreast. Initially, he selected the 1st Battalion, commanded by LTC Robert Douglas, to serve as the division reserve. Douglas's battalion occupied an assembly area behind the regiment at a small, rural train station known as Forest Buchholz Station.

Riley placed his 2nd Battalion in the north, starting at the town of Udenbreth and then running south just above the Losheimergraben Crossroads. A weak officer commanded this battalion. The battalion executive officer, CPT Ben W. Legare, did most of the commander's work. The major concern in the 2nd Battalion's area was the Weisser Stein Trail which ran through the battalion's northern flank. The trail presented a viable avenue of approach to the west, but not nearly as effective as the avenue to the south. That avenue was the main east-west road that originated in Germany and intersected the north-south boundary road commonly referred to as the International Highway, or, as the troops called it, "California Road." This intersection, the Losheimergraben Crossroads, was the real prize in Riley's sector. He gave the mission of defending this junction to his 3rd Battalion, commanded by the capable MAJ Norman Moore.

Initially, the mission of manning the outpost in Lanzerath went to the reserve battalion at Buchholz Station. LTC Douglas's Company C occupied the outpost until 10 December, when the Regimental Intelligence and Reconnaissance (I&R) Platoon, commanded by 1LT Lyle Bouck, replaced them. The next day, 11 December, the 1st and 3rd Battalions switched roles, the 1st now assuming the responsibility of division reserve at Buchholz Station.[9] This rotation gave all battalions in the line the opportunity to conduct patrols into enemy territory. Many were reconnaissance patrols led into Losheim.

There was a lot of night movement across the Siegfried Line by mid-December. Senior intelligence officers wanted to know whether German units had replaced others in the enemy line. Patrols tried to capture prisoners who would be interrogated for answers. Other patrols were ambushes. Soon, the men became accustomed to the sound of sporadic artillery fire. Many had seen actual enemy soldiers, eliminating the mythical notion of Germans as "supermen." The GIs also became accustomed to the familiar overhead roar of V-1 unmanned rockets, fired at Antwerp and other logistical high payoff targets. The men of the 99th Division soon christened their sector "Buzz Bomb Alley."[10] The division's antiaircraft units even succeeded in knocking a few of these terror weapons out of the sky as they raced westward.

The days between 14 November and 11 December were valuable for the regiment. COL Riley's men experienced great success in their patrols. When a 394th patrol went looking for a prisoner, it usually returned with several. The disposition of the regiment didn't change. The regimental command post (CP) was in the small hamlet of Hunningen while the regiment's Service Company operated from another town, Murringen, to the north. According to the equipment allocation for an infantry regiment in 1944, Riley was fully equipped for combat. His Cannon Company had a full complement of six organic 105mm howitzers and the Regimental Anti-Tank Company had nine 57mm anti-tank guns. His three battalions were fully equipped as well. Each battalion had an Ammunition and Pioneer (A&P) Platoon, an anti-tank platoon with three 57mm guns, and a mine platoon. In addition, each battalion had three full infantry companies and one heavy weapons company consisting of six 81mm mortars and eight .30 caliber machine guns. Each rifle company had three platoons of three squads each, two .30 caliber machine guns, and three 60mm mortars. Each battalion had its own company letter designations: the 1st had companies A through D, the 2nd had E through H, and the 3rd had I through M.[11] All battalions were close to full strength in both men and equipment, making the entire regiment a powerful force to be reckoned with.

By mid-December, the fighting north of Monschau prompted a deliberate attack on the Roer River Dams. General Hodges feared the Germans might flood the valley by opening the dams, thus making much of the terrain impassable by armored or wheeled vehicles. The 2nd Infantry Division had the task of seizing these dams in concert with increased activity to the German front by the 99th Division. The 106th Division had relieved the 2nd in the line south of the 99th, freeing them for the planned offensive. The 395th Regiment received additional support assets, making it a Regimental Combat Team. MG Lauer then detached it to the 2nd Division for the attack. The 393rd and 394th planned to step up artillery fire and limited engagements against the Germans to their front, a feint intended to dupe the Germans into thinking the attack was of a much greater scale. The date set for the attack was 13 December and the 2nd Division was moving to attack positions from the southwest to the northeast, placing many of their combat units directly behind the 99th Division's defensive positions. In addition, one company and a half went to the 395th from the 3rd Battalion, still in reserve at Buchholz Station.

The attack on the dams began as scheduled. Fierce fighting erupted to the north near Monschau. The 394th began conducting more aggressive patrols forward, firing occasional artillery rounds at the German positions as harassment. This activity continued as the attack progressed, up until 16 December, when Hitler's great counterattack, "Wacht am Rhein," went into effect.

CHAPTER 3

Germany's Last Warriors

The main effort of the entire German counteroffensive rested firmly on the shoulders of SS-Oberstgruppenfuehrer Sepp Dietrich. Dietrich commanded the 6th SS Panzer Army, a force that would strike along the northern shoulder of the penetration. With four SS panzer and five infantry divisions at his disposal, Dietrich was to spearhead the German offensive, reach the Meuse quickly, and then move on to Antwerp. Like others in the German High Command, Dietrich felt he would be lucky to reach the Meuse, the "small solution."

Dietrich proved a highly successful SS commander throughout the war. He served as one of Hitler's bodyguards in the 1920s, during the early days of the Nazi movement. He later commanded Hitler's prestigious bodyguard unit, the Leibstandarte-SS "Adolf Hitler." But many in the Wehrmacht still thought him an ignorant crony, prone to heavy drinking and smoking. With a pug nose and rough features, he fit this image perfectly. Most Army officers had little use for him and firmly doubted his command and military abilities. His only military experience before the war was as a sergeant in World War I. When the Second World War broke out in Poland, Dietrich's bodyguard unit participated as a regimental-sized element. Surprisingly, he met with great success. He was regarded highly by his men and officers, many professing an undying loyalty to him. The Leibstandarte-SS "Adolf Hitler" later grew into a full-sized panzer division and served as a "fire brigade" for Hitler, cleaning up "messes" in places like Greece and the Eastern front. Although Dietrich met with much success on the battlefield, senior officers like Generalfeldmarschalls von Rundstedt and Model doubted his abilities to command a unit larger than a division. When the order of battle for "Wacht am Rhein" was slated, both field marshals made certain that Dietrich had a capable and intelligent chief of staff, SS-Brigadefuehrer Fritz Kraemer, to rely on. Kraemer's assistance to Dietrich in the coming battle would be immeasurable.

The 6th SS Panzer Army consisted of three corps. The first, the panzer army's main effort, was the I SS Panzer Corps commanded by SS-Gruppenfuehrer Hermann Priess. Next came SS-Obergruppenfuehrer Willi Bittrich's II SS Panzer Corps followed by the LXVII Corps commanded by Generalleutnant Maximilian Otto Hitzfeld.[1] The deployment of these corps for the counteroffensive was as follows: Hitzfeld's LXVII Corps would conduct a supporting attack in the north near Monschau in concert with a limited parachute drop intended to prevent enemy reinforcements from attacking the army's right flank. The I SS Panzer Corps would attack along a front from Hollerath in the north to Lanzerath in the south, using its three infantry divisions to punch holes in the American defenses, thus allowing free passage for the two SS panzer divisions. The II SS Panzer Corps would wait in reserve, prepared to exploit the anticipated success of its sister panzer corps. Dietrich's intent was to clear five lanes in his sector for rapid exploitation. These routes (rollbahnen), the key to the success of Dietrich's attack, were labeled from A to E. Dietrich placed the responsibility of opening these routes squarely upon SS-Gruppenfuehrer Priess and the I SS Panzer Corps.

The I SS Panzer Corps consisted of three infantry divisions and two SS panzer divisions. The panzer divisions were two of the best; the 1st SS Panzer Division Leibstandarte-SS "Adolf Hitler" was commanded by SS-Oberfuehrer Wilhelm Mohnke and the 12th SS Panzer Division "Hitlerjugend" by SS-Standartenfuehrer Hugo Kraas. Mohnke was responsible for Routes D and E, and Kraas had Routes A through C. Both divisions would exploit the penetrations made by the three infantry divisions in the enemy's defensive lines. All three infantry divisions would attack on a broad front, with the 277th Volksgrenadier Division in the north, the 12th Volksgrenadier Division in the center, and the 3rd Fallschirmjaeger Division in the south. The main effort among these units was the 12th Volksgrenadier Division in the center, considered by Dietrich to be his best infantry. They would take the most crucial objective, the improved road intersection at Losheimergraben. This road intersection was the starting point of Route C, the best and fastest avenue leading directly to the west and the Meuse beyond. Without this key intersection, the panzer columns would be paralyzed. The grenadiers had to take it quickly—within the first hours of the offensive. As far as Dietrich was concerned, the crossroads were vital.

The 277th Volksgrenadier Division, slated to attack in the north, had only a brief history in the war to date.[2] In 1942, the division existed as a special-purpose divisional staff in Stuttgart and received its first infantry units only in December 1943. Most of these units were from Austria and did not contain the best trained soldiers available. After a brief stint in Croatia and southern France, the division moved to Normandy in mid-June and replaced the 9th SS Panzer Division in the front line. Now a part of the II SS Panzer Corps, the division performed well in July during the Battle of Caen. However, a little later, they suffered heavy losses in the Falaise Pocket. The new division com-

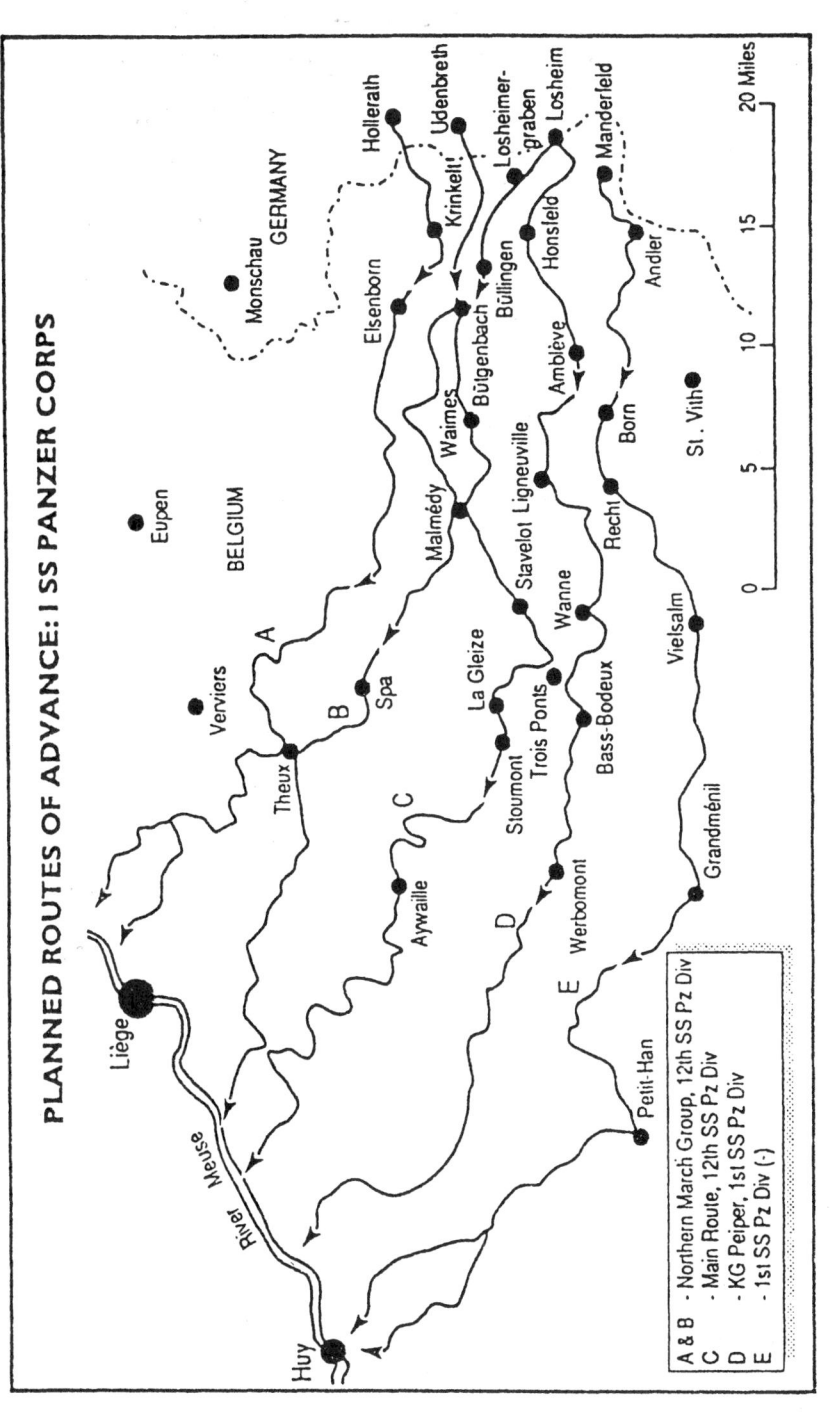

Planned Routes of Advance for the I SS Panzer Corps. Note the absence of Lanzerath, which would be just southwest of Losheim. Reprinted by permission, from James R. Arnold, *Ardennes 1944: Hitler's Last Gamble in the West*. Osprey Publishing Ltd., 1990.

mander, Oberst Wilhelm Viebig (who replaced Generalleutnant Albert Praum), could muster only 2,500 men, 1,000 of whom were actual combat troops.

Because of staggering losses in Normandy, the division was sent to Hungary where it ingested elements of the 374th Volksgrenadier Division. An order dated 9 September allowed the 277th to maintain its original numerical designation; on 5 November the division returned to the Western front. The 277th took over part of the Siegfried Line defenses in the Losheim area and remained there until the German counteroffensive began, disengaging from the line only a few days before the actual attack.

Oberst Viebig and his very capable chief of staff, Oberstleutnant Horst Freiherr von Wangenheim, had grave concerns about the upcoming battle. Viebig was aware that the quality of his replacements was poor. While in Hungary, he had received many young Austrian men as replacements, all poorly trained. Von Wangenheim was skeptical about these recruits as well, fully aware that the average Austrian male lacked the basic infantry training experience common to all Germans.[3] Many recruits barely knew how to use their rifles and, in some cases, even lacked firing pins. These men would have to wait and see what they could scrounge from the battlefield before they could put their weapons into action. While in the West Wall positions, the division received more replacements, many from the Kriegsmarine (German Navy) and the Luftwaffe. These men had only served in support roles in their original service branch, with little or no knowledge of basic infantry weapons or tactics.[4] By this point in the war, the Kriegsmarine was nearly defunct, as was the Luftwaffe, and the surplus men from these services began to see front-line combat service on all fronts. The Luftwaffe men usually came from airfield support crews while the Kriegsmarine personnel were trained to operate ships and port facilities. Because of this severe deficiency in experience and training, Viebig and von Wangenheim would have to rely almost solely on the expertise, experience, and courage of their regimental and battalion commanders. Many of these men were capable, well-trained leaders, who would have to lead from the very front to make certain the grenadiers reached their objectives and fought with some sense of unity and purpose. Among these leaders was Oberstleutnant Josef Bremm, one of the most highly decorated infantry officers to emerge from the war. Bremm had seen a tremendous amount of combat on the Eastern front and had some experience fighting the Allies in the West. As a distinctive symbol of his battlefield success, he wore the Oakleaves to the Knight's Cross of the Iron Cross around his neck. His 990th Fusilier Regiment, one of three in the division besides the 989th and 991st, lacked leadership ability and experience at lower command levels. If Bremm were to have success in the coming battle, he would have to personally be at the very front of the attack.

In the few days preceding the attack, Oberstleutnant von Wangenheim was frustrated by the refusal of his corps headquarters to allow reconnaissance patrols forward of the lines. As an experienced veteran of the Eastern front, von Wangenheim knew a unit that blundered into enemy positions was at a severe disadvantage. He knew the 99th Division was in the line opposite the 277th, but he wasn't certain of the disposition of their defense. He was also unaware that the attacking 2nd Division was right behind the 99th, driving on the Roer Dams in the north. The 2nd Division was attacking from the southwest to northeast, putting many of its combat elements directly behind the defending 99th Division. This knowledge would certainly have been a useful consideration for von Wangenheim in the planning phase, but he would never have the benefit of reconnaissance. This lack of reconnaissance would later cost the division heavily.

Another consideration for von Wangenheim was the necessity of quickly and adequately clearing the dense, coniferous forest of American troops. He learned in Russia that small bands of soldiers with anti-tank weapons could create havoc for advancing armored vehicles and other formations. If his infantry didn't eliminate the anti-tank threat early in the battle, then the 12th SS Panzer Division's panzers would face considerable risk in the advance west.[5]

As Viebig and von Wangenheim worked out the final plan, their division disengaged from its forward positions and occupied assembly areas two or three kilometers east of the West Wall and northeast of Udenbreth. The units that replaced them in the line were slow. On 15 December, the day before the offensive, one battalion of the 277th had yet to be relieved in the line. More than likely, this battalion would have to come forward after the attack began.

In the division CP, Oberst Viebig, Oberstleutnant von Wangenheim, and the regimental commanders worked out the final plan that would go into effect the next morning, 16 December. The division's objectives were clear: open Routes A and B for the 12th SS Panzer Division "Hitlerjugend." Once these routes were open, the division's next objective was to seize the main road junction in the twin villages of Krinkelt-Rocherath seven kilometers to the west. These two villages were the converging points of two main trails through the 99th Division's positions. The first, opposite Hollerath in the north, was called the Schwarzenbruch Trail. The other, just opposite Udenbreth in the south, was the Weisser Stein Trail. Both of these trails represented, from north to south, the start points of Routes A and B. Viebig's concept of the operation was to have the 989th Grenadier Regiment attack in the north to seize the Schwarzenbruch Trail opposite Hollerath. In the center, the 991st Grenadier Regiment would attack the central defensive positions of the 99th Division's northern sector, and then Oberstleutnant Bremm's 990th Fusilier Regiment would seize the Weisser Stein Trail in the south opposite Udenbreth. Bremm would be the main effort, employing in his area the division's only sturmgeschutzen, six assault guns from Sturmgeschutze Company 1277. This company also had several Jagdpanzer 38(t)s, another type of assault gun, but these would attack elsewhere.[6]

On the eve of the offensive, Oberst Viebig and Oberstleutnant von Wangenheim had accomplished all the necessary preparations for the battle. They reported to the corps chief of staff, SS-Brigadefuehrer Fritz Kraemer, that they were at 80 percent strength and ready to attack.[7] Viebig and von Wangenheim could hear the 12th SS Panzer Division occupying assembly areas behind them.

The panzers moved only under cover of darkness to avoid American aircraft attacks. The SS soldiers placed hay on the roads to help muffle the sound of their tracks, but many panzers could still be heard. Viebig had one battalion in the line yet to be relieved by its replacing unit. Viebig would have to attack without this battalion, combat power that could make a difference in the battle. Both Viebig and von Wangenheim were skeptical of success, however. The state of their division was far below that of a trained and cohesive fighting force. The 277th was nothing more than a hodgepodge of young, inexperienced men with superb leaders, an unusual mix at best. The division's only hope lay in Bremm's fusiliers making a quick and successful push along the Weisser Stein Trail. Bremm had the combat power and the experience, but would his soldiers prove capable? If the division could get at least one route open quickly, the SS panzers would take care of the rest. But even this hope, as both Viebig and von Wangenheim realized, was more than the officers could count on. But hope they did, determined to do their very best when the offensive began in a few short hours.

South of the 277th Volksgrenadier Division, the 12th Volksgrenadier Division would attack as Dietrich's main effort. Although Dietrich specifically labeled them his best infantry, the 12th was in a state no better than the 277th.[8] They too had absorbed numerous, untrained recruits. Their advantage lay in the quality of equipment the division commander, Generalmajor Gerhard Engel, obtained for them. Still, the 12th had a cadre of experienced and capable officers, many more than its sister division in the north.

The 12th Division was a unit that had fought with distinction in Poland, France, and Russia. In France, as part of the II Corps, 4th Army, the division prevented a French effort to cut the "panzer corridor" in an futile attempt to relieve the British and French armies trapped in Belgium. In Russia, the 12th Division began Operation Barbarossa as part of the 16th Army, assisting in the capture of Dvinsk. The following year, again part of the II Corps, the division was trapped in the Soviet encirclement of Demjansk but broke out after several months of repelling Red Army attacks. The 12th Division spent much of the Russian campaign in the north. In July 1944, the Russians encircled the division and Army Group Center in the Minsk-Vitebsk area. The commanding general at the time, Generalleutnant Rudolf Bamber, had no choice but to surrender the division. Except for some command headquarters and staff members, few escaped Russian captivity.[9]

By late summer of 1944, the division was rebuilt in East Prussia under the command of Hitler's former adjutant, Generalmajor Gerhard Engel (at that time still an oberst). As a man with "connections," Engel made certain the division received the best equipment available, such as the new and highly effective automatic assault rifles, the Sturmgewehr 44 (StG 44). The division was brought up to a strength of 14,800 men and received a full complement of equipment, something unusual for a German division that late in the war. Engel joined the ranks of a division cadre that had survived the disaster with

Army Group Center, to include two very highly decorated and capable majors, Wilhelm Osterhold and Heinz-Georg Lemm. These men were the best choices to command two of the three new regiments in the division.

By September, and on the Western front, the division excelled in the defensive and costly fighting around Aachen and Dueren. On 9 October 1944, the division received the honorific title, Volksgrenadier, or people's soldier, a term designed to instill elitism. On 2 December, the division, already slated for the Ardennes Offensive, withdrew from the fighting around Juelich and Dueren for a short refit and rest near Blankenheim. The 12th Division was next sent to assembly areas around Scheid, Kronenburg, and Frauenkron, where replacements began arriving to make up for losses in the recent defensive fighting. As the troops assembled, the plan for the upcoming offensive unfolded.

Highly experienced and successful officers led the three regiments. Oberstleutnant Wilhelm Osterhold (promoted in October) commanded the 48th Grenadier Regiment. His long-time personal friend, Oberstleutnant Heinz-Georg Lemm, commanded the 27th Fusilier Regiment, and Oberstleutnant Gerhard Lemcke commanded the 89th Grenadier Regiment. Although experienced leaders, all three had grave concerns about the upcoming battle. Reconnaissance was not allowed. Many recruits were trickling in by ones and twos, which didn't allow the commanders to train their regiments as a whole. Like the 277th, these new replacements would need experienced leadership up front if they were to succeed.

On 14 December, the 12th Volksgrenadier Division occupied forward assembly areas in the vicinity of Kronenburg. The 48th Grenadier Regiment was in the town itself, while the 27th Fusilier was in the forest to the south. Behind the 27th to the east was the 89th Grenadier Regiment. Here, regimental and battalion commanders were told of the plan. In the two days preceding the offensive, all three regiments would receive 20 to 30 percent of their new replacements.[10] Many commanders wouldn't even learn the names of their soldiers before they had to lead them into battle.

All three commanders managed some input into the planning process. Generalmajor Engel was very competent and capable, but he lacked the specific experience and knowledge found among his regimental commanders. After a long discussion with them, he developed a concept of the operation that appeared most likely to succeed. His objective was to open the vital route in the center, Route C, for the 12th SS Panzer Division "Hitlerjugend," a division that would be spread out between Routes A and B in the north. Route C began at the most improved road intersection in the 6th SS Panzer Army's area of operation, the Losheimergraben Crossroads. Losheimergraben was the prize, the main effort of the army, and the main effort of the division. Dietrich wanted this highly improved road taken quickly. That meant gaining immediate control of the vital crossroads. Once Losheimergraben was taken, the division could assist in taking Routes D and E in the south. Subsequent objectives were the villages of Hunningen and Murringen in the west, but the Losheimergraben intersection was the most important man-made terrain feature needed to get the attack moving.

The 48th Grenadier Regiment was responsible for taking the crossroads. The 27th Fusilier Regiment would move on line to the south of, and in concert with, the 48th. The 27th Fusiliers would provide support by moving along the southern rail line to below the crossroads, then flanking the junction from the south. Both regiments would envelop the crossroads quickly. Major Gunther Holz, commander of the division's assault gun detachment, offered six 75mm Sturmgeschutze IIIs from his Sturmgeschutze Company 1012 to the 48th to support the attack. The assault guns would attack directly from the road leading from Losheim into Losheimergraben.[11] Since the bridge over the railroad tracks was missing, destroyed by the retreating German Army several months before, the assault guns would have to find trails through the forest to get into Losheimergraben. This concept made the assault gun portion of the plan very dubious.

Oberstleutnant Lemcke's 89th Grenadier Regiment made up the final portion of the plan. Lemcke would follow Lemm's 27th Fusiliers as the division reserve, prepared to reinforce any successes or to protect his sister regiment's northern flank while it penetrated quickly into the enemy's lines.

The plan was set and agreed upon by all. Oberstleutnant Osterhold was satisfied but disgruntled by one aspect: the lack of reconnaissance. Osterhold's experience in Russia taught him that breaking the principle of reconnaissance was a cardinal sin in the infantry. He had no idea where the 99th Division's frontline positions were. He didn't know how much resistance he would face at the crossroads, or if the enemy was defending them at all.

The three regimental commanders returned to their command posts to formulate their own plans. They would, in turn, brief their battalion commanders.[12]

To the south of the 12th Volksgrenadier Division, the 3rd Fallschirmjaeger Division moved into assembly areas near the small town of Hallschlag, 10 kilometers east of Lanzerath. The division marched 30 kilometers to these positions on 15 December via Kronenburg and Stadtkyll. Since paratroopers had few motorized vehicles, they moved essential pieces of equipment on hand carts and baby carriages.[13] This hastily reformed unit comprised the southern wing of Dietrich's attacking infantry. They were responsible for opening up Routes D and E for the 1st SS Panzer Division Leibstandarte-SS "Adolf Hitler." Commanded by Generalmajor Walther Wadehn, the division could only move two regiments into position for the offensive; the 15th Army needed the other regiment to plug a defensive gap farther north.

The division had been formed in Rheims, France, in October 1943 and had been commanded by the veteran paratrooper Generalmajor Richard Schimpf. When the Allies landed in Normandy, the division was immediately sent into the fighting to prevent the invading forces from rapidly advancing inland. Like most parachute units formed after 1941, the 3rd Fallschirmjaeger Division never participated in an airborne operation. Most of the "paratroopers," save for a few veteran sergeants and officers who framed the division's cadre, had never jumped from an aircraft. Hitler had learned a hard lesson in Crete where the airborne operation had cost the Germans dearly. After Crete Hitler played down the significance of paratrooper operations; he considered them too costly for Germany where manpower waned daily. The 3rd Fallschirmjaeger would operate as ground troops in infantry-type operations.

At St. Lô, the 3rd Fallschirmjaeger suffered heavily during their attempt to halt advancing American forces. By 11 July 1944, the division had lost 35 percent of its 17,000 men. Later that same month, the division lost more men in the Falaise Pocket, where the newly promoted Generalleutnant Schimpf was severely wounded. Schimpf had to be evacuated during the breakout. Although greatly reduced in number, the division was tough and remained in action until relieved in October. The division withdrew to Oldenzaal, Holland, where it received numerous low-quality replacements, to include poorly trained commanders and staff officers. These replacements came from Luftwaffe ground units and airfield support crews and had little or no experience in infantry training or tactics. The veteran paratroopers hastily whipped them into shape. Now commanded by Generalmajor Walther Wadehn, the division was earmarked for the Ardennes Offensive.[14]

By mid-December, the division moved to its forward assembly areas south of Hallschlag. Logistical problems and excessive casualties caused one regiment to remain north to assist the 15th Army's defense. Equipment problems plagued the entire division. Gefreiter Walter Wittlinger, a member of the 2nd Battalion, 9th Regiment since the Normandy fighting, received one of the new StG 44s for the offensive. However, when he checked the weapon, it had no firing pin. When he raised the issue with his battalion adjutant, the officer told him to wait until someone was killed in action. Then he could take that person's firing pin. Dumbfounded by this answer, Wittlinger returned to his unit.[15]

The poor quality of operations personnel became an issue as well. The chief of staff of the I SS Panzer Corps quickly realized that his counterpart in the 3rd Fallschirmjaeger Division knew absolutely nothing about ground operations. He moved rapidly to have the man replaced with someone a little more experienced.[16] The division was only a shell of its former self; it no longer had a full complement of well-trained and experienced fighters. Parachute units were considered "elite," but this division did not qualify. Instead, young, inexperienced men were led by officers who had, at best, staff experience in rear-echelon units. Experienced veterans were distinguishable by the paratrooper helmets they wore, helmets missing the traditional flared rim of the standard German helmet. Others wore standard issue blue-gray overcoats and helmets, occasionally camouflaged with a white sheet for the snowy Ardennes.

Oberst Helmut von Hofmann, the commander of the 9th Fallschirmjaeger Regiment, was one such example of inexperience. Von Hofmann, a staff officer from a rear-echelon unit who had no knowledge of infantry operations, had the mission of clearing Route D—the crucial avenue from Losheim west to Honsfeld and beyond. A battle group from the very impatient and aggressive 1st SS Panzer Division was to pass along this route. If von Hofmann didn't accomplish his mission quickly, the 6th SS Panzer Army's plan would fail. Von Hofmann wanted his 1st Battalion to move along the main roads to seize Lanzerath. The 2nd Battalion would serve as a reserve. The regiment to his south, the 5th, was to move along Route E, but its members lacked experience as well. The division was underequipped and poorly led, but they had to move forward with what they had. They lacked assault guns, and SS-Brigadefuehrer Kraemer, the Corps chief of staff, listed them at only 75 percent strength.[17] Through no fault of their own, these men would be expected to perform as though they had trained and fought together for years.

In the 48th Grenadier Regiment's command post in the town of Kronenburg, Oberstleutnant Wilhelm Osterhold called his two battalion commanders together to plan the operation. He had a concept in mind, but he wanted their input and the benefit of their experience.

As Osterhold waited for the men to arrive, he considered the size of his regiment and how he would array them for the attack. A long-time veteran of Poland, France, and the Eastern front, Osterhold had been with the division since the beginning of the war. He had distinguished himself, earning the coveted Knight's Cross of the Iron Cross on the Eastern front in March 1944. Germany's highest award for valor and leadership identified the most distinguished officers and men in the German Armed Forces. Osterhold had two battalion commanders who held the same decoration. Major Siegfried Moldenhauer commanded his 1st Battalion, and Major Gerhard Kruse his 2nd. Osterhold considered himself fortunate to have two such distinguished soldiers leading his battalions. Osterhold, a commander who liked to associate with his men, tried to get to know them as they arrived, but his effort soon proved impossible. Even as he sat at his CP waiting for his battalion commanders to arrive, new replacements were still pouring in. And the offensive was to begin in a matter of hours. Even talking to the officers proved fruitless. They were too many, and there was not enough time. The new officers lacked confidence, and he gauged his few brief discussions with them to bolster their morale.[18]

Aside from the regiment's two battalions, Osterhold had an Infantry Howitzer Company with six M42 12cm heavy mortars, two 15cm heavy infantry guns, and two platoons of 7.5cm PAK light infantry guns (standard organization called for only one platoon). Normally, one platoon went to each battalion for support. Most of this equipment was horse drawn. Osterhold used a captured American jeep instead of a kubelwagen as his command car. Each grenadier battalion had four numbered companies; the 1st Battalion had companies 1 through 4 and the 2nd had numbers 5 through 8. The 4th and 8th Companies were Heavy Weapons Companies, consisting entirely of MG42 or MG34 machine gun crews. This company normally had two heavy machine gun platoons, an infantry howitzer platoon, and one mortar platoon. Each regular line company had two sub-machine gun platoons (MP40 or StG 44) and one rifle platoon (KAR 98). All of these elements had the equipment specified by the table of organization, but many platoons were mixed and matched with different types of rifles and automatic weapons. Even the actual battalion-level organization was increased or reduced based on available personnel and equipment. However, unlike most other infantry units during this late stage of the war, the 48th Grenadier Regiment had a full complement of equipment.[19]

The other regiments in the division were organized in the same manner. Some lacked the leadership Osterhold enjoyed, but they were well-equipped. In an assembly area to the south, Oberstleutnant Lemm's 27th Fusilier Regiment looked the same as Osterhold's except he had fewer experienced leaders to rely on. Still, he had some distinguished, experienced officers in command positions. The battle-proven Hauptmann Claus Breger was a holder of the Knight's Cross of the Iron Cross like his regimental commander, Lemm. The 12th Volksgrenadier Division would go into battle with some highly qualified infantry leaders.

Osterhold's two battalion commanders arrived early in the evening. The attack would begin in less than 12 hours. The planning had to be fast and simple. The officers set to work. Osterhold informed Major Moldenhauer and Major Kruse of the regiment's augmented support. He told the two men of the sturmgeschutze assault that would support their attack on the crossroads. Osterhold explained that the regiment also had priority of artillery fires; two dedicated Volksartillerie Battalions would fire exclusively in support of the regiment's attack once the army's initial preparatory barrage ended. Within minutes, the three commanders agreed to move north of the east-west Losheim-Losheimergraben road in column formation. This movement formation was for speed and noise discipline, allowing them to orient their movement on a major terrain feature, the road, for ease of navigation. Considering the experience of the new soldiers, this plan would make things easier. Strangely enough, Osterhold had actually been told to follow a specific compass azimuth of 48 degrees, roughly due west from Frauenkron, and that this azimuth would put him right at the crossroads. Since the 1st Battalion would lead the attack as the regiment's main effort, Osterhold told Major Moldenhauer to follow this compass heading when he moved out the next morning. It might help them get through the American positions with more ease. Osterhold decided to employ his heavy weapons along the Losheim-Losheimergraben road in a support position east of the crossroads and north of the east-west road to Losheim. The heavy weapons, the mortars and infantry guns, would support the regiment by suppressing any American position that threatened attack.

Osterhold made it clear to the officers that the 48th was the division's, the corps', and the army's main effort; their success was critical. They not only had to take the crossroads quickly, but the villages of Hunningen and Murringen needed to be in their hands before nightfall the next day. Considering the inexperience of the replacements, all three men decided that the key to success was to lead from the front, to show the raw recruits how to attack. This type of leadership didn't bother these officers because it tended to be their usual style, especially on the Eastern front. Osterhold also made clear his anger over the lack of reconnaissance. Under usual circumstances, he would have had patrols out looking for the enemy's frontline disposition. All he had now was a compass heading and speculation. He hated the thought of blundering into an enemy's defenses. All of his experience and training told him that stumbling blindly into the enemy wasn't the key to a successful operation. His commanders agreed. They felt uncertain about the situation, too. Osterhold and Generalmajor Engel also voiced concern over the preparatory fire plan but had no say in it whatsoever. All Osterhold knew was that the planning and execution of the artillery preparation would come from higher command levels. His concerns were where the artillery would land and if it would be adequate to support the attack. The artillery preparation was scheduled for 0530 and would last two hours, with all artillery assets firing steadily for that length of time. The duration and scope of the preparation made Osterhold even more skeptical about the entire plan.

Osterhold concluded the planning session by discussing a few control measures. The regiment would move to a forward assembly area two kilometers west of Frauenkron at 0200. Once there, they would wait one hour before crossing the line of departure. This delay was a traffic control measure installed to ensure the regiment moved smoothly without getting backed up. Osterhold told his commanders to make sure the men got some sleep. The next few days would be long ones, and the men were living in relative comfort for the moment in the houses of Kronenburg. Osterhold forced a smile and wished his commanders luck. They thanked him and the meeting ended without comment. Moldenhauer and Kruse returned to their battalions and quickly issued oral orders to the men. They were brief so that all could capitalize on some much-needed sleep. The 16th of December would be a challenging day.[20]

At his panzer army headquarters, SS-Oberstgruppenfuehrer Sepp Dietrich, the man responsible for the counteroffensive's success, slept restlessly. The operation was no longer in his hands; Dietrich had placed his trust and confidence in the officers and men of his command. Only the courage and determination of the soldiers in the 6th SS Panzer Army would bring victory in the coming days. In a few short hours, the battle would begin, and Dietrich would find himself an impatient and anxious observer.

CHAPTER 4

Seize the Crossroads!

At 0530 on the morning of 16 December 1944, the great German artillery barrage began. Hundreds of German artillery batteries erupted in a thunderous cacophony. The bombardment opened up a massive front over 20 miles wide. On the north shoulder, the barrage fell on the American rear positions, including the service and support areas first, then began to creep slowly toward the east. Thirty to forty flak searchlights, originating east of the Siegfried Line, lit up the sky. The Germans arced the searchlights upward, reflecting off the hanging gray clouds, creating a faint glow on the ground below. The searchlights were supposed to assist the German infantry move forward, but the light was so faint it only added to the confusion of shapes and shadows running through the thick, coniferous Ardennes forest.

The artillery pieces flashing in the east created a brilliant aura in the night. The noise was deafening. Scores of projectiles whizzed through the air in search of an Allied target. This barrage was perhaps the most ominous display of German firepower the Americans would see. The magnitude of the attack stunned American veterans of North Africa, Sicily, and Normandy. For those who lacked combat experience, it would be unforgettable.[1]

At approximately 0400, Oberstleutnant Wilhelm Osterhold moved his 48th Grenadier Regiment forward. He wanted his two battalions close to the jump-off point so that they could exploit the artillery. Osterhold's battalions were the key to the attack. In addition to his division's artillery, he had two Volksartillerie Battalions in support. As soon as the initial preparatory barrage finished, Osterhold would command priority of the combined artillery. However, his only link to the gunners was a single strand of field wire that led to the radio relay positions in the rear. His artillery officer used this line to contact a radio operator who would relay the fire request up to the battalions and then the batteries.[2]

Osterhold wanted to move his troops forward in the darkness before the preparation fires began, primarily because he knew fear might paralyze his younger recruits. He wanted to take advantage of the silent, pitch-black morning to position them near their objective. Once the artillery barrage lifted, he could capitalize on the rush of adrenaline many of them would experience. A clear objective would encourage his men to concentrate on seizing that objective and allow them to forget their fear. He moved his battalions in column formation, primarily for speed and to reduce noise.

The 1st Battalion, commanded by Major Siegfried Moldenhauer, took the lead. Osterhold and his command group followed. Major Kruse's 2nd Battalion brought up the rear. Behind them the heavier infantry weapons, the 7.5cm light and 15cm heavy infantry guns, some of which were horse-drawn, some of which were pulled by men, lagged. These heavy weapons needed to be in place, along with the regiment's mortars, near the Losheim-Losheimergraben road to support the grenadiers' attack. The regiment moved swiftly through the darkened forest, with Major Moldenhauer following the prescribed 48 degree azimuth (roughly due west).[3] Osterhold was still unaware of the 99th Division's specific positions; the lack of reconnaissance left him and his commanders uncertain of the enemy's strength and position.

Just short of their line of departure, Osterhold told Moldenhauer to stop. The regiment halted. The grenadiers sought cover near a tree or simply took a knee. Osterhold's radio operator called division headquarters and asked if the artillery barrage would begin on time. He also inquired about Major Holz's sturmgeschutze assault. So far, things went as scheduled.

Osterhold instructed his heavy weapons to move to the southwest and establish support positions. They moved out quickly. For now, Osterhold could do nothing but wait.

Combat experience taught him nothing would go as planned. Major problems would develop; he would have to react. He had faith in his battalion commanders, but they were handicapped by the inexperienced men they commanded. He had to take the Losheimergraben Crossroads quickly, or all would fail. He knew how vital his mission was and that he might have to set an example for his men to accomplish it. The personal risk didn't bother Osterhold; that was his style. Human error bothered him. Would the others do their part? On time? His friend, Oberstleutnant Lemm, would be on time. He wasn't so sure of the others.

He sat against a tree and waited. He turned the flashlight buttoned to his left shoulder board on and shone the beam at his watch. It was 0530; the artillery would begin in seconds. He turned his head upward as the first artillery rounds whistled overhead. A thunderous roar echoed from behind as scores of guns fired at the American positions to the west. The great German counteroffensive had begun.

The men of Company B, 1st Battalion, 394th Infantry, watched as the German artillery soared overhead. Many climbed from their holes to watch the

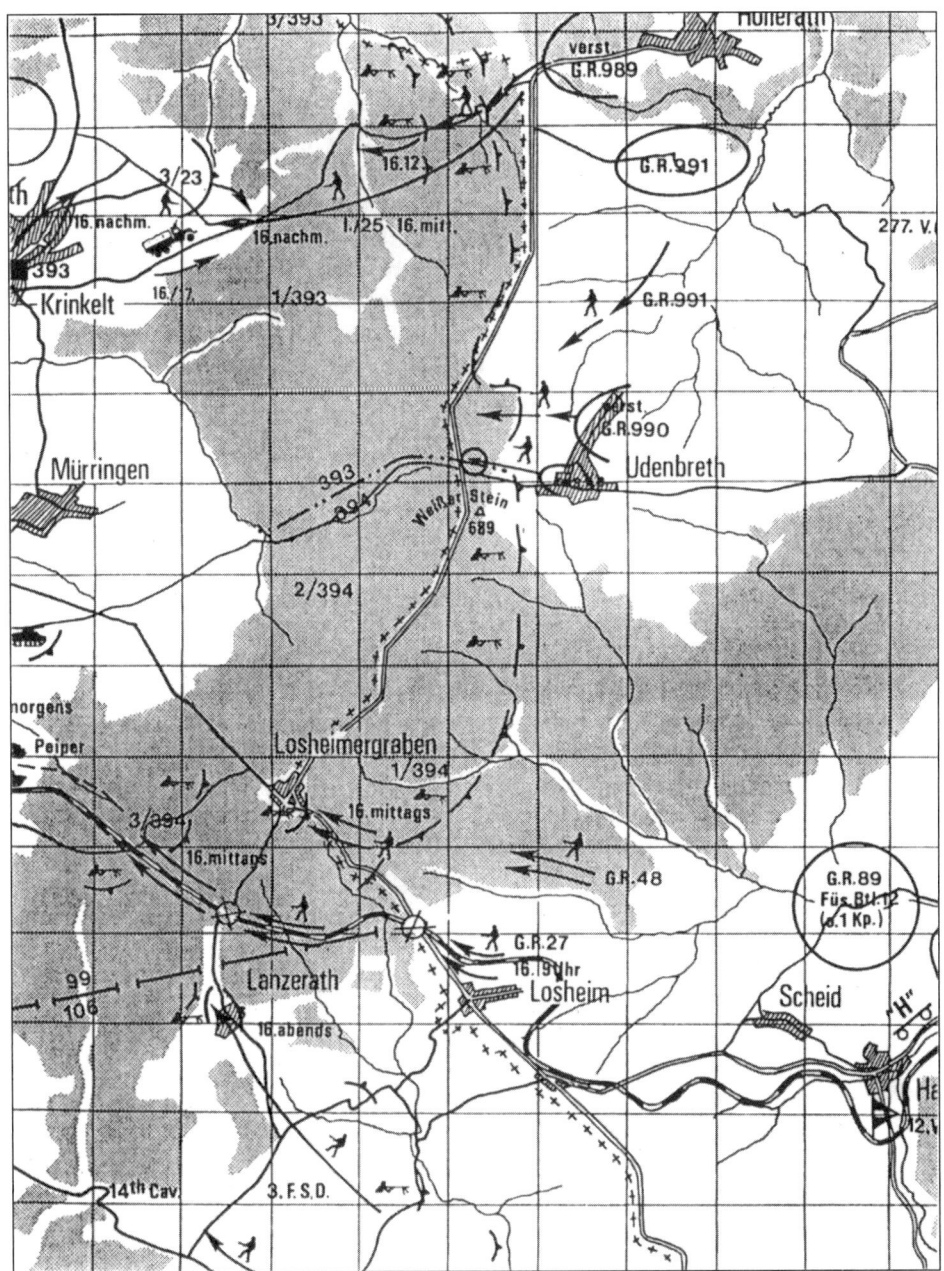

An excellent German graphic of the terrain and troop disposition of the battle area as found in Hubert Meyer's *Kriegsgeschichte der 12. SS Panzerdivision "Hitlerjugend."* Although Meyer intended the dates, times, and dispositions portrayed to be general, they are relatively accurate. *Mittags* means midday, *abends* is evening, and *uhr* is hour. Courtesy Hubert Meyer.

spectacle, more amazed than frightened. Some joked a little, wondering how "those guys in the rear" were enjoying the wake-up call. Some watched in stunned silence.

Company B, commanded by CPT Sidney A. Gooch, was the sole American unit that stood between the 48th Grenadier Regiment and the Losheimergraben Crossroads. Bordered on the north by Company C and on the south by Company A, the Company B foxhole line sat firmly astride the east-west road that led to the crossroads. CPT Gooch had deployed his company with two platoons on line and one platoon, fragmented into squads, either on the flanks or serving as observation positions. The company weapons platoon, complete with heavy machine guns and 60mm mortars, supported the two line platoons. The men had constructed excellent fighting positions with overhead cover.

The fields of fire were limited by the dense forest, however. Deep ravines and the spurs that fed them were too numerous to cover with firepower and made observation difficult, if not impossible. An attacking enemy could get within small-arms range of their positions before the GIs would be able to detect them. The actual foxhole line was 1,200 meters or so east of the crossroads. The customs houses located at the crossroads offered the men a place to wash up and get resupplied. The Americans had the best position the terrain offered them. They would soon learn, though, that it wasn't enough.

Oberstleutnant Osterhold looked to the west. The artillery shells were landing too far behind the American positions. He fully expected the barrage to start with the forward positions and then creep westward to hit the rear-echelon units. The opposite was taking place, giving the Americans in the forward lines an opportunity to prepare for the attack. The artillery would have little effect without surprise. Osterhold shook his head, disgusted. He had had no say in the artillery plan. Now he regretted not speaking out.

The darkness surrounding Osterhold, save for the searchlights' strange glow, was frightening and claustrophobic. Osterhold could barely see anything in the forest. The eerie blackness was almost certainly compounding the fears of his recruits.

The artillery continued to fall far to the west. Osterhold looked for his 2nd Battalion commander. It was still very dark. The shadows created by the searchlights made his regiment seem twice its actual size.

"Kruse! Kruse!" shouted Osterhold.

"Here, Herr Oberstleutnant!" A shadowy figure approached the regimental commander.

"Tell me, Kruse," began Osterhold, "have you ever experienced anything like this?"[4]

"What do you mean?" answered Major Kruse.

"The damned artillery is falling too far away!" exclaimed Osterhold. "We won't reach the American rear for another few hours. What about the forward positions? This fire plan must have been drawn up in Berlin!"

Osterhold's comments were met with silence from the battalion commander. Although it was dark, he could feel the man's eyes glaring at him. The sarcastic reference about the German High Command had irritated the young major. Osterhold checked himself. Kruse was a former member of the Hitler Jugend (Youth) and firmly believed, unlike Osterhold, in Hitler's leadership. People like Kruse could make trouble, even for their commanders. Osterhold didn't fear his subordinate, but he wanted to maintain a positive relationship with him. Kruse was good-natured and Osterhold liked him. He was unlikely to turn anyone in, but Kruse usually met any jabs or sneers about Hitler or the High Command with a cold stare. Osterhold dismissed the comment and continued to speak.

"This artillery isn't working in our favor," he began. "We have to move now. Tell your men to get ready. I'll inform Moldenhauer."

"Yes, Herr Oberstleutnant," replied Major Kruse.

Osterhold walked to the front of his regiment's column in search of Major Moldenhauer. Unlike Kruse, Osterhold could speak openly with Moldenhauer, who was much less an idealist. The regimental commander found Moldenhauer looking upward at the searchlights reflecting off the gray clouds overhead.

"What do you think of those lights?" Moldenhauer asked Osterhold.

Osterhold looked up and laughed. "I think they're ridiculous. Listen, Moldenhauer, the artillery isn't working in our favor. We need to move now if we're going to have any element of surprise. It looks like we won't even get an artillery prep on the enemy's forward positions. We'll have to hope our infantry weapons get set in time."

"Fine, Herr Oberstleutnant," said Moldenhauer. "We'll move at once."

By now, the artillery barrage had been going for 45 minutes, steadily raining deadly artillery rounds on the American rear, pausing only occasionally for a few minutes before starting up again. Osterhold stood in silence with his command group as his lead battalion got to its feet and began moving to the west. For the most part, he was impressed by their stealth and quiet. Even the new recruits did well. Soon, his heavy infantry weapons, the 7.5cm PAKs, the 15cm light infantry guns, and the 20mm guns, would be in their designated support positions. So far, save for the artillery fire, things were going smoothly. He fell into formation behind the 1st Battalion, while Major Kruse and his men picked up the rear. The men moved quietly through the forest to the west, heading directly for the Losheimergraben Crossroads and the GIs of Company B.

Many of Company B's men who left their foxholes to watch the barrage suddenly became worried about their situation. It was apparent that the artillery was steadily moving eastward, toward their positions. On the northern, or left, flank of Company B, SSG George Ballinger, a machine gun section leader from the weapons platoon, told his men to get back inside their holes. He occupied a log hut with three other men. One of his machine gun teams was in a hole to the right. Just as the men got back inside their holes, artillery began landing with ominous force directly on their positions. The trees overhead cracked and splintered as the German artillery rounds impacted on top of them, raining wood splinters and hot metal shrapnel on the foxholes below. Since the men had built strong overhead cover, everyone in Ballinger's section fared well, except for one. The weapons platoon leader, LT Charles E. Butler, received a direct hit on his dugout. He died instantly.

Butler's position was behind Ballinger's, and the force of the rounds landing nearby created such a vacuum that the men felt as though their heads would either cave in or explode. SSG Ballinger felt like his vision was being distorted and his eyes squeezed out every time a round landed.

Back near the platoon's CP, PFC Danny Dalyai, one of the weapons platoon's mortar men, ran to Butler's smoldering log hut to help. When Dalyai stuck his head into the dugout, the grim sight of splattered blood and bodies met his eyes. Among them was the torso of LT Butler, both legs blown completely off. He wished he had never looked in.[5]

South of SSG Ballinger's position, artillery wounded a GI who didn't make it back to his foxhole in time. LT Harvey F. Williamson, a platoon leader from Company D in support of the B Company men, saw the man fall and cry out in pain. Artillery rounds landed everywhere, barely missing the injured soldier. Williamson, without thinking, jumped from his foxhole and made for the wounded man. An artillery round landed nearby, knocking the officer's helmet from his head. Men in other foxholes cheered Williamson on. Williamson reached the wounded man and, placing him over his shoulder in a fireman's carry, ran back to his dugout. Once inside, he administered first aid to the soldier. When a medic took over, Williamson sat back to catch his breath. He looked himself over, searching for shrapnel wounds. His uniform and field jacket were full of holes. But he didn't have a scratch. He breathed a sigh of relief.[6]

Farther south, on Company B's right flank near the east-west road leading to Losheim, the artillery had its most devastating effect. Company B lost three mortar squads to direct hits. SGT Lilly, a mortar section leader, told PFC Ralph Gamber, two men nicknamed "Pap" and "Big Moose," and others from his section to stay inside their gun position. The men crouched low, hands clamped over their ears to stifle the deafening roar of the German 105mm and 150mm rounds. Since the mortars were in a forest clearing, the artillery had few treetops to hit. The rounds landed with full force next to the mortar men. Besides the three mortar squads, two lieutenants (including the unfortunate LT Butler, their platoon leader), the platoon sergeant, and many of the gunners were wounded or dead. In essence, the entire Company B complement of 60mm mortars failed to survive the German guns. Only SGT Lilly and his men managed to keep safe. SGT Kermit Ball, in charge of the 1st Mortar Squad, took charge and kept the survivors together. His section sergeant, SGT Lilly, was still in a daze from the artillery.[7] Aside from these glaring casualties, Company B's men withstood the bombardment well and found safety within their log huts or foxholes.

The artillery barrage shifted eastward as the 48th Grenadier Regiment moved west through the forest. Major Moldenhauer, the commander of the 1st Battalion, could see flashes from artillery rounds only 2,000 meters away. The ground rumbled and shuddered with each impact; Moldenhauer could feel the tenseness of his new recruits.

Suddenly, the column stopped and everyone took a knee. A small explosion sounded to Moldenhauer's front. He waited for a report from his lead company commander. The shadowy form of a messenger appeared in the morning twilight. The soldier informed Moldenhauer that the lead company had encountered a series of mines and trip flares, emplaced by the defending American units. Moldenhauer sent the messenger back with instructions for the lead company to clear a path. He sent his own runner to inform Osterhold of the obstacles. As the runner departed, Moldenhauer moved forward to examine the trip wires the Americans employed. He walked west in the dim morning light with his radio operator, fully aware that the artillery barrage was creeping closer to his battalion. As he approached his lead company's location, he saw soldiers spread out everywhere, carefully feeling for trip wires with their bare hands. Anxious over the delay, he helped the men find and disarm the booby traps.

Several minutes after Moldenhauer began checking for trip wires, Oberstleutnant Osterhold approached from the east with his radio operator and artillery liaison officer. Osterhold could see the soldiers of his 1st Battalion on their hands and knees, cutting away every wire in sight. He moved to where Moldenhauer was kneeling and asked for a situation report.

"How long will this take?" asked Osterhold. "We must get going. The heavy infantry weapons are moving into support positions now."

"I don't know, Herr Oberstleutnant," came the reply. "There are a lot of them. If we trip another one, the Americans will know exactly where we are."

Just then, Osterhold looked up and west. The sound of artillery fire now seemed closer. Many of the younger soldiers looked up nervously, bothered by the loud roar of the rounds impacting nearby.

"That artillery should have lifted by now," said Osterhold. "If it keeps moving, it'll fall on us in a few minutes."

"Did it hit the American infantry positions?" asked Moldenhauer.

"Yes, thankfully," answered Osterhold.

Osterhold turned and called for his artillery officer. The man quickly came forward carrying a field phone with wire dangling from it. He looked worried.

"Call the gun batteries and tell them to lift fires," said Osterhold. "Wait, what's wrong?"

"The men cutting the trip wires cut my land line to the guns," came the reply. "I have no way to contact them..."

Before the man could finish his sentence, the ground around the 1st Battalion erupted in a fury of dirt, snow, and bodies. The German artillery now landed directly on Osterhold's men, throwing them like rag dolls. They had no overhead protection. The rounds impacted in the trees and sprayed the men with hot, burning shrapnel. Osterhold, Moldenhauer, and the artillery officer dove for the ground, covering their heads with their arms. The barrage was tremendous. The pine trees overhead snapped and splintered like small sticks. Within minutes, the artillery fire lifted, leaving scores of moaning, writhing grenadiers scattered on the forest floor.

Osterhold lifted his head and listened. Miraculously, he appeared uninjured. He realized the entire German artillery preparation must be over now. The forest was strangely silent. A loud groan emanated from a small depression a few feet from Osterhold. Osterhold crawled to the wounded soldier. It was Major Moldenhauer, severely wounded in the back by shrapnel. Osterhold stood and looked around him. The 1st Battalion was in chaos. Nearly 60 percent of the grenadiers lay wounded on the forest floor. Five or six men appeared dead. Osterhold called for a medic to assist Moldenhauer. Then he moved off to the east, in the direction of his 2nd Battalion. He wanted to make sure they were intact.

Osterhold found his 2nd Battalion and Major Kruse. Kruse informed him that the artillery came very close but lifted at the last moment, leaving his men unscathed. Osterhold was relieved that he had combat power available.

"Listen to me," said Osterhold quickly. "Moldenhauer is wounded and so is most of his battalion. I want you to take the lead while I try to get the remainder of Moldenhauer's battalion moving. You must take the crossroads. Do you understand?"

"Yes, Herr Oberstleutnant," came the response. "I'll find a gap in the enemy lines that will get me to the crossroads quickly."

"Good," said Osterhold. "Remember, Major Holz should be moving on the crossroads with his sturmgeschutzen at any minute. I want you there for infantry support. Take your battalion to the right of the 1st Battalion. The sight of Moldenhauer's wounded might demoralize your younger soldiers."

Kruse departed to brief his company commanders. Osterhold looked at his watch. It was 0745 and things were going badly. He had to get his artillery support under control, and he had to make the 1st Battalion into a cohesive fighting force again. With a sigh, Osterhold walked back to his wounded men.

As the artillery barrage lifted, LTC Robert Douglas, the commander of the 1st Battalion, 394th Infantry, left his command post to check on the companies in the line. His CP location was 1,200 meters west of the Losheimergraben Crossroads and south of the main road. Six feet tall, confident and capable, Douglas struck an impressive figure. He was a brave man, personally willing to accept risk. Firm but good-natured, he enjoyed an excellent reputation with his battalion.

As Douglas moved from company CP to company CP, he was glad to learn that his men had not suffered heavily from the big guns. Well-prepared foxholes offered sufficient cover; those who failed to build adequate protection suffered during the barrage. Company B had the most casualties, especially among the mortar men.

Douglas made his way through the dense forest to Company C's location. The ground had large shell holes blasted into the frozen earth. Fantastic spray patterns of soil and splintered wood lined the snow around the craters. CPT Jim Graham greeted Douglas as he approached the log hut that served as the company CP. Graham, the company commander, was a big Texan. Douglas asked how Graham's company had fared. Graham told him Company C had come through relatively unscathed.

"What did you do while it was going on?" asked Douglas.

"Hell, Colonel," came the reply, "I just stayed under cover till it was over. Wasn't any use getting my head blown off."[8]

Douglas laughed. He lingered to talk to CPT Graham, not realizing a large German attack was under way. Douglas—and for that matter, the other American commanders in the area—thought the German artillery was a response to the ongoing attack on the Roer River Dams to the north. They were wrong.

PFC Carl Combs was the assistant squad leader of the 1st Squad, 1st Platoon, Company B. He shared a foxhole with SGT Fred Robertson on the extreme right flank of Company B's defensive line. From their foxhole, the two men could observe the main east-west road into Losheim and the 57mm anti-tank gun position that covered the road. The 57mm gun position was to their right front, well dug in near the road. Once the artillery lifted, the men of Company B emerged from their foxholes to assess the damage. Combs saw the anti-tank men checking their gun. He didn't know the men because they were from the regimental anti-tank company and kept pretty much to themselves.

Combs looked around his area. The effects of the artillery barrage seemed negligible. Save for a few cuts and bruises, everyone was fine. Suddenly, Combs saw the anti-tank men scramble to their gun position. The sound of a vehicle moving up the road from Losheim reached his ears. Combs yelled to his fellow GIs. Everyone jumped into their foxholes. To their astonishment, an American jeep, driven by a couple of German soldiers, drove by them toward Losheimergraben. No one fired. As quickly as it came, the jeep stopped, turned around, and drove back to the east. Still, no one fired. Everyone remained puzzled.

The roar of the jeep's engine again became audible. The jeep came into view again, this time leading a 75mm sturmgeschutze (assault gun). The anti-tank men yelled "Tank!" and jumped behind the blast shield of the gun. They let the jeep pass. The crack of the anti-tank gun broke the silence of the forest. The projectile hit the sturmgeschutze just above the left-side track, causing it to unravel from the road wheels. The assault gun lurched to a halt, the gears grinding as the vehicle spun its wheels. The jeep slowed. Company B's foxholes, located near the road, crackled with rifle fire. The two Germans in the jeep died instantly, one slumping over the wheel, the other falling onto the road. The jeep moved backward erratically before settling in a ditch on the north side of the road.

The anti-tank men had already reloaded their gun and fired, hitting the assault gun just above the front glacis plate. By now, the vehicle was smoking and flames emerged from several apertures. The gun crew reloaded and fired a third and final shot at the smoldering vehicle, again hitting the front hull. A German crew member tried to climb out from a top hatch, but he was quickly cut down by an American sharpshooter. He fell from the top of the vehicle into the ditch beside the road, severely wounded. Just then, the entire vehicle began to shudder as the ammunition inside caught fire and exploded. The assault gun literally jumped on the road as 75mm rounds exploded inside. In seconds, the entire vehicle was completely in flames, finally sliding into the ditch on the north side of the road.

PFC Combs and SGT Robertson watched the smoldering wreck in amazement. The sight of a German vehicle coming down the road had shocked them. Aware that there might be more, the two men settled themselves in their foxhole and waited for the inevitable German attack that would follow.[9]

After receiving his orders from Oberstleutnant Osterhold, Major Kruse acted quickly. He gathered his company commanders. Kruse explained the 1st Battalion's mishap and said the 2nd had to take the lead. He told his commanders to form the battalion in march column for immediate departure.[10] He also instructed them not to mention the fate of the 1st Battalion to their soldiers. The sight of wounded comrades might break their already strained fighting spirit. Kruse led the 2nd Battalion to the north, around the 1st Battalion, avoiding the wounded. The battalion moved rapidly for 30 minutes before Kruse called a halt. He sent runners to find the company commanders. Once the commanders arrived, he spread his map on the forest floor.

"We're here," he began, "approximately 500 meters north of hill 664 and 1,000 meters east of the road intersection at Losheimergraben. I intend to lead Companies 5, 6, and a part of Company 8 up to the customs station at the intersection to probe the position. If I see a chance for success, I'll attack."

The young company commanders listened intently. Major Kruse, a well-decorated veteran of the Eastern front, was being very specific. Their confidence in the major was high, his capabilities represented by the Oakleaves to the Knight's Cross he wore around his neck. Kruse continued the briefing.

"As you well know," he began again, "the forward observer has no contact with the guns, so we'll have to depend on our own firepower. If an attack fails to develop, I'll move behind the intersection and cut the retreat route of the Americans."

Kruse turned and looked into the eyes of his 7th Company commander, Oberleutnant Kurt Steinhofel. Steinhofel had taken command of the company on 22 September 1944, during the defensive fighting around Aachen. He replaced the original commander, who was wounded, and became the youngest company commander in the regiment. He listened intently as Kruse spoke to him.

"Steinhofel," continued Kruse, "I've chosen you and your 7th Company to block the enemy's retreat to the west if they choose to move that way. Because you'll be operating alone on the right wing of the regiment, I'm giving you a machine gun group from the 8th Company. I'll be in the woods north of the customs station at Losheimergraben. I will receive all reports there. Report when you have crossed over and secured the north-south boundary road."

Steinhofel acknowledged the plan. A few commanders asked questions, to which Kruse responded quickly. The officers returned to their companies. Kruse and his command group posted themselves at the head of the 5th Company.

Oberleutnant Steinhofel returned to his company and gathered his platoon leaders. He quickly briefed the leaders on the plan, emphasizing that it was essential to avoid engagement and subsequent delay by American fire. Steinhofel, because of the sparse forest and rolling terrain, chose to split his company into two groups. He created a small security group to move ahead of the main body. This advance guard would make contact with the enemy first, allowing Steinhofel time to maneuver his main force and quickly eliminate any resistance.

The 2nd Battalion soon began moving west, with the main body led by Major Kruse traveling parallel to the Losheim-Losheimergraben road. Steinhofel's 7th Company, with the machine gun section from the 8th Company, moved north to look for an undefended gap in the American lines. Unknown to him, Steinhofel was heading directly for the seam between Companies B and C while Kruse was moving directly for the center of Company B's foxhole line. It was now 0820. The artillery barrage had been over for an hour. The Americans would almost certainly be waiting.

SSG George Ballinger checked his machine gun section after the barrage to ensure that all was well. His positions faced a north-south ravine that extended 500 to 600 meters and stopped at the road to the south. He was in a dugout with three other men, among them SGT Guy Mathena and SGT George Grimm. The third, PVT George Boggs, operated a .30 caliber machine gun. To their right, PFC Alphonse Sito and PVT Clarkson occupied two corners of a three-man position that looked down the ravine on the right. Satisfied everyone was unharmed, SSG Ballinger returned to his dugout.

Ballinger talked to the men in his dugout, speculating on the purpose of the bombardment. He thought he heard voices in the woods to his front. He poked his head out of the dugout and looked around. Ballinger noticed a figure walking in the woods. The German scout moved through the woods as though no danger existed. The scout was a member of Kruse's 5th Company, now on the left flank of Company B. Ballinger watched the scout carefully. The German paused and looked in Ballinger's direction, locking his gaze on the sergeant's eyes. Suddenly, the German disappeared.[11]

"Okay, you guys," said Ballinger, "here comes the attack. Wait till I tell you to fire."

But the attack didn't materialize the way Ballinger envisioned it. Six German soldiers, one carrying an MG42, appeared from the morning mist directly in front of the GIs. They were no more than 60 meters away.

"I can get them," said PVT Boggs. "I've got 'em in my sights."

"No, wait," said Ballinger. "Let's see what happens."

The six Germans milled around, oblivious to any danger. They talked among themselves. Then one of them placed a tripod on the ground. Another set the MG42 on top of it. The MG42 alarmed Ballinger. He ordered Boggs to open fire. The .30 caliber machine gun broke the silence as it ripped into the Germans. The Germans fell. The men in the foxholes around Ballinger took their cue and opened fire.

German troops moving with the machine gun crew now attacked, yelling as they charged. Other Germans took cover in the ravine next to Sito's position. To the right, the Germans attacked Ballinger's machine gun section with a withering hail of small arms fire. Only a two-man team with a Browning Automatic Rifle (BAR) covered the right flank.

Within minutes, attacking German soldiers filled the forest to the front of Ballinger. Major Kruse and his command group were directly behind the attackers, pushing them into the assault. The German grenadiers set up an MG42 machine gun nearby. The steady rate of fire from the MG42 chewed the wood on top of Ballinger's hut into sawdust. But the Company B men still put up a fight. Ballinger, Grimm, and Mathena popped up long enough to get several rounds off with their M1s before the machine gun fire forced them back inside.

As SSG Ballinger came up to fire a second time, he saw a German medic tending a wounded grenadier not five meters away. The man seemed oblivious to the firefight; he shook his fist at Ballinger as the section leader watched him perform first aid on the man. Ballinger's men respected the medic's position. No one fired at him.[12]

Soon, PFC Sito, in the foxhole on Ballinger's right, called out to the section leader.

"Hey," he yelled, "most of the krauts' fire is comin' from my right. I think they're behind us!"

"How many are there?" asked Ballinger.

This time the response came from PVT Clarkson. Clarkson said a German sharpshooter had just killed PFC Sito. He also shouted that the Germans were at the perimeter of his position, yelling and firing from their hips. Ballinger could hear heavy machine guns and mortars from Company D firing behind him, so he knew the Germans must have encircled his position. Ballinger's dugout was on the receiving end of the heaviest concentration of German fire. He couldn't even rise to fire anymore. The wood parapets overhead continued to disintegrate. Ballinger realized the battle was over. He had to surrender or die. Before he could say anything, he heard SGT Mathena speak to him.

"Hey, Ballinger," he said, "look at your pitcher."

SSG Ballinger looked up at the 10-inch ledge of the dugout, created by wood parapets that had been set back. A silver cream pitcher that Ballinger had picked up from somewhere and cleaned sat on it. The pitcher had a German bullet hole in it. Rounds had penetrated the position. Mathena showed him where one of his boot heels had been shot off.

"Listen, you guys," said Ballinger, "this is it. We've gotta give up or we're dead. We did our best."

The men agreed but decided that the Germans wouldn't get their money or valuables. Inside the shelter, the men used a five-gallon can as a heater. They moved it and dug a small hole into which they stuffed personal letters and about $200 in French francs. They quickly buried these items and put the heater back over the hole. SSG Ballinger then took a machine gun cleaning rod and tied a white undershirt to it. He stuck it out one of the openings, and the German small-arms fire stopped instantly.

The Germans shouted for the GIs to come out. SGT Grimm decided to go first. As soon as he emerged, a shot rang out. Grimm dove back inside. A German voice speaking broken English said that it was a mistake, that Grimm should come out again. Grimm ventured forth once more, and Ballinger and Mathena followed. The grenadiers didn't fire. Instead, the Germans milled around, looking for booty and helping their wounded. As Ballinger looked around, he realized some of his men had gotten away. He thought they had been the last to resist in Company B. Apparently he had been wrong. A German soldier approached the three men and spoke to them in excellent English.

"Who are you?" asked the grenadier.

"Americans," answered Ballinger.

The man turned and spoke to several other soldiers behind him. He pointed at the GIs and said "Ami." Several of the Germans smiled and approached the three men. One put his hand on Ballinger's shoulder and nodded approvingly.

"Ami," he said. "Gut soldaten!"

Ballinger suddenly realized that the enemy respected him and his men. They did nothing to harm them and seemed to mingle casually with the GIs. Ballinger turned to Grimm and Mathena and spoke.

"We should see if Sito's still alive," he told them.

The men agreed and attempted to move to Sito's foxhole. The Germans stopped them, though. Ballinger pointed to the foxhole and said he wanted to help a comrade. The German responded in broken English, saying they would take care of it. The three men acquiesced and stood by as instructed. Despite the good treatment, their state of affairs was not good. Capture by the enemy is demoralizing, and Ballinger's men were demoralized. The men had done their best, but they didn't feel that way. The GIs looked up and saw a large group of Germans continuing west. Ballinger and his men were now in enemy-held territory.

Oberleutnant Steinhofel's 7th Company continued northwest, just above the main body of the 2nd Battalion. The 7th had heard the battalion's contact with SSG Ballinger and his crew but avoided the area. Steinhofel knew that if he were to succeed, he would need to avoid decisive contact with any of the

American units. He moved his company quickly, the ground solid despite 10 centimeters of snow. Unknown to Steinhofel at the time, he was moving through an undefended seam between Companies B and C of the 394th Regiment. Called "Creepy Corner" by the Americans, the gap was 200 to 300 meters wide. After moving for several hundred more meters, the ground rose, forming a slight hilltop just east of the main north-south boundary road, known to the Americans as the International Highway, or "California Road."

The company's security element climbed this hill. Steinhofel saw them disappear into the forest 150 meters to his front. Suddenly, the sound of individual rifle shots echoed through the forest. Steinhofel, aware that his security element had made contact, turned and quickly shouted for his men to get down. A messenger sprinted down the hill, arriving at Steinhofel's location short of breath.

"What's going on?" asked Steinhofel.

"There's an enemy position ahead," said the young grenadier.

Steinhofel looked, squinting to see the enemy's defenses. He realized the Americans were probably defending the top of the small hill. Perhaps he could encircle them. He turned and called his 2nd Platoon Leader forward. He gave him very detailed instructions.

"Listen," he began, "there's an enemy position on the rise just up ahead. Move around to the right and attack to the left with a turning movement. Use machine guns and automatic weapons to hold them down. I'll move forward with the rest of the company and do the same from here."

The man nodded, fully understanding. He sped back to his platoon, issued brief instructions, and moved out to the right. The platoon leader's men stayed low as they approached the hill from its northern side.

Steinhofel assembled his 1st Platoon and assigned a machine gun group from the 8th Company to them. He moved the platoon forward within range of the enemy. Within minutes, his 2nd Platoon opened fire on the American foxholes, now visible on the forward slope of the hill. There appeared to be few foxholes judging by the rate of fire. This was in fact true. The withering hail of small-arms fire forced the GIs back inside their holes. The GIs could not return effective fire. Steinhofel ordered his group to open fire. Within seconds the American foxholes were caught in a well-coordinated crossfire. After 10 minutes of continuous fire, the first American soldiers emerged from their holes, hands held high. Steinhofel ordered an immediate cease-fire and got to his feet. He walked forward to the surrendering GIs, waving for them to move from the foxholes. Several grenadiers came forward and searched the men for weapons. They found none.

Oberleutnant Steinhofel consolidated his position on the hill, checking for casualties and counting POWs. There were at least 15 Americans, and the GIs seemed pleased they had made it out alive. The 2nd Platoon Leader approached Steinhofel with a negative casualty report, stating that all of his men were fine. Suddenly, a lone shot rang out. A small hole appeared in the platoon leader's head, right before Steinhofel's very eyes. Everyone took cover, including the American POWs.

"What is it?" yelled Steinhofel.

"Sniper in a foxhole off to the right," came a reply.

A few more shots rang out, barely missing some of the prone grenadiers. Steinhofel looked at two of the American prisoners. He couldn't speak English, but he wanted to tell these two men to get their sniper friend to surrender. The determined and highly irritated look on the German company commander's face convinced them. Both shouted to the sniper in English, saying something incomprehensible to Steinhofel. Within seconds, the sniper emerged from his hole with his hands up. Steinhofel gathered the American prisoners and the lightly wounded Germans and sent them to the rear with two gefreiters. He told the gefreiters to find Major Kruse at the crossroads and inform Kruse that he had reached the boundary road. Steinhofel's plan was to cross the boundary road and turn left behind the crossroads after a brief search of the captured enemy positions. The gefreiters nodded and took their charges east into the forest.

Steinhofel sent a small security force to the boundary road. He wanted to make certain there were no American positions covering the avenue. Crossing the road would be dangerous, for the movement would expose the company to enemy fire. They would be sitting ducks. Steinhofel had to take precautions. As the security element departed, Steinhofel reformed the rest of the company. They moved west a few hundred meters to wait for the security element to return.

As they moved, Steinhofel found, to his surprise, a large tent and several small ones near the captured American foxholes. A quick inspection by his men indicated they were mess tents. There was also a field kitchen overflowing with food. The Americans he captured must have been the guard force for this field kitchen. Steinhofel recognized, at that moment, that he was well to the rear of the enemy's positions.

He had to watch everything around him. His men quickly pilfered the food, stuffing it into their mouths to sate their ravishing hunger. The quality of food in the German Army was poor, and Steinhofel's men hadn't eaten for over 24 hours. Steinhofel partook of the small feast himself. To his astonishment, he drank grapefruit juice from a can, something he had never seen in Germany before. He ate until he was full and then gathered his blissfully stuffed men once again for the movement west.

The security element returned. The element's leader reported that all was quiet on the boundary road. The security force once more in the lead, the 7th Company moved west, hitting the main boundary road within minutes. Steinhofel sent his men over in small teams. The men dashed across the road into the safety of the dense underbrush on the other side. Within minutes, the entire company was across, reformed, and moving west. Oberleutnant Steinhofel warned his men to be cautious. They were now behind enemy lines. Loose bands of American soldiers, separated from their units by the fighting, might be wandering the forest. Steinhofel wanted to avoid encountering Americans at all costs.

The company passed the Losheimergraben Crossroads. The intersection was clearly visible down the road to the south. Steinhofel's movement paralleled the east-west Bullingen road. He encountered no opposition from American forces. He stayed to the left of his formation and looked back at the road and intersection with his binoculars to make sure the enemy wouldn't deploy reserves against him. So far, all was quiet and trouble free. At noontime, the company reached a position 800 meters west of the crossroads. Steinhofel placed a platoon on each side of the road. He told them to prepare defensive positions oriented east. Their mission was to prevent the Americans from retreating. Steinhofel was confident that he had the Americans encircled along the Bullingen-Losheimergraben road.

Steinhofel quickly formed a reconnaissance patrol from one of his platoons. He intended to probe the enemy positions from behind. The patrol would move back east toward the crossroads. While he briefed the patrol, a small group of Americans suddenly appeared on the road. The GIs moved directly toward his positions. Strangely enough, men from his platoons, positioned on either side of the road, waved at them and called them over. The Americans, curious to see who waved, walked over to one of the platoons and into captivity. This same scenario repeated itself for about a half hour. Steinhofel captured over 30 American prisoners.

The recon patrol departed east. The early afternoon sky became darker. Dusk was not far off.

Steinhofel sat by a tree with some of his men, waiting and hoping that Major Kruse and the rest of the battalion would arrive shortly. If they didn't, he and his men would have to spend a dark, nervous night deep within the American lines. The young company commander found this thought unappealing.

After taking SSG Ballinger's positions, Major Kruse and the main body of the 2nd Battalion pushed through to the rear of Company B's foxhole line. Once there, Kruse sent his 5th Company south to attack the American positions down to their right flank. Other elements from the battalion moved north, searching for remaining enemy soldiers.

The 5th Company slammed into the American foxhole line from the north, systematically moving south from one foxhole to another. Several Company B soldiers left their foxholes and headed west, many in small, organized groups. Kruse realized that they might attempt to reestablish another defensive line by the boundary road. Many Americans stayed in their foxholes, however, fighting with a determination that awed the young German grenadiers. Germans crawled forward and stuffed grenades inside individual foxholes to eliminate the opposition. The Germans suffered heavy casualties.

The retreating GIs sprinting to the west looked back over their shoulders to witness incredible acts of bravery. Young German grenadiers risked their lives rushing the foxholes, firing their StG 44s from the hip. Many never made it.

The GIs saw Americans like T/SGT Edward Dolenc, from an attached heavy machine gun platoon, firing his machine gun with 20 or more Germans piled up in front of it.[13]

On Company B's right flank, the Germans faced the fury of SSG James F. Murray, Jr., as they approached the crossroads from the north. SSG Murray had his entire squad wiped out by German fire. In desperation, he grabbed a BAR from a wounded man and charged the attacking grenadiers from the 5th Company. Murray made it within 10 feet of the Germans before they cut him down with machine gun fire.[14]

The assault was a slow and deadly process, but the Germans finally managed to reach the main east-west road a few hundred meters east of the intersection. By this time, Company B had lost over 60 percent of its combat power. The company commander and those of his men who escaped established a hasty defensive line back near the boundary road concentrated on the crossroads. SGT Lilly's 60mm mortar section from Company B's weapons platoon managed to avoid German contact. The remnants of a rifle platoon, with the help of one of the mortar sergeants, SGT Kermit Ball, protected Lilly's section while the mortar men set up their guns. SGT Lilly gave PFC Gamber and "Big Moose" a field phone and several sets of aiming stakes. Within minutes, Lilly was giving fire commands at the request of one of the attached Company D machine gun section leaders. The men managed to fire, but the results were unknown.[15]

The men of Company B had taken the full brunt of a German battalion and managed to have something left to fight with. The survivors remained in the area long enough to give the German grenadiers more problems, specifically with the taking of the road intersection and the customs houses.

Major Kruse moved his command post to the northeast corner of the intersection. His 5th Company established hasty defensive positions in the forest. He could see the customs houses across the street, full of American soldiers willing to fight. But Kruse had shot his bolt. He had taken too many casualties. He needed time to consolidate and reorganize.

He desperately needed to move the rest of his battalion across the boundary road and link up with Steinhofel's 7th Company. Kruse could hear small-arms fire. His battalion was clearing American pockets of resistance missed earlier. Exhausted, Kruse looked at his watch. It was nearly noon. His men had fought for over two hours in the Company B foxhole line. And it wasn't over either. Others were still in contact to the north.

On Company B's left flank to the north, PFC Charles Kent and SSG Bill Sears occupied foxholes that overlooked a small field in the forest. Sears was a rifle squad leader in the 3rd Platoon, and Kent was his assistant. Several other men were in foxholes nearby. Once the 3rd Platoon lost contact with Company C on their left, T/SGT Wesley Kibler, the platoon sergeant, repositioned the platoon to watch the field. The positions were several yards from each other. Both Kent and Sears had listened intently to the battle raging north, south, and east of them. They clearly heard the Germans engaging SSG Ballinger's position and then moving down the line. Strangely enough, the German attack down the Company B foxhole line had missed them. But they knew the Germans would return to finish the job. Sears and Kent nervously awaited their own encounter with the grenadiers.[16]

Soon, the small-arms fire abated. No attack came. The Germans, who had overrun most of their platoon's area, withdrew into the forest. The men waited for nearly two hours, wondering what was happening. Besides Sears and Kent, only a few Americans remained. This small group of GIs fought an eerie sense of isolation and fear. Suddenly, PFC Kent heard something in the forest nearby. From his foxhole, he saw a column of 50 to 75 men walking behind Company B's foxhole line to the southeast, straight across the field they were watching.

"Hey, SGT Sears!" yelled Kent. "Who are these guys? Are they ours?"

"I dunno," returned Sears. "Their helmets are awfully dark."

Suddenly, both men realized the men were Germans. Sears and Kent leveled their rifles and fired into the column. Each man hit a few Germans.

But the grenadiers moved quickly to the east and out of sight. Within minutes, the Germans reappeared, screaming and yelling at the tops of their lungs. The grenadiers fired their rifles and machine guns into several foxholes. This tactic killed many of the Company B men. German mortar rounds, hastily employed by the grenadiers, impacted near the dugouts. The rounds fell dangerously close to the attacking Germans.

Several shards of hot shrapnel hit SSG Sears, wounding him severely. He felt as though his entire right side was paralyzed. Kent emerged from his position, moved to the rear of the foxhole line, and took cover behind a tree. Kent could see other GIs had done the same. He saw the familiar face of a character nicknamed Mudcat.[17] Both acknowledged the other's presence with a nod, then remained silent. Kent watched the Germans take several of his comrades prisoner, including the wounded SSG Sears. The grenadiers pulled Sears from the same foxhole which they shared earlier that morning and stripped Sears of his field equipment.

Kent saw the major German force withdraw east with their prisoners, forward of the foxhole line. They didn't bother with stragglers, like him, who were hiding in the underbrush. Suddenly, a German soldier appeared on top of Kent's old foxhole, the one Kent and Sears had previously occupied. The grenadier was taking one last look. Kent put the man in his sights and fired. The German dropped instantly. Several Germans rushed to the area. They searched for stragglers, checking the foxholes.

By now, PFC Kent's hands were too cold to reload his rifle. He waved his arms to warm them. Suddenly, he heard the sound of someone rushing up behind him. His weapon was empty. He knew he was going to get shot or take a bayonet in the back. He rolled over onto his back and expected the worst. To his surprise, it was Mudcat who jumped down beside him. The man had just risked detection by the probing grenadiers.

"Why in the hell did you run up on me like that?" demanded Kent.

"You were slinging your hand, and I thought you were signaling me to come," he replied.

"No," said Kent, "I was trying to get my hand warm enough to jam another clip in my rifle."

"Oh," said Mudcat.

The Germans, after an unsuccessful search, moved off to the west. Kent, Mudcat, and the remaining GIs formed a small group and moved southwest. The GIs avoided enemy encounters in the German-infested forest. They later took refuge in the customs houses near the crossroads.

These men represented the last of Company B from the original foxhole line. Kruse's 2nd Battalion had either killed or captured 60 percent of these men and driven the rest back several hundred meters to the boundary road. Kruse accomplished this task in a few hours, without help from Moldenhauer's depleted battalion. Oberstleutnant Osterhold was still near the start line with the 1st Battalion. Osterhold tried to organize the 1st Battalion's survivors to assist the 2nd Battalion, but with no luck. Too many 1st Battalion men were wounded or in shock. Despite Kruse's success, the battle was far from over. The 394th's 1st Battalion remained for the Germans to contend with.

CHAPTER 5

Fusiliers in the Flank

Company A of the 1st Battalion, 394th Infantry, endured the German artillery barrage rather well. Company A's men had constructed large log huts with very solid and thick overhead cover, but a few had not. Men became casualties as a result. Company A's GIs initially thought the bombardment interesting, mainly because for the first hour or so the rounds landed far to the west, on the American rear positions. But when the artillery found its way to Company A, the men no longer thought the barrage interesting; instead, they found it terrifying.

LT Willard W. Clark, the commander of Company A, planned his defense with two platoons on the line, the southernmost platoon bent slightly to face the area of Losheim in the southeast. Clark kept an additional platoon in reserve west of the north-south Losheimergraben-Lanzerath road, 200 meters southwest of the road intersection. Company A was on the southern flank of the 1st Battalion; their right limit was the east-west railroad cutting that originated in Germany. Company A, along with the 3rd Battalion to its rear, formed the forward right flank of the entire 99th Division. Company D's 81mm mortar platoon, led by 1LT John W. Vaughan, supported Company A. Company D also offered some heavy machine gun support; these machine guns were mixed in among the Company A fighting positions. In addition, two 57mm anti-tank guns from the regimental Anti-Tank Company, commanded by CPT Harold Z. Moore, covered the logging trails and fire breaks that ran through Company A's defensive sector. One 57mm gun covered the Losheim-Losheimergraben-Lanzerath road network between the company's main foxhole line and the reserve platoon. Several forward observation posts from Cannon Company protected Company A from surprise attacks. When the barrage ceased, Company A and their cohorts would have their fair share of contact with the enemy.

Behind Company A, 200 meters southwest of the Losheimergraben intersection, sat the 81mm mortars of Company D. 1LT Vaughan, the mortar platoon leader, used a small, battered forest house nearby for a command post. A few meters north was a wooden shack where men from the mortar platoon rotated guard duty. LT Vaughan was inside when the artillery began. He sat and listened to the roar of distant guns. He turned to LT William Vacha, a forward observer attached to the platoon, and asked, "What do you make of this barrage?"

"Damned if I know," answered Vacha. "Seems pretty intense. It seems to be coming closer."

"Yeah," said Vaughan glumly. "It's definitely creeping toward us."

Vacha rose and walked to the front door of the house. He stepped outside and looked east. He moved quickly back inside and closed the door. It was 0630 in the morning and still very dark outside.

"Geez," he said as he sat back down, "it definitely is closer. I hope everyone's in his hole out there."

"They should be," said Vaughan. "Word went out for everyone to stay put until this passed."

"What do you make of those searchlights bouncing off the clouds outside?" asked Vacha.

"Don't know," answered Vaughan. "Maybe the Germans are trying to spook us with a light show."

Outside the command post, near the wooden guard shack, PFC Bob Newbrough and two other privates from the platoon stood guard. They watched the flashes of artillery against the western horizon. The men shuddered slightly in the cold as the roar of each impact hit their ears. The searchlights filled the sky to the east. The glow formed bizarre and eerie shadows on the hanging gray clouds.[1]

"Boy," said Newbrough, "that artillery's lasting a while."

"Yeah," returned one of the privates, "but what about those lights?"

"Who knows?" answered Newbrough. "Wow, that artillery seems to be coming our way. We might have to make a run for the holes pretty soon."

"Nah," said the other private," the krauts are just goin' after the guys in the rear. They want to spoil that show with Marlene Dietrich in Honsfeld, that's all."

"They don't know about her," jeered the other private.

"Oh, yeah," he returned, "them Jerries know everything."

Suddenly, the ground around the men erupted in a cascade of dirt and snow. All three soldiers fell backwards. Several more German artillery rounds landed nearby. The trees splintered and cracked. Newbrough saw the rounds landing around him clearly as the sky brightened with the light of morning.

"Hey!" yelled Newbrough. "Head for the shack!"

The men jumped to their feet and bolted straight for the old shack that served as their guard post. The artillery fell around them. The men ran through

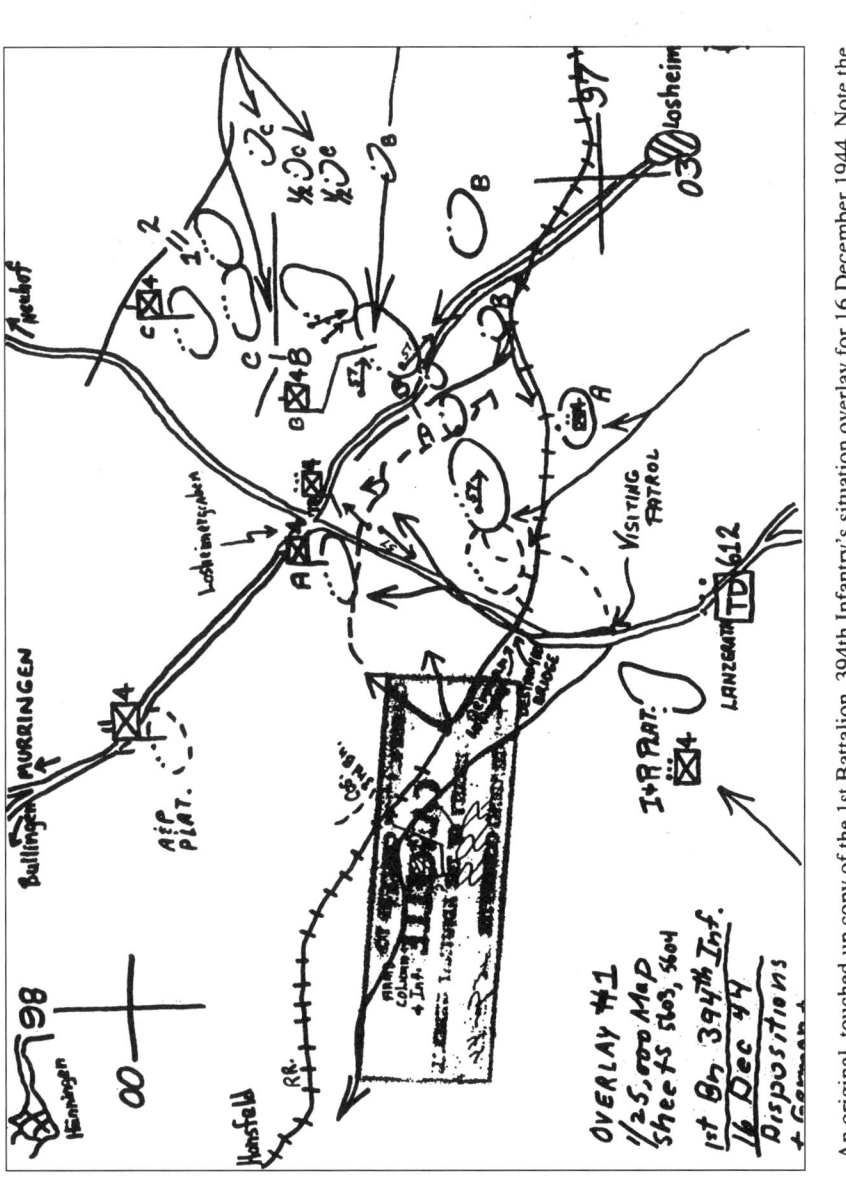

An original, touched-up copy of the 1st Battalion, 394th Infantry's situation overlay for 16 December 1944. Note the designation of the tank destroyer unit in Lanzerath, which reads 612 instead of 820. Elements of the 820th replaced a similar element of the 612th on 10 December. Courtesy Richard Byers/National Archives.

a gauntlet of flying snow and dirt. They made it safely to the shack where they discovered a cellar and took refuge.

Inside the battered forest house, LTs Vaughan and Vacha lay flat on the floor with other members of the platoon. They hoped the CP would not receive a direct hit. Rounds landed within meters of the old building. It shuddered from the impact. The rounds fell for several minutes, spraying dust and dirt on the prostrate men. CPL George Bero got up to check the platoon's radio, which sat on a table nearby. He pulled the radio onto the floor to protect it from damage. Just then, an artillery round landed directly outside the back wall of the house. Tiny fragments perforated the wall. Hot metal splinters flew about the room and made a tinkling sound as they landed around the men. Some of the hot metal fell on the back of LT Vacha's neck. He swore under his breath. Suddenly, he heard a gurgling sound to his right and looked up. CPL Bero rolled over onto his back. Blood flowed from a severe shrapnel wound to his throat.

"Hey!" yelled Vacha. "Bero's hurt!"

Vaughan and Vacha crawled to him. Both men flinched as the artillery shells continued to land outside.

"Stop the bleeding!" shouted Vacha. "He'll die in a few seconds if we don't!"

Bero lay on his back, eyes slightly open. He made an occasional gurgling sound as the blood interrupted his breathing. The two officers, with the help of other soldiers from the platoon, tried vainly to stem the flow of blood from the wounded man. Both men clamped hard on his throat with their hands, but the blood continued to flow, forming a large pool. LT Vacha realized that Bero had stopped breathing.[2]

"I think he's dead," said Vacha.

"You're right," mumbled Vaughan. "Damn!"

Their anger at the soldier's death was short-lived. Another artillery round burst outside. They decided the cellar would be safer and quickly crawled down the basement stairs for refuge. The barrage continued for another hour. The bombardment forced everyone to seek cover.

The barrage hit Company A's positions as well. The log huts built with strong overhead cover proved effective. Most of these foxholes stood the artillery's test, but men became casualties in the foxholes that lacked this overhead protection. Unfortunately, a few men built dugouts with their comfort, not protection, in mind.

LT Clark, the company commander, realized that phone communications with the platoons had ceased to exist. The artillery had destroyed all wire lines. Clark received an occasional radio report from his platoons; he learned they were fine save for some minor casualties. Clark told the platoons to keep down until the artillery passed. The German rounds were well-placed and landed directly inside the company sector. Anyone who ventured forth from the dugouts would be dead in seconds.

Oberstleutnant Heinz-Georg Lemm, commander of Fusilier Regiment 27, left his assembly area southwest of Frauenkron with no problems. His axis of attack was south of and parallel to Oberstleutnant Wilhelm Osterhold's Grenadier Regiment 48, which moved in the north. Lemm chose to move his 1st Battalion along the high ground north of the railroad cutting before the artillery even lifted. His 3rd Battalion traveled on the railroad tracks below. Lemm had his battalions attacking abreast, with only a small company reserve following behind. He wanted to speed his men along to exploit any success made by either battalion. He had only two battalions, the 1st and 3rd, when the regiment reformed in July; there was no 2nd Battalion.[3]

Lemm's intermediate objective was Losheim, about 2,500 meters southeast of Losheimergraben. His men took Losheim quickly and without a fight. The 394th had established observation posts there, but none was manned when the fusiliers entered the town. Lemm kept moving west. He hoped to reach a point south of the Losheimergraben Crossroads and then swing north and envelop the intersection in concert with Osterhold's attack. His battalions made swift progress. The fusiliers moved straight toward the thunderous artillery.

A long-time veteran of the Eastern front, Lemm couldn't remember such a fierce barrage. The power of the German artillery attack put spirit into his heart. He wanted this operation to succeed so Germany wouldn't suffer as much when the war ended. He knew Germany was certain to lose, but he voiced his opinion only with his close friend, Oberstleutnant Osterhold; both Lemm and Osterhold shared the same belief. They served together in the division as young officers in every campaign, even competing, in a lighthearted way, to see who would get what decoration first. Lemm received his Knight's Cross of the Iron Cross before Osterhold, but Lemm's friend quickly caught up to him.[4] As close, personal friends, their confidence in each other was immeasurable. They only wanted to win this battle so Germany might force the Allies into a position that would forego the previously stated notion of "unconditional surrender." This term struck both Lemm and Osterhold to the core. They didn't want the innocent of Germany to suffer for the crimes of the few.

Despite the difficult terrain north of the rail line, Lemm's 1st Battalion made excellent progress. His only experienced officer, Hauptmann Claus Breger, commanded that battalion. Like Lemm, Breger was a veteran of the Eastern front who realized he had to lead raw recruits from the front. He was there now, in the lead element.

Breger guided the battalion swiftly through the forest. Despite their inexperience, the battalion remained silent. Breger passed a small ridge on his right which overlooked Losheim to the southeast. The ridge normally hosted an observation post from the 394th's Cannon Company during the day. At night, and on this night, the OP team, led by 2LT Bernard Epstein, was in one of the customs houses at the crossroads where the GIs spent their nights. If the observers had been there, they would have been able to reach out and shake hands with Hauptmann Breger as he and his men passed by.

Lemm moved directly behind Breger's battalion. He occasionally looked down into the railroad cutting to check the progress of his 3rd Battalion. Lemm could hear the artillery beginning to wane. The barrage had lasted nearly two hours. According to his map, he was close to the crossroads. He wanted to swing northwest quickly and take the intersection. He was 800 meters away, and the going was smooth. He located Hauptmann Breger and instructed him to swing his battalion north. The artillery had lifted at this point; Lemm now wondered when the sturmgeschutzen (assault guns) would move against the crossroads to his north. Lemm wanted to attack in concert with the sturmgeschutze assault and the 48th's attack, but his radio operator couldn't contact either Oberstleutnant Osterhold to the north or Major Holz's assault guns in the east. Lemm chose to move forward, hoping to bypass any American opposition. The 1st Battalion swung north.

Several pairs of eyes observed their movement, however. These eyes belonged to the platoon observation posts from Company A. The GIs immediately reported the German formation to their platoon leaders, who in turn notified LT Clark. It was now 0745. The battle was set to begin.

Hauptmann Breger heard his men come into contact with the American positions to the northwest as he moved through the forest. To Breger, it sounded as though the firing came from his right near the main road. He moved forward to get a report from his lead company commander. As he moved, the rest of his battalion followed. The fusiliers also heard firing to their right; they moved with caution. The element of surprise was gone. The new recruits knew the Americans would be waiting for them. The fusiliers were frightened; most had never seen combat.

Hauptmann Breger looked for his lead company commander as he moved north through the snow-covered forest. Some of his men took cover behind some trees. He approached their position. Small-arms fire erupted to Breger's left. He could hear the roar of Browning Automatic Rifles (BARs) and machine guns. The Germans had stumbled onto Company A's hastily dug alternate foxhole line south of the main road. Breger dove for cover. He crawled forward to see how the Americans had arrayed their positions. He rushed next to his lead company commander, who shouted orders to move forward. But the Germans indicated no desire to rush the foxholes. Breger realized that his lead company had blundered into the enemy's primary engagement area.

The withering flurry of small-arms fire continued. A young soldier from Company A, PFC Arthur Mings, popped his head up from his fighting position to look for the Germans.[5] Satisfied he had a target, Mings took aim and fired. The men in Ming's platoon had suffered a few light casualties in the early morning artillery barrage. But they caught Breger's unit completely by surprise.

News of the impending German attack came first from the forward OP. The GIs had left their well-prepared positions and occupied alternate, partially completed backup positions to meet the assault. The deadly hail of bullets coming from the men of Company A made it difficult for the Germans to return fire. The fusiliers took tremendous casualties. Many wounded Germans moaned in agony.

Mings took his time and fired well-aimed shots with his M1. He noticed a man crawling forward from behind the German formation. The man shouted in German as he moved. Mings surmised he was an officer trying to get his soldiers moving. Most Germans were hiding behind trees. Mings took aim with his M1. Just then, the man got to his feet, turned, and sprinted to the rear. Mings hesitated to shoot a man in the back. Suddenly, a shot rang out from a foxhole nearby. The German fell forward onto the snow. The man screamed as he hit.

Several Germans jumped up, firing from the hip as they moved back. The rest took a cue and fired at the American positions as well. The GIs ducked down in the shallow foxholes. As soon as the firing stopped, the GIs popped their heads up. The German fusiliers were gone, save for several wounded, and the dead leader. The Americans emerged from their foxholes and went forward to help the soldiers moaning in the snow.

PFC Mings approached the body of the dead officer. Mings turned him over. He wanted to make certain the man was dead. The German was fairly young. Mings opened the man's jacket and searched for documents. He found several pieces of paper in a pocket of the man's tunic. He noticed that the man's uniform was covered with impressive looking medals and ribbons. Mings recognized an Iron Cross. Mings sorted through the various papers. He found a typed message in German which appeared to have been freshly printed. He couldn't read the text, but he noticed the name "von Rundstedt" on the bottom. He had heard the name before, and the document looked important. He examined a small, brown passbook with the word "Soldbuch" on the cover. Inside, he saw a picture of the dead officer in his uniform, an excellent likeness. He couldn't read the German text, but the man's name was on the first page.

"Claus Br-Bre-ger," he muttered to himself. "Looks like an officer."

Mings stuffed the papers in his pocket to give to his platoon leader. He looked at the small passbook again, shrugged, then dropped it on the man's chest.

"Probably a nobody," he mumbled.

PFC William Kirkbride was a 57mm anti-tank gunner in the 1st Platoon of the AT Company.[6] His platoon, commanded by LT Gifford Benson, had established three gun positions with three 10-man squads. The platoon sergeant, T/SGT Arthur C. Piar, deployed the guns to cover the roads into the 1st Battalion sector. Because the platoon supported the entire battalion, only two guns were with Company A. Kirkbride was with a gun crew forward of Company A's reserve platoon, east of the north-south Losheimergraben-Lanzerath road. Kirkbride and his gun crew covered a firebreak in the woods, the Lanzerath road to the south, and part of the Losheim-Losheimergraben road to the north. Company A's main defensive line, consisting of two platoons, was forward of Kirkbride's gun position.

When the artillery fire subsided, Kirkbride and another crew member, PFC Angelo Esultante, returned to their position to check the gun. The two men had waited out the barrage in a log hut several meters to the rear of the gun position.

"How's she look?" asked Kirkbride as Esultante looked at the breech.

"It's okay," answered Esultante. "No damage. We're damn lucky, too. That artillery was everywhere."

"No kidding," said Kirkbride. "Do you see anything happening on the road? I'm sure the Germans have gotta try something after all those fireworks."

"Nope, not a thing...," came the answer, but the man's voice trailed off.

Both anti-tank men turned and looked toward the eastern woodline.

"Did you hear something?" asked Kirkbride.

"Yeah," said Esultante quietly.

Both men listened. They could hear the sound of sporadic rifle fire coming from the direction of Company A's foxhole line. The firing subsided within minutes. The puzzled men looked at each other.

"What was that?" asked Kirkbride.

"I don't know," answered Esultante. "Maybe the guys are gettin' jittery 'cause of the artillery."

Both men shrugged. They checked and oiled the 57mm gun. Kirkbride inspected the ammunition supply to make sure the artillery hadn't damaged any rounds. The morning was cold. The men rubbed their hands together and stuffed them into their pockets to keep them warm.

Suddenly, an entire platoon of Germans from Lemm's 1st Battalion appeared from the woods to the south. The fusiliers tried to avoid the foxhole line by circling Company A's right flank and driving straight for the crossroads to the north. This route paralleled the Lanzerath-Losheimergraben road. Both parties paused for a moment, stunned. The Germans opened fire. MP40 and StG 44 rounds sprayed Kirkbride and Esultante. Several fusiliers took cover in a gully south of the main road and set up an MG42 machine gun. Kirkbride and Esultante dove behind the 3/8-inch steel shield on the anti-tank gun. Both men covered their heads with their arms as rifle and machine gun fire pinged off the metal plate.

"We've gotta run for it!" yelled Kirkbride.

"Well, let's go!" shouted Esultante.

Both men sprinted for the woods to their rear, dodging German bullets that severed small twigs from the trees around them. Kirkbride and Esultante headed straight for their section's dugout, shouting at friends as they approached.

"Grab your rifles and move out!" shouted Kirkbride. "The krauts are right behind us!"

Kirkbride followed the others who ran toward Company A's reserve platoon positions. Most of the men only had .45 caliber pistols; there were only six M1s between them. Kirkbride looked over his shoulder as he ran. He saw three German soldiers hot on his heels. Kirkbride sped up. Suddenly, to his front, he saw a foxhole with two GIs looking out. Kirkbride prepared to yell when one of the men manning a BAR aimed it directly at Kirkbride. Kirkbride inhaled. A moment of sheer terror overcame him. The machine gunner fired. The rounds missed him. They went high and over his left shoulder. Kirkbride spun around. The three Germans fell backward. Blood streamed from the fusiliers' wounds as they landed on the thin layer of snow in the forest. One appeared to be an officer. The other two were a machine gun crew, complete with an MG42 and ammunition belts strapped across their chests. Kirkbride, wide-eyed and exasperated, turned and looked at the machine gunner. The man smiled with a big grin.

"We knew they were coming," said the man. "OP told us."

Kirkbride nervously resumed his retreat west. He passed through the Company A reserve platoon's foxhole line where he saw his crew stopping for a quick rest. Kirkbride approached and, somewhat recovered, addressed the men.

"The platoon leader and the platoon sergeant aren't around," began Kirkbride. "The section sergeant's missing, so I'm gonna take charge. Got any problem with that?"

The men shook their heads, glad someone was taking control. The actual gunner in the crew was a corporal, who outranked Kirkbride, but both the gunner and the missing section sergeant had made it clear before the battle that they would not give orders that might cost a life. And the corporal silently accepted Kirkbride's leadership. The men rose and followed their new leader to the rear, hoping to find someone in charge from Company A or D.

PFC Bob Newbrough emerged from the cellar of his guard shack when the artillery lifted. He and the other two men shook themselves off. They noticed that many of their fellow platoon members were carrying wounded men to the command post.[7] Newbrough decided to help. He walked to the house that served as CP and looked around. Several men from Companies A and D lay near the old, battered house. The men groaned from shrapnel wounds. Newbrough heard the door of the house open. Two men carrying a covered body struggled through the doorway. They set the lifeless form next to a tree, away from the wounded men.

"Who's this?" asked Newbrough.

"CPL Bero," came the answer. "He got some shrapnel in the neck. Bled to death."

Newbrough moved his hand to his throat. He knew Bero. It stunned him to see the corporal's corpse under the tree. He turned away and surveyed the damage. Most men had left their 81mm mortar positions and milled about, trying to be of help to the wounded. He could hear LT Vaughan inside the house. Vaughan was giving a casualty report to the company commander on the radio. LT Vacha, the platoon's forward observer, and LT Marion McQuarry, another officer from Company D, ventured from the hut. Newbrough walked slowly toward the wounded.

"Hey, McQuarry, I think we should check the gun positions for damage, don't you?" asked Vacha.

"Good idea," said McQuarry.

Both men walked south. The officers looked into each gun pit and checked the condition of the mortars. Most of the tubes were near firebreaks to allow for ease of firing. As McQuarry and Vacha walked, they tried to determine the caliber of the German artillery rounds by analyzing their craters.

"Not all of these rounds were 105s," said Vacha. "I'd say some probably came from those big rocket launchers the Germans have. These craters are pretty big."

"Yeah," said McQuarry, "it's a wonder they didn't do more damage."

Both men continued through the forest. Two of the platoon's jeeps, each with a trailer, took direct hits. The vehicles and trailers were rendered inoperable. Twisted hunks of metal in grotesque shapes were all that remained.

"Well," sighed Vacha. "I'd better go back and tell Vaughan that we lost some vehicles."

Suddenly, both men heard firing to their left front. They paused and listened again. The sound of small arms fire echoed through the forest. It was very distinctive.

"Who do you think that is?" asked Vacha.

"Don't know," answered McQuarry, "but I thought I saw something over there..."

The officer never finished his sentence. A German fusilier jumped from the underbrush and fired from the hip with an MP40. The rounds struck McQuarry in the chest and stomach. McQuarry pitched forward and then backward.[8] His body slammed into Vacha. The impact knocked Vacha to the ground. The Germans, assuming they had killed both men, stepped over them and fired in the direction of the CP. Although the GIs at the CP hadn't yet seen the Germans, they ran for cover, diving for their foxholes. Well over 30 Germans emerged from the forest from the south. The fusiliers fired as they moved.

LT Vacha struggled from under LT McQuarry's body. All too quickly he realized the young officer was dead. McQuarry's lifeless eyes stared blankly into space. Vacha shook his head sadly. Behind him, the Germans were moving against the mortar positions. He could hear still other Germans shouting in the bushes to his front. Vacha was trapped between them. He jumped upright and dashed into the bushes, circling back to the old, dilapidated house that had served as LT Vaughan's CP.

PFC Newbrough heard the firing coming directly at him and dove for cover. Many of the wounded could do nothing except lie flat on the ground to avoid further injury. Disregarding the incoming fire, Newbrough got to his knees and looked around. He saw several GIs making for their foxholes, and he decided to do the same. An unoccupied gun position next to a firebreak was his best choice. But the Germans were only a few meters away from the hole and moving parallel with the firebreak. Newbrough took the chance and sprang to his feet. He dodged German bullets as he ran beside the approaching formation and dove into the gun pit. To his surprise, a sergeant and a corporal joined him. Up to now, Newbrough hadn't seen the Germans. He knew where they were by their fire and their shouts. But they had remained an invisible enemy to him.

Suddenly, a German face popped from the underbrush not three meters from Newbrough's gun position. Both men stared at each other, surprised by the proximity of their encounter. Newbrough noticed the man had a stick grenade in his hand. The German disappeared within seconds. Newbrough breathed a sigh of relief. It was the first German he had seen in the war, and Newbrough must have been the first American the German had seen as well. Newbrough fired a few token rounds into the bush. By now, he could see Germans moving all around him. The Germans were intertwined with the mortar platoon's positions, firing as they moved. Some GIs behind Newbrough opened fire. But the Germans kept moving.

"Does that field phone work?" Newbrough asked the sergeant with him.

The sergeant turned the handle of the phone. The man reached a radio operator in LT Vaughan's CP.

"We're under attack!" yelled the sergeant into the receiver. "What does the lieutenant want us to do?"

The sergeant listened for a moment. He strained to hear over the din of small arms fire. He put the receiver down and faced Newbrough and the corporal.

"The lieutenant's gonna call in artillery," he said above the noise. "It'll be close. We've gotta watch out."

"Are you kidding?!" shouted Newbrough. "We'll all get killed! What about our mortars? I'd feel safer with them!"

The sergeant called the suggestion in. The man could hear voices talking on the switchboard.

"The LT's telling SGT Stumpff to fire his mortars in front of our position," said the sergeant. "He wants us to adjust. He musta read your mind, huh?"

"Who knows?" shouted Newbrough.

Back at the CP house, LT Vaughan told Section SGT Delbert Stumpff to fire mortars onto the German formation south of the platoon's position. Their gun positions were just behind Newbrough and the others, so the guns' elevation would have to be maximized. Since the tubes faced east, Stumpff ordered his men to swing them around to the south. SGT Stumpff barked orders to his men.[9]

"C'mon, hurry up!" yelled Stumpff. "Pull all the increments off the rounds. We only want 'em to land a few feet from here!"

"What elevation?" asked a gunner.

"89 degrees!" came the response.[10]

"Gun one up!" shouted a gunner.

"Gun two up!" came another.

"Fire!" yelled Stumpff.

The rounds popped from the tubes. Stumpff yelled "Incoming!" to those around him. The mortar rounds impacted five meters from Newbrough's position. The ground shook as the rounds hit. Newbrough and the others heard a distinct popping sound as the rounds left the tubes. Newbrough felt secure, however; he had trained with these men and trusted them completely. He much preferred a barrage from them to one from an artillery unit firing from the rear.

The mortar rounds fell among the attacking Germans with deadly accuracy. The fusiliers dispersed in all directions. When some attempted to return fire, shrapnel quickly wounded or killed them. Many fusiliers sought safety in the forest, but the mortars found them there as well. The sergeant with Newbrough talked incessantly on the field phone, adjusting the mortar rounds as necessary. To the sergeant's rear, SGT Stumpff continued to bark out fire commands to his gun crews. The gunners performed magnificently. The German attack was completely off balance.

In the forest to the west of the mortar platoon and Company A's position, 1SG Lyle O. Frank, the Company A first sergeant, was returning through the woods from a mission in the rear support area.[11] He had three other GIs with him who had served on the detail. Frank heard firing to his front and chided the men to hurry. To his left, he heard mortar rounds impact 300 meters away. The men broke through the dense underbrush. Suddenly, the GIs stumbled upon an entire company of Germans from the 1st Battalion, 27th Fusilier Regiment. The fusiliers were moving north to reinforce comrades in contact with Company D's mortar platoon. Frank motioned the men to stop and be silent.

"Do you guys remember marching fire?" he asked.

They nodded apprehensively.

"I don't know what's happening, but we're gonna get these Germans," Frank said in a low voice. "I want you to get on line. When I say 'go,' start firing your rifle from the hip every time your left foot hits the ground."

The men nodded and lined up next to Frank. They made sure their M1s were loaded.

"All right," said Frank, "let's go!"

The men stepped off and immediately fired into the German formation's flank. The Germans looked to their left, stunned by the small group's surprise attack. The four GIs maintained a steady rate of fire as they moved. The volume of fire created the illusion of a much larger force. Several Germans fell to the ground, the wounded screaming in pain. Instead of going to the ground, the fusiliers withdrew to the south. In their haste to flee the Americans' small-arms fire, the Germans bumped into each other. As the last German disappeared into the forest, 1SG Frank held up his hand. The men ceased fire. The four men stood near the wounded and dead Germans lying on the ground, about 10 in all.

"Well, what do you think, fellas?" asked Frank, with a nervous smile on his face. "We just routed a whole bunch of krauts!"

The men smiled back but quickly turned their attention to the wounded men at their feet. They administered first aid and tried to make the wounded men as comfortable as possible.

"We'll stay here," said Frank. "I still hear mortars to the north. Just lie low until I find out what this is all about."

The men nodded and then bandaged the wounded German soldiers, who smiled gratefully at the concerned GIs.

By the time 1SG Frank attacked the rear of the German formation, the fusiliers at the mortar platoon's position had withdrawn under extreme pressure from the deadly mortar rounds. Many simply turned tail and retreated to the southwest. Some fusiliers sought refuge on the high ground north of the railroad tracks. Within minutes, all that remained of the German attack were the dead and wounded bodies of Lemm's fusiliers. The sergeant in Newbrough's gun position called SGT Stumpff and told him to stop firing. The forest fell silent except for the occasional groan or gasp of a wounded soldier. The smell of cordite was strong.

Newbrough emerged from his gun position and walked among the dead and dying Germans. Many writhed in pain. Their hideous facial contortions forced Newbrough to look away. He felt sick to his stomach, but he suppressed his nausea. Other soldiers assisted the wounded Germans. He joined them. Miraculously, no Americans were wounded by the mortar fire. But the carnage among the German ranks was incredible. Newbrough counted over forty Germans on the ground around him, a staggering loss for Lemm's 1st Battalion.

PFC Kirkbride and his gun crew finally made it to Company A's CP. They moved quickly, spurred on by their near catastrophic encounter with the Germans. Kirkbride saw a GI walking to his dugout and asked the man where the command post was. The soldier pointed to a log hut with several land line wires running into the top. Kirkbride told the men to lay low while he and PFC Esultante spoke to the company commander. As both men approached the dugout, LT Willard Clark, the company commander, emerged from the CP. Clark, surprised to see the men, asked Kirkbride what was happening.[12]

"Well, sir," began Kirkbride, "Germans attacked my gun position. They came out of the woods from the south and started shootin'. We had no choice but to run back here for protection."

"You said they came from the south and not the east?" asked Clark.

"That's right, sir," answered Kirkbride. "I've got a perfectly good 57mm anti-tank gun still sittin' back there with a Dodge 6x6 truck."

Just then, both men heard footsteps crunching through the snow. They turned to see CPT Harold Z. Moore, the AT Company commander, approaching.

"What's going on?" asked Moore.

Kirkbride repeated his story to his company commander, who listened intently. When Kirkbride finished, the man shook his head.

"Where's LT Benson and your platoon sergeant?" asked Moore.

"I don't know, sir," responded Kirkbride. "They might be stuck in Company B's positions."

As Kirkbride finished the sentence, intense small-arms fire crackled to the north and south, and mortar rounds impacted nearby. The ground shuddered. A radio operator from inside Clark's dugout thrust his head through an opening, stating that the platoon near the railroad tracks was under fire from lots of German troops. He also said that Company D's mortar platoon, located only 400 meters away, was under heavy German attack.

"Damn!" said Clark. "They're takin' us in the flank! They're already behind my main defensive line. I've gotta reshuffle some of my positions."

"Then the firing north of us must be coming from B and C Company's areas," said Moore. "They must be trying to take the crossroads."

"My gun is still functional and only 300 yards from here," said Kirkbride.

"Well, we need it back," said Moore. "If they want these crossroads, they'll use tanks. Clark, can you give him some support in retaking that gun?"

"Yeah, I can," answered Clark, "but not right now. I've gotta deal with this mess."

Clark disappeared into his dugout. Moore, Kirkbride, and Esultante heard him giving orders over the radio. Clark told his platoons to concentrate their efforts to the south and to be aware that the Germans were already in their rear.

"When you get your gun back," Moore told Kirkbride, "I want you to make sure you can fire east and north of the intersection. Cover those crossroads! They're vital to our defense!"

"Will do, sir," answered Kirkbride. "Can you send me more ammo?"

Moore nodded and turned to go. He paused for a moment, then turned back around and faced Kirkbride.

"By the way, you did good," he said. "Remember, I don't have many guns down here. LT Anderson's platoon went north to the 2nd Battalion to serve as riflemen."[13]

Instantly, the officer disappeared into the thick underbrush and headed north, probably to check his other gun positions.

"Well," said Kirkbride, "let's get to it."

"I'm right behind you," answered Esultante.

Oberstleutnant Lemm had left the 1st Battalion just before they attempted their flanking movement to the north. He withdrew to consult with Oberstleutnant Gerhard Lemcke, the commander of Grenadier Regiment 89. Lemcke's regiment followed Lemm's 27th. Lemcke wanted to know what Lemm's plans were. Lemm told him he wanted to find a weak spot in the American defense, but he might need some flank protection to his north.[14] Since Lemcke's regiment was the reserve, Lemm thought the 89th could provide the protection. But before the discussion could continue, Lemm heard small-arms and mortar fire to the north. He decided to see what happened. Lemm left Lemcke on the railroad tracks. They would have to consult later.

Lemm climbed to the top of the northern rail line embankment with his aide and radio operator. The men made for the sound of the firing, just in time

Fusiliers in the Flank 59

to greet their own soldiers, survivors of the devastating mortar attack, withdrawing through the forest to the southeast.

"Stop!" yelled Lemm. "Where's Hauptmann Breger?"

A young officer approached the regimental commander. The officer told Lemm that Breger was dead and that sniper fire from the American foxholes had pinned down one of the 1st Battalion's other companies. In essence, the 1st Battalion had hit a stalemate. Much of the battalion's combat power remained trapped in the woods by the American foxholes. Lemm put the young officer temporarily in charge until he could better determine the situation.

"Can the men see the American foxholes?" asked Lemm.

"No, Herr Oberstleutnant," came the answer. "The Americans are dug in well. But some of them have these enormous huts that are nearly useless."

The officer stepped aside to reveal an abandoned log hut, possibly used by an observation team to observe the rail line to the east. Lemm thought the hut looked strange. The position seemed designed more for comfort than for fighting. Lemm expected more from the Americans, especially considering the length of time they had been on the Siegfried Line.

"Stay here and come up with a plan to extract the rest of the battalion," Lemm told the officer. "I'm going to find the 3rd Battalion. They must have decided to keep moving down the railroad tracks to the west."

Lemm slid down the steep, snow-covered embankment with his aide, his radio operator, and a messenger. The young officer watched silently as Lemm disappeared into the mist along the tracks. He quietly turned and gave instructions to the fusiliers.

LTC Robert Douglas, commander of the 394th's 1st Battalion, went out to check his company positions after the artillery barrage ended. A tough, brave man, Douglas wanted to comfort his men with his presence. He wasn't the type of leader who gave orders from the rear. He was a man of action, and his soldiers knew it.

Douglas had just left Company C's position and was moving south when he heard small-arms fire to the southwest. He told the radio operator to contact battalion headquarters, but no luck. Douglas hurried back toward the CP, afraid something big might be happening. Just then, a tired and disheveled private burst out of the woods and into Douglas's path.

"Sir," gasped the soldier, "the XO wants you back at the command post. Company A and Company B are under attack, and the Company D mortars have Germans to their south."

"Let's go!" shouted the battalion commander.

The three men sprinted back to the command post, 1,200 meters west of the crossroads. When Douglas asked for a situation report, his executive officer and S-3 (operations officer) briefed him quickly. They considered the most significant action to be the one south of Company D's mortars. Douglas listened intently. He instructed the S-3 to have the companies hold in place. If there was an attack, his men were doing a good job of repelling it for the time being. But most of the pressure was on Company B, some of whose men had been forced to move west.

The executive officer also carefully admonished his battalion commander for disappearing for so long. He told LTC Douglas they needed a live leader and not a dead one.[15] The executive officer then informed Douglas that they had several German prisoners outside. Douglas told the man to bring one in for questioning. A young German medic entered the command post. He was five feet, six inches tall, and his helmet was far too big for his head. Douglas had studied some German in school and decided to question the man himself. He raised himself to his full six-foot stature and bellowed at the man.

"Wie heissen sie, dummkopf?" he roared.

"I'm sorry, sir," returned the German in excellent English. "I don't understand a word you say. By the way, sir, I have a cousin, Hans Schmidt, in Milwaukee. Do you know him?"[16]

Douglas turned red in the face. The men in the CP tried not to laugh. Flustered, Douglas ordered the man out and sat down to monitor the situation to the front of Companies A and B. It was now 0900 and the day was only beginning.

By late morning, PFC Kirkbride and his gun crew had recaptured their gun.[17] LT Clark, the Company A commander, supplied Kirkbride and his men with the reserve platoon for security. The men checked the condition of the gun and found no damage. Kirkbride thanked the infantrymen, who now returned to their foxhole line. Some men from the reserve platoon had moved their positions farther forward to give the gun crew more security.

Just then, T/SGT Arthur C. Piar, Kirkbride's platoon sergeant, arrived on the scene and told Kirkbride what was happening in the battalion's sector.

"The Germans have pushed Company B back several hundred yards," he began. "They're in alternate positions close by. If you look real hard in the woods across the road by the intersection, you'll see krauts sneaking around. Company B's casualties are terrible. You need to watch this road for another attack."

"Who's in those customs houses?" asked Kirkbride.

"There's a mix of our anti-tank people, soldiers from Companies A and B, and, I think, some artillery FOs," he answered. "That seems to be the focus of our defense. I think the colonel may reinforce the crossroads later with guys from Company C. They didn't get hit as hard as we did."

Kirkbride acknowledged all that Piar told him. Piar told Kirkbride to stay alert, that he and LT Benson would help reorganize the defense of the crossroads. Piar then disappeared into the forest. Kirkbride prepared for action.

LTC Douglas continued to receive reports at the command post. Since the morning artillery barrage had destroyed all landline communication, Douglas could make only sporadic contact with his companies via radio. The battalion commander was dismayed to see the new copper wire outside his CP torn and shredded. The Battalion Communications Platoon had expended a lot of effort to lay that wire.[18]

It was late morning. The first German attacks from the south and east were several hours old. Companies A and B took the brunt of the German attacks, with Company B losing 60 percent of its troops in a few hours. The German attacks pushed Company B back 400 meters to positions close to the international highway and the road intersection.

Company A took many casualties as well, perhaps 30 percent of its total strength. Company A still held its original positions, but LT Clark had to consolidate some of his platoons and draw them in closer to the crossroads, away from the rail line in the south. The Company D mortar platoon, which defended itself so well earlier that morning, displaced to a new location 300 meters northwest of the Losheimergraben Crossroads. CPT Jim Graham's Company C had much less enemy contact than the others. Douglas considered sending some of Graham's men to reinforce the other companies. He told his S-3 to look at the possibility of sending one platoon each to Companies A and B. Douglas considered the protection of the crossroads as the focus for his defense.

LTC Douglas still did not have a clear grasp of the big picture. He had limited radio contact with MAJ Norman Moore of the 3rd Battalion, located behind him at Buchholz Station. The 3rd Battalion also had enemy contact, but Douglas didn't know to what extent. Far to his north, CPT Legare's 2nd Battalion fought back an enemy attack that morning. Douglas also had limited radio communications with Regiment and COL Riley. He managed to send a few reports to COL Riley, who couldn't offer him much information. Riley gave him only one order that morning: detach one of Company C's platoons to Company G of the 2nd Battalion in the north. Riley also sent the 2nd Battalion one anti-tank platoon to serve as infantry. Apparently, large enemy patrols were probing Company G, patrols which probably originated from the 277th Volksgrenadier Division attack farther north. Any success by the 277th would severely threaten the 1st Battalion's defense of the intersection. The Company G commander positioned the Company C platoon slightly north of its original position, allowing the platoon to remain in limited contact with its parent unit in the south.

The most significant thing LTC Douglas was unaware of was Oberleutnant Steinhofel's 7th Company, Grenadier Regiment 48. Steinhofel had slipped through a seam between Companies B and C and now sat quietly, with other attached elements, in the forest 800 meters west of the crossroads, north and south of the main road. Steinhofel's element was a mere 300 meters from the new positions occupied by Company D's mortars. Steinhofel waited there for Major Kruse to bring forward the rest of the 2nd Battalion in the next few hours.

Kruse finished searching Company B's defensive line for prisoners before leading his battalion's main body across the highway to Steinhofel's location. After Kruse linked the rest of his battalion with Steinhofel's force, he returned to the crossroads and remained there with his 5th Company in order to make contact with the rest of the incoming regiment.

Steinhofel's element in the American rear made no trouble for Douglas in the interim, other than taking about 30 American prisoners as they stumbled into the German positions. The grenadiers remained incredibly quiet. They blocked any withdrawal by American soldiers to the west by commanding a small part of the main Losheimergraben-Bullingen road. In fact, the grenadiers were so quiet that the men at the 1st Battalion CP, including Douglas, didn't even hear them. They were practically neighbors now, with the nearest German element only 500 meters away. This position represented Oberstleutnant Osterhold's farthest advance, and he was able to forward a report through division headquarters to the commander of the I SS Panzer Corps, SS-Gruppenfuehrer Hermann Preiss, that he had seized the crossroads but not secured them. Securing them would take more time.

CHAPTER 6

Buchholz Station

Forest Buchholz Station sat astride the east-west railroad line that originated in Germany. The station itself was typical of most railroad depot stations; it had a large concrete loading dock and a roomy, open interior for freight storage and offices. The building was constructed of brick and wood and appeared to be at least 40 to 50 years old. A dirt road ran south of it, well-packed and very capable of supporting armored vehicles. This improved dirt road led to the tiny villages of Lanzerath in the south and Honsfeld in the west. The station was approximately 1,000 meters southwest of the Losheimergraben Crossroads. Part of the improved road connected to that east-west strip as well. Across the road from the station was a farmhouse and other small, stone buildings. The family who owned and operated the station occupied them.

The railroad tracks leading east into Germany had very high slopes on either side. These slopes created the illusion that the railroad tracks were sunken into the ground by 20 to 25 feet. As the tracks neared Buchholz Station, the high banks leveled off and became less steep. Several old boxcars, intended for freight use but now empty, sat along the tracks 200 meters from the station. Six to seven inches of snow carpeted the entire area. The snow accented the already serene beauty of this small pastoral paradise hidden in the Ardennes. Before long, the sights and sounds of a horrific battle would shatter this peace and beauty.

The 3rd Battalion, 394th Infantry Regiment, initially located at the crossroads area, relieved the 1st Battalion of its reserve mission on 11 December. The 3rd Battalion, commanded by the highly competent and worthy MAJ Norman Moore, had conducted aggressive patrolling forward of the Losheimergraben area. They had performed this mission ever since they relieved the 1st Battalion, 60th Infantry of the 9th Infantry Division of that same location on 14

November.[1] The 3rd Battalion moved to Buchholz Station and became the division's mobile reserve. MG Walter Lauer, the 99th Division commander, believed that his southern flank, which sat in the middle of the Losheim Gap, was the weakest part of his defensive line. When he established the division's defense in sector, Lauer ordered COL Don Riley, the regimental commander, to establish a division reserve to the south with one of his battalions. For unknown reasons, Lauer didn't hold Riley in high regard, but he thought him capable of successfully defending this open flank.

The 3rd Battalion's mission at Buchholz Station was to occupy assembly areas and serve as the division mobile reserve. They had to be ready to move at a moment's notice to reinforce any divisional unit in the defensive sector. MAJ Moore used the farmhouse by the road junction as his headquarters. He felt uncomfortable about having his companies occupy assembly areas, especially since a potential enemy avenue of approach, the railroad, ran right through his area of operations. Moore had Company L occupy security positions along the railroad line facing east. The rest of the battalion remained in fortified assembly areas north of the station and railroad line.

On 13 December, the 2nd Infantry Division began a planned attack to seize the Roer River Dams in the north. The 2nd Division, recently pulled from the line farther south, attacked to the northeast, directly behind the 99th Division's defensive positions. The 395th Infantry Regiment, now a regimental combat team, was detached from the 99th to support this drive. The 393d Infantry Regiment, which defended the northern part of the 99th's sector just above the 394th, was tasked to support this offensive by conducting small, limited attacks forward of its sector. Late on 15 December, MG Lauer ordered COL Riley to detach Company I and one machine gun section from Company M from the division reserve, the 3rd Battalion, to support the 393d in its limited attack mission. Lauer warned Riley and Moore to prepare the rest of the battalion to support the 393d should they need it. Only Companies K, L and part of M remained in the division reserve position at Buchholz Station. These companies would represent the 3rd Battalion's strength when the German offensive struck in three days, on 16 December.

At 0535 on the morning of 16 December, members of the 3rd Battalion awoke to the deafening roar of thousands of German artillery pieces firing into Allied positions to the west. At first, many of the battalion's members thought it was "outgoing mail" from the American artillery. They soon realized they were wrong. During the course of the two-hour barrage, rounds dropped in and among their positions at Buchholz Station. The rounds landed at Buchholz Station and the Losheimergraben Crossroads simultaneously. Two men, presumably an anti-tank gun crew from Company A, 820th Tank Destroyer Battalion (part of Task Force X, 14th Cavalry Group, VIII Corps), bolted from their gun position just east of Buchholz Station. Their platoon was farther south across the corps boundary in the village of Lanzerath. Both men had failed to prepare good defensive positions with overhead cover. Running west through the forest for several hundred meters, they desperately sought cover from the torrential rain of German shell bursts that impacted in the trees overhead. The gun crew reached the assembly area of Company K in a panic, frantically looking for a place to hide from the artillery. Screaming in terror, the frantic men ran up to a foxhole from Company K's 3rd Platoon and tore the overhead cover from it. The two soldiers inside became frightened. Thinking they were under attack by fanatical German soldiers, the GIs shot and killed the two AT men. It was an unfortunate and demoralizing incident of "friendly fire," a harsh lesson for the men of the 3rd Battalion.[2]

At 0730, the barrage ended, and life in the division reserve area went back to normal. The consensus among the officers and men was that the German artillery was a response to the ongoing attacks on the Roer River Dam area in the north. Few realized that a great German offensive was aimed directly at them. The barrage killed no one from the battalion except for the AT men who abandoned their position at the crossroads.

1SG Elmer Klug of Company L decided it was time to feed the company breakfast, however late, and the company commander, 1LT Neil Brown, agreed. Klug organized a chow line by the station building, sending runners to bring the platoons to eat in numerical order. The line wasn't set up until 0800. Just then, Klug heard small arms and mortar fire about a mile to the east.

"I wonder what that's all about," he mumbled.

What the unsuspecting first sergeant heard was the struggle of LT Vaughan's Company D mortars to prevent the 27th Fusilier Regiment from flanking the 1st Battalion from the south. Major Moore, inside his CP, had just learned of this incident. Moore received a report indicating that the 1st Battalion had encountered German soldiers to their front and that they were now engaged in a firefight. Moore thought about this news for a second. He realized that, as the division reserve, he had to avoid decisive contact with the enemy. Contact with the enemy would completely eliminate MG Lauer's flexibility; Lauer would not have a reserve to work with in a crisis. But Norman Moore was a man of initiative and was cautious about taking unnecessary risks. He knew the 1st Battalion was only 1,000 meters away. If they were in contact now, he would be next. Moore didn't want to leave himself open for a catastrophe. He sent a messenger to Company K's assembly area, instructing the commander to move a rifle and weapons platoon to the small hillock south of the station and to the right of Company L. Then MAJ Moore sat back and pondered the situation further. He considered the possibilities should the enemy attack.

Captain Wesley Simmons, the commander of Company K, received the message and moved the two platoons to the specified location.[3] He sent LT Charles Spencer's 1st Platoon and LT Richard A. Ralston's weapons platoon to occupy the small hillock south of the station. CPT Simmons went along with them. He was always in the forefront with his soldiers. Of medium build and with a small, black mustache, Simmons always had a smile for his soldiers. His men absolutely loved him. After the war, one of his men indicated that Simmons was "tops in my book," very high praise indeed.

Simmons left the other two platoons in the assembly area with his executive officer, 1LT Joseph P. Rose. He then moved through the dense, coniferous forest to the small hillock identified a few days earlier by Major Moore and set up a hasty defense facing southeast. He tied into the right flank of Company L with LT Spencer's 1st Platoon. Simmons moved the light machine gun section from LT Ralston's weapons platoon up with the 1st and had Ralston set up the company's 60mm mortars in defilade to the rear of the small rise. His men dug hasty fighting positions in the cold, hard, snow-covered ground. At 0830, Simmons still had men moving into position, but he was only moments from reporting his company as "set."

Back at the Company L chow line, 1SG Klug continued to feed his company. Only one platoon had passed through the chow line, and he wanted them to hurry up. Klug observed the chow line's progress from a window inside the station house. 1LT Brown was beside him.

"Now who is this?" asked Klug as he looked east at the railroad tracks. Klug saw figures moving toward the station house in the morning haze.

"Is that 4th Platoon?" he asked.

"I don't know," said Brown.

"Somebody go and tell those guys it isn't their turn to eat yet!" he roared from the window at a soldier. Suddenly, the figures in the mist didn't seem familiar at all.

"Hold it," he said. "Something ain't right here."

The figures became clearer in the mist. The appearance of a large column of German soldiers moving down the railroad tracks stunned Klug. They were heading straight toward his chow line and Buchholz Station. There were at least two companies of them. Before saying anything, he picked up his M1 carbine and ran outside.

"Krauts!" he yelled. "Dammit, take cover!"

Klug raised his carbine and fired. The German soldiers, members of Oberstleutnant Heinz-Georg Lemm's 27th Fusilier Regiment, dove for cover on either side of the railroad tracks. The padded overwhite jackets and pants they wore made them difficult to see in the snow. A power line relay tower afforded them shelter. The Germans were surprised when 1SG Klug yelled and then fired. Almost 60 of them took immediate refuge inside and under the closest of the abandoned boxcars.[4]

The members of Company L split from the chow line and dove for cover. Others fired at the Germans located near the boxcars. Technician 5th Grade (T/5) George Bodnar, the Company L armorer-articifer, ran back and forth from the station house with ammo for the soldiers. The small arms fire was deafening, but he could hear the painful groans of a wounded German soldier sprawled in the open near the station. The German had been one of the closest to the station when the firing began. He lay now severely wounded in the snow, one of the first casualties.

Bodnar couldn't stand to hear the man groan. Right near the wounded man, PVT John Claypool was firing a bazooka at the boxcars. The rounds went

Buchholz Station 67

either short or high. Bodnar moved next to Claypool carrying a shelter half for a pup tent.[5]

"Watch out for me, will ya?" he asked.

Claypool nodded as Bodnar ran into the open amidst a gauntlet of small arms fire. He quickly realized he couldn't possibly drag the wounded German back to the station because of the shooting. He covered the wounded man with the shelter half and turned to leave.

"Sorry, buddy, but I've gotta go," he told the man. "I'll be back later."

The man probably had no idea what Bodnar said to him. If he knew, perhaps he was grateful someone cared. Suddenly, 81mm and 60mm mortar fire from Company's M and K rained down on the Germans. Bodnar returned to the station building and got down next to Claypool.

"Haven't you hit anything with that bazooka yet?" he asked.

"No, I keep missing," said Claypool. "I thought I was good with this thing, too."

"Give it here," said Bodnar. "Let's see what I can do."

At the same time, members of the regimental Anti-Tank Company attached to the 3rd Battalion put two 57mm anti-tank guns into action against the boxcars. The anti-tank men positioned the guns behind the southeastern corner of the station house. They fired at the boxcars and scored some direct hits.

"All right, load me up," said Bodnar.

Claypool loaded one of the bazooka rounds into the launcher and slapped Bodnar on the back.

"Okay, fire!" he yelled.

Bodnar fired and missed, short by three meters. Claypool quickly reloaded the bazooka and Bodnar fired again. This time he scored a direct hit on the first boxcar. By now, Germans streamed out of the freight cars and sought cover outside. Bodnar and Claypool repeated the process and scored another hit on the roof of the boxcar. The combination of bazooka and 57mm AT fire set the boxcars ablaze. The voices of screaming, wounded Germans echoed in the cold, morning air. Several dove onto the tracks and nearby embankments. Many Germans continued to fire, but others simply gave up. Suddenly, German artillery rounds impacted around the station. T/5 Bodnar ran back into the station to seek shelter from the hail of rounds. Seconds later, the station took a direct hit. A shell splinter bounced off of Bodnar's ammo bandoleer and into the head of a medic, PVT Joe Ryan. It killed him instantly. PVT Joe Genovino, sheltered in the station along with Bodnar, decided to run outside and take his chances under the concrete loading bay.[6] The artillery stopped after a few minutes. The GIs soon realized that the fusiliers were withdrawing back to the east along the railroad tracks. Several NCOs from Company L yelled for the men to stop firing. Almost abruptly, the groans of wounded Germans replaced the sound of rifle fire. Several men from Company L and the Ammunition and Pioneer (A&P) Platoon, who had moved up with and augmented Company L on the right during the engagement, approached the boxcars and demanded that the remaining Germans surrender. The GIs rounded up 30 prisoners and moved them back to the station area. Company L suffered only 25 to 30 casualties in the fray.[7]

MAJ Moore knew this was an attack in force. The Germans thought they had the element of surprise by moving in the mist along the railroad cut. They had little or no forward security, which caused them to become decisively engaged with their main body immediately. Moore believed that this German force was trying to outflank the 1st Battalion after Company D's mortar platoon repelled them. He knew they would come back in strength and with a better plan. Moore also knew that his battalion's presence came as a surprise to the Germans, mainly because they were moving in a close-knit formation designed for speed. It was clear to him that they wanted to use their own rapid advance as their security. He sent a messenger to CPT Simmons with instructions to bring the rest of Company K to the hillock where the 1st Platoon now sat. Simmons complied and sent a message to LT Rose to get moving. Moore instructed the 81mm mortars of Company M to remain in their assembly areas and to offer fire support from there. Just then, the Germans sent a patrol straight into Company K's position. Elements of the A&P Platoon now shared the left side of this position. The Germans were obviously looking for a weak flank to exploit. A brief exchange of gunfire ensued. Casualties were heavy for the Germans. The survivors quickly withdrew but not before killing the A&P Platoon leader with a well-placed round from an StG 44.

LT Rose soon arrived with the remaining two platoons. CPT Simmons instructed LT Ray Thibadeaux, the 2nd Platoon Leader, to occupy a position on the right flank of 1st Platoon, oriented in the same direction. He then told LT Norman C. Schlemmer to take his 3rd Platoon and establish a defensive position behind the company facing south. Simmons didn't want to take any chances of being hit in the flank. The purpose of the initial German assault had been clear: the Germans wanted to circle behind the GIs and cut them off. The men of Company K dug in. They anticipated future contact with an enemy force waiting to strike again.

Oberstleutnant Heinz-Georg Lemm, commander of the 27th Fusilier Regiment, came forward just in time to see Company L and the A&P Platoon bring withering fire down upon his 3rd Battalion.[8] His 3rd Battalion, hoping to avoid resistance, had sped ahead of the 1st Battalion, which was now pinned down by Company A of the 394th's 1st Battalion. Lemm made his intent clear to his commanders: move quickly and open a gap for the SS panzers to exploit. But the 3rd Battalion had moved too quickly. Despite MAJ Moore's suspicions, the fusiliers' tactic of speeding ahead in a tight formation was born of inexperience and nothing more. This tactic and the 3rd Battalion's collective inexperience resulted in a shocking surprise at Buchholz Station.

He watched as the remains of the 3rd Battalion withdrew and went to ground. They remained just outside of small-arms range of Company L. Lemm was with his command group: an aide (an oberleutnant), a radio operator, and a messenger.

"What do you think is happening?" he asked his aide.

"I'm not sure, Herr Oberstleutnant," he responded. "The remnants of the battalion appear to be encircled."

Although encirclement was not the case, Lemm agreed with his aide. He feared the worst. He told his radio operator to send a message to the 1st Battalion. He instructed the 1st to disengage from the 1st Battalion, 394th Infantry's positions and move west and to the left. Lemm wanted them to conduct a flanking attack against the southeast position of the Americans at Buchholz Station. He hoped to relieve quickly his besieged 3rd Battalion. Lemm informed the acting battalion commander that he would link up with him and further explain the situation. Lemm knew he would have to give these young, inexperienced recruits assistance if they were to succeed. He could no longer rely on one of his best officers and the commander of the 1st Battalion, Hauptmann Breger. Breger had fought his last battle in front of Company A's position.

The 3rd Battalion, in fact, was not surrounded. They were simply scattered and disorganized, a result of inexperienced and unseasoned leadership. Lemm only had a few good officers left, and they couldn't be everywhere. After withdrawing from the battle at the boxcars, the remainder of the battalion backed away and set up a hasty defense in the woods on either side of the railroad tracks. They were frightened and uncertain of what lay ahead.

Lemm moved east along the tracks and met the 1st Battalion disengaging from the 394th's 1st Battalion. The men quickly rallied around Lemm and his command party on the railroad tracks. He told a young, unknown officer, now in command of the battalion, what he wanted.

"I think part of the 3rd Battalion may be encircled ahead by an unknown American force. It's too dangerous to get close enough to see, but we can't let the attack stall. I want you to move left and find a weak flank. Try it first with a recon patrol. If you succeed, quickly attack in strength. It's best if you stay in small battle groups, which will allow you to quickly exploit small successes. You'll have mortar support as soon as I can arrange it. Any questions?"

The young officer, with barely a few months in the German military, shook his head. As the acting battalion commander, and replacing the experienced Breger, he would have to lead this assault. It was a great responsibility, and it had to happen quickly. The attack must continue.

Lemm moved into the woods to the left. He remained behind the 1st Battalion, which moved to an assault position in the dense, coniferous forest. Lemm coordinated for mortar support on his radio. Lemm then instructed the young officer that the mortars were at his command. It was now 1040 hours.

Captain Wesley Simmons, commander of Company K, made certain that his men improved their positions. The size of the force that Company L engaged told him the enemy would try another assault. At 1050, soldiers from the 1st Platoon reported movement to the front. CPT Simmons passed this report on to MAJ Moore and then sat and waited. Suddenly, small-arms fire broke the chilly, late morning silence as men from the 1st and 2nd Platoon engaged a small group of German soldiers who appeared 100 meters away in a small ravine. This group was the patrol Lemm had ordered his 1st Battalion to send out. The density of the forest forced the Germans to get very close before being able to see anything. By getting so close, they compromised their location, but they did discover Company K's front line. Many of Simmons's soldiers couldn't see the enemy. The GIs responded with sporadic small-arms fire. The German patrol interpreted this sporadic shooting as a weakly manned position. The patrol broke contact, and neither side suffered casualties. Simmons reported the event to the battalion CP and once again waited. He knew this German patrol was only probing Company K's positions for a weak flank. He alerted LT Schlemmer of the 3rd Platoon to be aware of a possible deep flanking movement by the Germans. If the enemy succeeded in such a move, the fusiliers could envelop the entire 3rd Battalion. The service and support elements of the battalion, the trains, lay directly behind the 3rd Platoon's defenses. These trains included the attached Anti-Tank (AT) Platoon, who had helped Company L so well in the battle for the boxcars.

At 1100, the expected attack began with a German mortar barrage that fell on the Company L and Company K positions at Buchholz Station. Simmons yelled to his men to keep down but to watch their front since an assault would surely follow. His prediction proved true. Two full companies of German infantry assaulted his position. Small-arms fire crackled from both sides. Some German soldiers came as close as 100 meters. The young American and German soldiers fought valiantly and persistently. LT Ralston's 60mm mortars inflicted severe damage on the assaulting German formation, but the attack continued. Schlemmer's 3rd Platoon position also received fire from the small German assault groups. These Germans took the Anti-Tank (AT) Platoon under fire. The AT men quickly joined the fight on the flank.

SGT Savino Travalini, the AT Platoon leader, moved his men next to the 3rd Platoon and exchanged fire with the German infantry. A small stone roundhouse, part of the farm located across the road from the station, sat directly in front of Travalini's and Schlemmer's position. The Germans managed to get inside the roundhouse, which provided a good foothold from which to engage Company K's flank.

Outside the roundhouse, a German machine gun team set up an MG42 and poured heavy grazing fire over the heads of the 3rd Platoon and AT platoon men. Travalini knew this machine gun team might spell success for the Germans. He had to eliminate the MG42 and its crew.

"Gimme some grenades!" he shouted to one of his men.

He took the grenades and stuffed them in his field jacket. He checked his M1 carbine to make sure he had a full magazine. He called to his men.

"I'm going forward," he yelled. "Don't shoot me!"

Travalini low-crawled toward the machine gun nest. He stopped periodically to fire his M1 carbine. He took two grenades from inside his jacket, pulled the pins, and rushed the machine gun nest. He threw the grenades on top of the surprised Germans and dove for cover. The grenades exploded in rapid succes-

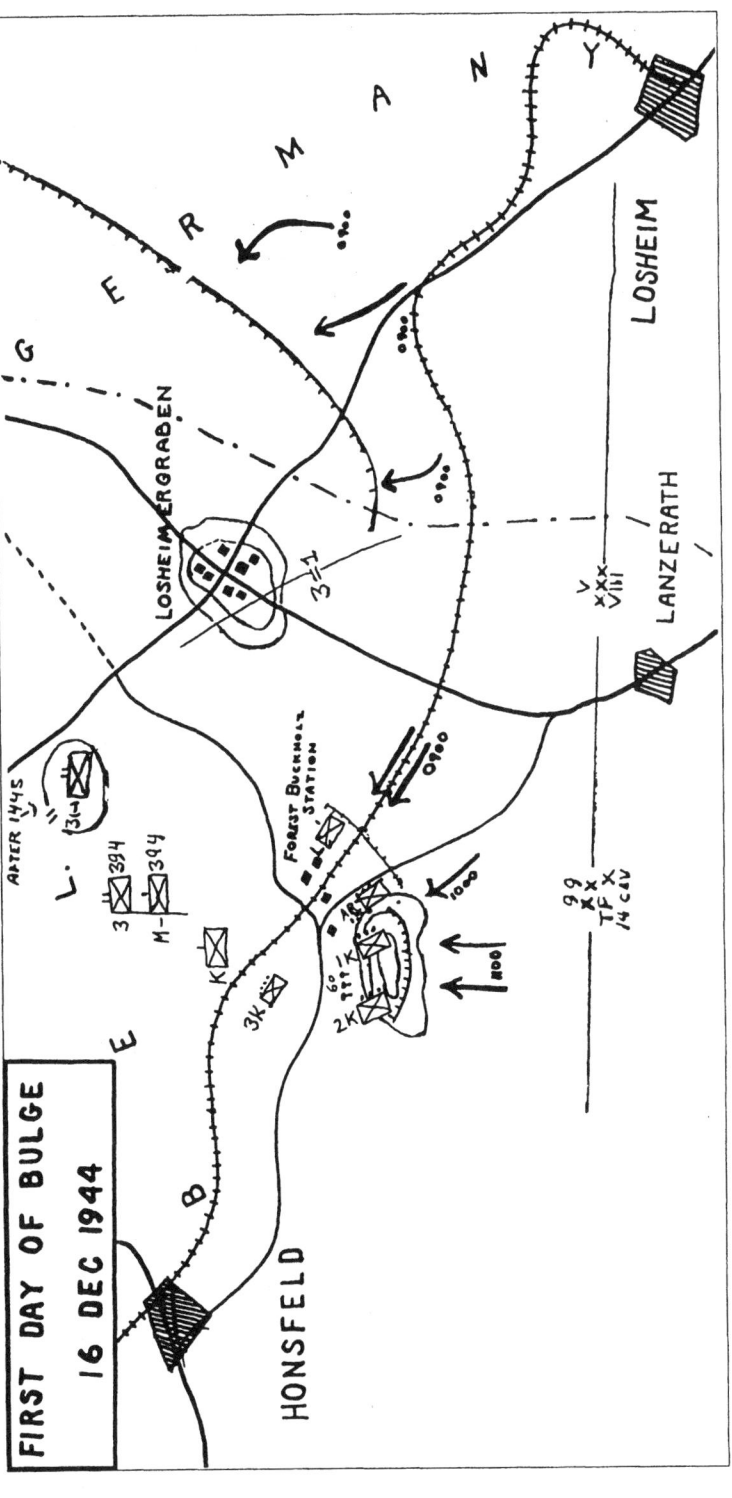

Hand-drawn map by Captain Wesley J. Simmons from his 1949 monograph portraying the 3rd Battalion's disposition at Buchholz Station on 16 December 1944. Courtesy U.S. Army Infantry School.

sion. The screams of the three dying Germans followed. Travalini jumped up and ran back to the 3rd Platoon position. The incoming fire had slacked off. But the Germans in the stone roundhouse still continued to pour murderous and well-aimed fire at Travalini's and Schlemmer's men. Travalini called back for the platoon's bazooka.

"I've got it here!" yelled one of the AT men.

The young soldier pushed the bazooka toward Travalini, along with two rounds. Travalini grabbed it, loaded one round, and sighted in on the roundhouse. He fired the bazooka. The projectile whizzed toward the very center of the building. The round impacted with a loud crack, followed by a thin haze of smoke. Two Germans staggered out in the haze and headed back to the southeast, toward a small ravine. Travalini picked each German off with his M1 carbine. At this point all assaults ended near Schlemmer's platoon position, thanks largely to SGT Travalini's heroism. His leadership and heroism earned him a Silver Star and a battlefield commission as a second lieutenant.[9]

The 1st and 2nd Platoons of Company K performed well in the fight. The Germans got no closer than 100 meters and took severe casualties from the well-coordinated fires of both platoons. CPT Simmons himself participated in the fray. He realized that most of the small-arms fire was coming from his own men. He ordered a cease-fire and waited. The Germans were withdrawing. They moved back down the ravine where the assault had begun. Simmons reported to the battalion CP that the Germans had withdrawn. He asked LT Spencer and LT Thibadeaux for a casualty report. In the fog of battle, Simmons couldn't see if any of his men were wounded or killed. Those near his position seemed in good shape, but he couldn't see to his extreme left or right. He feared the worst. The battle had been intense, and both sides dished it out to each other. He knew his men had probably suffered as much as the Germans had. As both platoon leaders made their way to his location, he braced himself.

"Our total casualties include one dead, two wounded," said LT Spencer.

These were unusually light casualties for an engagement of the magnitude they just experienced. Although one soldier died, Simmons breathed a sigh of relief, thankful that the casualty rate wasn't higher.

Oberstleutnant Lemm knew he couldn't make a penetration in this area. His 1st Battalion had suffered severe casualties in the assault, as had the 3rd Battalion in the boxcars and at the station. He would have to look farther south for a wider gap, one with little or no resistance. His strength was severely depleted. He couldn't afford costly battles like the one at Buchholz Station. He reassembled the remnants of his two battalions and moved south, looking for a gap in the lines to exploit. Lemm knew some very impatient panzer officers were "chomping at the bit" for a safe passage through enemy lines. This day had already proved very trying for Lemm and the 27th Fusilier Regiment.

MAJ Moore knew that his battalion's successes would be short lived. He was fully aware of the gap that existed to his south, on the boundary of the V and VIII Corps. The closest friendly unit was Task Force X of the 14th Cavalry Group. Task Force X only held a series of outposts on a nine-kilometer front. The Losheim Gap was wide open. The Germans would discover the gap soon, and when they did, the entire regiment would be outflanked. The Germans could easily envelop the 99th Division from south to north. German artillery had caused Moore's 3rd Battalion to lose contact with the 394th's regimental CP. The 3rd Battalion executive officer, MAJ George A. Clayton, was working hard to restore communications. Moore needed to report the 3rd Battalion's situation, to seek instructions, and to learn more about the friendly and enemy situation. Moore's only clear reports came from the 1st Battalion at the Losheimergraben Crossroads. The 1st Battalion indicated that the Germans had made numerous penetrations in their defense. Miraculously, the battalion still maintained most of its original positions. To further compound the news of the penetrations, a soldier from Company L had recovered, from the body of a dead German soldier, a message sent to all German units involved in the counteroffensive. It was a copy of the same message found on Hauptmann Breger by PFC Arthur Mings of Company A. It came from Generalfeldmarschall Gerd von Rundstedt, commander of all German forces in the West. The translated message read as follows:

Soldiers of the West[ern] Front. Your great hour has struck. Strong attacking armies are advancing today against the Anglo-Americans. I don't need to say more to you. You all feel it, everything is at stake. You bear in yourselves a holy duty to give everything and to achieve the superhuman for "Our Fatherland and our Fuehrer."

—von Rundstedt[10]

The situation suddenly became much clearer to Moore. The German assault was far more than a local attack. This German offensive was bigger than perhaps anyone realized. Moore knew he couldn't maintain his present positions. He would have to move, to do something, but what?

CHAPTER 7

Defense of the Weisser Stein

In the northern part of the regiment's sector, the 2nd Battalion stood up under the might of the enemy artillery barrage quite well. Like its sister battalions in the south, the 2nd Battalion's soldiers had constructed strong log huts and foxholes. All foxholes were equipped with solid overhead cover, which minimized any damage by incoming artillery rounds. The battalion headquarters, located in a small hunting lodge, quickly relocated to a log hut prepared to house the Command Post under combat conditions. As the German barrage began, CPT Ben Legare, the battalion executive officer, ran to the new CP location. As he entered the log hut, he heard the deafening roar of artillery impact in the trees overhead. Legare, shaken by the gauntlet he had run, asked if the CP still had contact with the companies. A private, working the switchboard, looked at Legare and shook his head.[1]

"No, sir," he replied. "All land lines to the companies are out."

"Okay," said Legare, "as soon as the artillery lifts, get a status report over the radio."

"Roger, sir," came the reply.

Legare scanned the CP. He tried to see through the dim, early morning light which officers were in the hut. He could still hear the sound of occasional artillery rounds. Larger groups of projectiles followed and struck the treetops overhead. Something seemed strange to Legare, though. The soldiers in the command post were strangely quiet, save for the low voice of the radio operator trying to contact the companies. As his eyes adjusted to the dim light, Legare saw the men looking at him strangely.

"What's wrong?" asked the officer.

"Well, sir," replied a sergeant, "it's the colonel..."

"What happened?" asked Legare. "Did he get hit?"

"No, sir," came the weak reply.

"Then where is he?" asked Legare. "I haven't seen him since the barrage started."

The sergeant stepped aside to reveal a shaking, quivering form in the corner of the hut. Legare looked at the figure, then at the other soldiers in the CP. He was astonished.

"W-What...?" he stammered.

"He got that way as soon as the artillery came close to us," responded the sergeant. "He hasn't said a thing."

Legare approached the cowering, shaking form of his battalion commander.

"Sir, " he said, "it's me, Ben Legare. Can you hear me?"

The man looked up at him with wild eyes. Hysteria radiated from those eyes. Legare looked away. His commander's condition shocked him. He swore softly under his breath. CPT Bob McGee, the battalion S-3, moved over to Legare.

"Ben," McGee said, "you're the commander now. We suspected the old man would crack the first time we slugged it out with the Germans. The colonel just couldn't handle the pressure."

Legare looked at McGee. Both men winced slightly as the German artillery rounds hit the tall pine trees outside the log hut. Legare knew McGee was right. The battalion commander had proven himself incompetent long before this artillery barrage. Every time a visiting senior officer, such as MG Lauer or COL Riley, arrived at the battalion's location, the battalion commander chose either Legare or CPT McGee as escort. When a visiting officer asked a question, the battalion commander never answered. Nor could he. He always deferred the questions to Legare or McGee. The man had never made a command decision; nor did he exercise any command authority over his battalion. He was a poor officer, clearly undeserving of combat command. Legare thought he should have acted more deliberately to have the colonel relieved. Officers like him cost young soldiers their lives.

"Okay, Bob," he finally said, "I assume command of the battalion... temporarily, anyway. Help me contact the companies to see how they're faring under this artillery."

The companies held their positions. The battalion's soldiers found safe refuge in their well-constructed log huts or foxholes. The companies were still arrayed in line, with CPT William G. Patterson's Company E on the left, 1LT John A. Goodner's Company F in the center, and CPT John Haymaker's Company G on the right. Company G was tied in with Company C of the 1st Battalion in the south. CPT Robert Mannheimer's 81mm mortars from Company H sat directly behind Company F in defilade positions. On the battalion's left flank, Company E sat astride the only improved road through the battalion's defensive sector, the Weisser Stein Trail. This trail ran through the forest to the west and came out several hundred meters east of the hamlets of Hunningen and Murringen. This route was potentially very desirable for German armor and would become one of the focal points of the battle that lay ahead.

Defense of the Weisser Stein

Meanwhile, several company commanders attempted to contact the battalion CP. They realized the artillery had knocked out the telephone lines in the area. These lines had taken several days to install. A German artillery barrage—only 30 minutes old—had completely wiped out their effort. Still, despite the damaged lines, several commanders managed to report that all was well in the forward positions. The men of the 2nd Battalion avoided needless casualties by keeping inside their foxholes.

CPT Legare contacted each company by radio himself. He speculated to the commanders that the artillery might be in response to the attack on the Roer River Dams in the north. But Legare wanted the company commanders to keep an eye out for a possible German ground attack following the barrage. He had nothing to base this fear on except a strong feeling that something big was imminent. His intuition would prove valuable, not only for the 2nd Battalion but for the entire 394th Infantry Regiment.

The artillery fell for nearly two hours. The shelling finally ended at 0730. Legare received a call from CPT Patterson of Company E, who reported large numbers of camouflaged German infantry, supported by several tanks, approaching his positions. The other two commanders reported infantry on their front as well but no tanks. Unknown to Legare, the lead battalion of the 990th Grenadier Regiment, 277th Volksgrenadier Division, was attacking his battalion's position. These grenadiers were Oberst Viebig's men, and their attack was supported not by tanks but by 75mm sturmgeschutzen. Viebig had also bolstered the 990th with the 277th Fusilier Battalion to increase its combat power. Viebig wanted the Weisser Stein Trail in his hands quickly.

The white-clad Germans approached Company E's position slowly. CPT Patterson ordered his men to fire. A withering hail of small-arms fire erupted through the German ranks. Many sought immediate cover. The German assault guns fired their 75mm projectiles at the entrenched infantryman of the 2nd Battalion but with little effect. The rounds simply impacted on the trees nearby. Lethal splinters of wood flew everywhere.

Patterson realized the German attack was concentrated on his company. The Germans were trying to gain control of the Weisser Stein Trail to move the tanks of the 12th SS Panzer Division "Hitlerjugend" forward. If the German's punched through Patterson's company, they could outflank the 394th from the north. Such a maneuver would threaten the regiment's defense of the Losheimergraben Crossroads in the south. Patterson called Legare at battalion headquarters and told him that the German infantry, with an assault gun detachment, was grouped in the area where preplanned artillery targets existed. If they fired the artillery now, they could severely damage the attacking German battalion.

Legare turned to the battalion Artillery liaison officer, CPT Joseph Knight, and told him to fire all concentrations in front of Company E. Knight immediately went to work. He called CPT Mannheimer's Company H mortars. Knight and Mannheimer had spent hours perfecting and fine tuning the battalion artillery and mortar fire plan in the days past.[2] Now was their chance to put the plan to the test. After contacting Mannheimer, Knight called the division general support artillery battalion and requested they fire all concentrations in front of Company E. The artillery commander acknowledged. Knight called CPT Patterson and told him that rounds were on the way.

Back at Patterson's position, the German infantry moved forward slowly. The tremendous flurry of small-arms fire from the men of Company E did not stop them. The assault guns crept forward as well. The vehicles used the contours of the rolling hills in front of Company E to prevent exposure to enemy fire. Finally, CPT Patterson got CPT Knight's call that the artillery was on the way. Patterson quickly relayed the news to his platoons. Suddenly, the first of CPT Mannheimer's 81mm mortars exploded among the German infantry. The German assault formation broke up. The Germans withdrew to the safety of the dense, coniferous forest. Most of Company E's soldiers sought shelter from the flying splinters inside their foxholes. The GIs relied on the thick overhead cover to keep them safe.

A loud whooshing sound could suddenly be heard overhead. The Germans paused for a moment and looked upward. The small-arms fire from Company E had stopped as the men took refuge inside their foxholes. CPT Patterson had just put down the radio after hearing CPT Knight's "Splash" when the ground to his front erupted. Dozens of artillery rounds landed directly in front of his company. CPT Patterson dove for the bottom of his log hut. He clapped his hands over his ears and opened his mouth wide to keep his ear drums from bursting. The artillery barrage was tremendous and fell murderously on the ranks of the German infantry. The assault guns tried to back up as the artillery came in. Each assault gun shuddered as the rounds impacted nearby. The crews inside were deafened as small pieces of shrapnel smacked and tinkled on the outside hull. The German infantry had no protection save for the forest. The artillery rained death on their ranks in a most unforgiving manner. German soldiers screamed as the deadly shrapnel rent and tore their bodies. The blasts sent many flying through the air. Those lurking in the forest saw the barrage destroy their comrades. In great haste, the Germans withdrew east, to the forest.

CPT Patterson received a call from one of his platoon leaders who informed him that the Germans were leaving with their assault guns. Patterson called Knight and told him to stop the artillery. The fires soon lifted. The GIs of Company E could now hear the moans of wounded Germans in the snow before them. Several soldiers emerged from the foxholes and went forward to help the injured men. Patterson instructed his medics to assist as well. When the medics arrived, they surveyed the carnage wrought by the mortars and artillery. Pieces of German bodies lay scattered about the dirty snow. The artillery had turned up the dirt underneath the snow, the blasts causing the soil to spray in odd and fantastic designs over the crisp, white carpet. Mingled with this dirt was the blood of the German infantrymen. Their bodies were strewn about the battlefield in grotesque positions. The artillery plan had paid off for the 2nd Battalion. The barrage had broken the back of the German attack.

Defense of the Weisser Stein 79

Oberst Wilhelm Viebig, the commander of the 277th Volksgrenadier Division, was shocked to learn that his 990th Grenadier Regiment's lead battalion had suffered nearly 50 percent casualties in the initial attack. Viebig's chief of staff, Oberstleutnant Horst Freiherr von Wangenheim, had warned him that new replacements might suffer in their first action. Obviously, von Wangenheim was right. These raw recruits, even though led by experienced leaders, were still learning about the infantryman's craft. Many of them came from Luftwaffe ground support troops, the Kriegsmarine (navy), and Austria. Most didn't even have their own weapons; they would have to wait until one of their comrades fell in battle before they could acquire one. It was painful for Viebig to send these men back into the fray, but he had to open the Weisser Stein Trail for the 12th SS Panzer Division. He instructed von Wangenheim to call the 990th Grenadier Regiment's commander, the highly decorated Oberstleutnant Josef Bremm, and order him to attack again. Bremm was an inspiring leader. His exceptional abilities were evident by the Oakleaves to the Knight's Cross of the Iron Cross he wore around his neck. Viebig hoped this time the new recruits would find some success.[3]

Back at the 2nd Battalion CP, CPT Legare considered the situation reports from his companies. Company E on the left had held well, despite intense pressure by the 990th Grenadier Regiment. Companies F and G had contacted only small numbers of German infantry to their front. The GIs quickly drove these small bands back with well-coordinated small-arms fire. Since the battalion held a large front, roughly 3,000 meters, the companies defended with small, well-integrated strongpoints that mutually supported each other. These well-prepared strongpoints allowed the GIs to maximize their fires. Most important, these strongpoints hindered the Germans' efforts to find gaps in their line. Enemy patrols to the south were very strong, however. Legare was concerned. He feared for the security of the battalion's right flank and stated his concern to Regiment. COL Riley understood and detached a platoon from the 1st Battalion's Company C to the 2nd Battalion's Company G. Riley also sent an antitank platoon to serve as infantry. Soon, all units were in place. The 2nd Battalion's line was intact. Legare was pleased with his men: They had stood their ground, and he happily reported this fact to COL Riley.

At 1000 hours, the Germans struck Company E again. This time the grenadiers hit on the deep left flank. Their attack brought them to the very left side of T/SGT Fred Wallace's platoon. Once again, the Germans came with sturmgeschutze support. The assault guns followed closely behind the attacking German infantry. T/SGT Wallace's platoon erupted with heavy small-arms fire, but the Germans breached his position. He called CPT Patterson and told him the platoon was being overrun but that the men were still in their foxholes and fighting. Wallace shouted commands to his platoon from his fighting position.

"Listen, you guys," shouted the sergeant, "stay put in your holes! I'm gonna bring the artillery right on top of us!"[4]

"You're gonna do what?" came a bewildered response.

"Just stay in your holes and you'll be okay," answered the sergeant.

German MP40 fire kicked up snow and dirt next to T/SGT Wallace's foxhole. Wallace called CPT Patterson and told him to bring the artillery down right on top of the platoon's position. If Patterson didn't do as he asked, the Germans would roll the whole battalion up from the left flank. Patterson called CPT Knight and told him to bring the artillery down quickly or the battalion would be in great jeopardy.

Within minutes, mortar and artillery fire again erupted around Company E's positions. Wallace and his men dove for the bottoms of their foxholes. They pulled their steel helmets down upon their heads. The artillery rounds impacted within the platoon's position. The noise was deafening. Wallace heard nothing but the constant roar of exploding rounds. Dirt shook loose from the walls of his foxhole. The soil nearly buried Wallace alive. Then, as quickly as it began, the artillery stopped. Wallace, visibly shaken, stiffly pulled himself up from the floor of his foxhole and looked outside. All he saw were wisps of blue smoke that hung in a dense fog around his platoon's positions. He could neither see nor hear any German soldiers or armored vehicles. He pulled himself from the foxhole and stood erect.

"Hey!" he called. "Is everyone okay?"

He received no immediate answer. He picked up his M1 carbine and walked forward. He stumbled as his foot hit something on the ground. He waved the mist and smoke away long enough to see the horribly mutilated form of a German soldier in front of him. He looked around and saw nothing but German bodies lying everywhere. The artillery had been tremendous. The bursts had splintered and shattered nearby trees. Suddenly, ghostlike figures appeared in the mist and approached the sergeant.

"Hold it!" he yelled. He leveled his M1 carbine at the approaching figures.

"Easy, Sarge," came a voice. "It's just us."

Wallace could see his men climbing slowly from their foxholes. There were no Germans left standing, only shaken American infantrymen.

"Okay," said Wallace, "get a count, squad leaders."

The squad leaders reported all present. Wallace was delighted. Calling the artillery on their position had been risky, but the squad had come out safe and sound.

"Who called for that goddamned artillery?" asked one flabbergasted soldier.

"I did," replied Wallace. "We were bein' overrun. What the hell else could I do?"

"You're nuts," answered the soldier. "But I'm sure glad you're on my side."

"Say, where are the rest of the krauts?" asked another soldier.

"Long gone," came another reply. "I saw 'em head for the hills when the artillery started comin'. Same for them tanks, too."

Defense of the Weisser Stein   81

"What a mess," muttered Wallace as he surveyed the dead Germans. "We've gotta move these bodies. They can't stay here. They'll stink up the place."

Just then, the sound of breaking brush and crunching snow echoed behind them. They wheeled around and leveled their rifles at an approaching form.

"It's the CO," said Wallace. "Hold your fire!"

"Holy...," mumbled CPT Patterson at the sight of the dead Germans. "You men okay?"

"Yes, sir, " replied T/SGT Wallace. "The Germans took off back east, except for these here."

"That was incredible, SGT Wallace," said the captain.

"I had no choice," came the reply.

Suddenly, the men detected movement to their north. Wallace's men scattered for their foxholes. Patterson joined Wallace in the sergeant's hole.

"They're attacking again," yelled Wallace to his men. "Hold your fire until you see who it is."

"Hey, Sarge," came a voice." They're GIs."

The men emerged from the foxholes. Several frightened and disheveled American soldiers approached.

"Where are you men from?" asked CPT Patterson.

"1st Battalion, 393rd, sir," answered one of the men. "Our battalion's been pushed back. We got left behind."

"Wait a minute," said Patterson, "you mean to tell me there's no one on our left?'

"That's about the size of it, sir," answered the soldier.

Patterson hurried to his CP and reported the success of SGT Wallace's platoon and the incident with the men from the 393rd. The last bit of news alarmed Legare. The 393rd was all that protected the 2nd Battalion's left flank. Legare called COL Riley. The regimental commander could only tell him that the 393rd was under tremendous German pressure. He didn't know how far back the Germans may have driven them. Legare wanted to find out for himself. He instructed CPT McGee to assemble a patrol from the Battalion Headquarters Company's men. He told McGee to have the patrol contact the 393rd's positions further north and gather any information possible. The patrol quickly departed for the woods north of the Weisser Stein Trail.

Legare was worried about his left flank now. He called CPT Patterson and told the Company E commander to put as many troops on his left flank as he could spare, to include support troops from the company's headquarters. Patterson called back within minutes and told Legare he had done as ordered. Thirty minutes after their departure, the patrol returned and reported to CPT Legare. They had found no American units. Only Germans were walking in the forest where the 393rd should be. Legare immediately informed COL Riley. Riley released the regimental Mine Platoon to the 2nd Battalion for use on the left flank. The Mine Platoon arrived at 1400, and Legare handed them over to CPT Patterson. Patterson placed them beside his support elements on the left flank.

The rest of the day remained quiet. Legare found out about the rest of the regiment. He knew that the 1st Battalion to the south had been hit hard but was still in place. The Germans had even probed some of Company G's positions. Concentrated small-arms fire quickly repelled them. Most of the company land lines had been replaced. These land lines effectively reestablished telephone communication within the battalion. Legare was satisfied. The battalion had succeeded in stopping the push of Oberstleutnant Bremm's 990th Grenadier Regiment.

Oberst Viebig now had to look for success elsewhere in the north.

The 394th Regiment's left flank, and the critical crossroads to the south, were safe for the moment. Legare's men had done well, and casualties were light. For the most part, his battalion's disposition remained the same as the day before. Everything looked good from his perspective, and everyone had performed quite well. Everyone, that is, except for the quivering mass of human flesh that pathetically hugged a corner of the CP's log hut. Shaking his head, Legare looked at his battalion commander.

"If only he kept his head," he muttered to himself. "He'd have a lot to be proud of now. What a damned disgrace!"[5]

CHAPTER 8

Lanzerath: "Hold at All Costs!"

From the hill overlooking Lanzerath to the northwest, the 394th's Intelligence and Reconnaissance (I&R) Platoon heard the first German artillery rounds land behind them to the west.[1] 1LT Lyle Bouck, the platoon leader, ordered his men into their foxholes. The artillery fell far to the west; it presented no immediate threat to the platoon. Bouck could see the western horizon brighten as the German shells impacted near the small hamlet of Honsfeld. The bright flashes bounced off the gray, early morning sky. To Bouck's east, German searchlights reflected eerily off the hanging clouds. The barrage had already lasted an hour and a half.

Suddenly, the trees above Bouck's position exploded. Wooden splinters sprayed the platoon's foxholes. The artillery landed directly on the I&R Platoon. A terrifying and deafening roar shook the ground. Bouck clamped his hands over his ears and closed his eyes. He prayed the barrage would soon lift. He got on his radio and spoke to the assistant regimental S-2, 1LT Edward Buenger. Buenger said the entire division was under bombardment. Bouck put aside the radio handset and waited for the artillery to end. After several minutes of sporadic but intense artillery fire, the barrage moved east. The artillery finally lifted a few minutes later. Bouck removed his hands from his ears and listened. It was over. The barrage lasted nearly two full hours. The final rounds landed on his hill and the area around Lanzerath.

Bouck slowly climbed from his foxhole and walked toward the other fighting positions. Large wood splinters from the damaged trees littered the white carpet of snow to his front. Smoke mixed with the early morning haze obscured his vision. He couldn't see farther than a few feet ahead. Everything seemed quiet, deathly quiet. Bouck feared that many, if not all, of his men were killed by the artillery. He called for his platoon sergeant, T/SGT Bill Slape.

"Sergeant Slape!" yelled Bouck.

"Right here, sir," answered Slape. "Keep it down. My ear drums are throbbing!"

T/SGT Bill Slape, the I&R Platoon sergeant, approached Bouck from out of the mist. Bouck heard the movements of other men as they clambered from their foxholes. Many muttered and swore under their breath. SGT Slape called out for a status report. He then turned to Bouck.

"You shouldn't holler so damn loud, sir," he said. "Didn't that damn artillery give you a headache, too?"

SGT Slape was a rough, ornery man, not very popular with the soldiers. He was firm and demanded discipline. But he got the job done better than other platoon sergeants, and the men respected him, especially Bouck. He solved many problems for his platoon leader, which made Bouck's job easier. Bouck took Slape's mild admonishment as teasing. He grinned as he watched the man dig in his ears with his fingers, trying to get the ringing out.

"Well, SGT Slape," answered Bouck, "I've got a headache, too. That artillery was pretty scary. I wonder why the Germans did it."

Just then, several platoon members called out to Slape and told him everyone was fine; the platoon suffered no casualties. Bouck sighed with relief.

"Well," said Slape, "that's all that artillery was: scary! It didn't damage our position. Good thing, too. The gun jeep doesn't have much overhead cover."

"Yeah," answered Bouck, "but why the artillery? What does it mean?"

Both men pondered this question. Meanwhile, soldiers of the 9th Fallschirmjaeger Regiment, 3rd Fallschirmjaeger Division, moved west to their first objective: Lanzerath.

Twenty-year-old 1LT Lyle J. Bouck was the youngest man in his platoon save for another, a 19-year-old named PVT William Tsakanikas. Despite his youth, Bouck had already accumulated over six years of military service.[2] He came from a struggling family of five kids, supported by a father who was a carpenter. They often lived in places with only one bedroom, no electricity, and no plumbing. Bouck lacked motivation in school. He repeated the fifth grade because he failed to pay attention in class. This shameful incident became a turning point for Bouck. He quickly applied himself academically and excelled at every subject. In 1938, just before his fifteenth birthday, Bouck's father convinced him to spend two weeks of the summer in the St. Louis National Guard. Bouck's father was an NCO in the National Guard in 1928 and saw an opportunity for a couple of his sons to earn some extra money. That two-week summer camp would net the young Bouck a dollar a day, big money in those days.

Bouck joined. His father influenced some of his old National Guard friends to bend the age rules a bit. Bouck enjoyed the summer camp and decided to stay since he only drilled once a week and earned $13 every three months. His father's old "contacts" saw to it that he stayed in the supply room, but from then on, Bouck was on his own. He spent his days folding wool blankets and counting canteens.

On 23 December 1940, Bouck's National Guard unit, the 138th Infantry Regiment, 35th Infantry Division, was activated and sent to Camp Robinson in Little Rock, Arkansas. He was only 17 then, but no one cared. Bouck's father insisted he return to school, but Bouck wanted to stay. He told his father he would complete high school when the division demobilized after a year. Bouck was promoted to buck sergeant and placed in charge of the supply room. As a young NCO, he made $60 a month.

Soon, the Japanese attacked Pearl Harbor, and America was in the Second World War. Bouck turned 18 just ten days later. He was now eligible for Officer Candidate School. Bouck applied, and his commanding officer recommended him. However, he had to falsify his educational records. Officers needed at least four years of high school; Bouck had had only two. He went to OCS at Fort Benning, Georgia, and graduated on 26 August 1942. By then, officer candidates were moved through rapidly because of the war. Instead of receiving orders to ship out, Bouck stayed at Fort Benning as an instructor for two years, where he grew a little and matured as an officer. A colonel took a liking to him and offered him a slot in the three-month officer advanced course located at Benning. In the advanced course, Bouck was the only lieutenant in a sea of captains, majors, and colonels.

After completion of the course, Bouck became company commander for a Basic Infantry Replacement Training Center at Fort Hood, Texas, which was commanded by a "screamer." The "screamer"—a little colonel—was so obnoxious and irritating that Bouck sought any chance to leave. At one of the command and staff meetings, Bouck heard about four first lieutenant slots opening in the 99th Division at Camp Maxey, Texas, in March 1944. Bouck volunteered. He soon became the weapons platoon leader and subsequently the company executive officer in Company C of the 394th Infantry Regiment. While in Company C, he made friends with the officers and men of the 1st Battalion.

During the 99th's training exercises at Camp Maxey, the I&R Platoon performed so poorly that the division commander relieved both the platoon leader and the regimental commander. The new regimental commander, upon his arrival, relieved the regimental S-2 and appointed a veteran of North Africa, MAJ Robert L. Kriz, in his place. The new commander requested Kriz, who received the Silver Star while serving with the 9th Division in Africa, to disband and then reform the I&R Platoon with hand-picked soldiers. Kriz reassigned all but four of the platoon's members. These men would form the basis for a new and efficient I&R Platoon.

While Kriz was rebuilding the I&R Platoon, LT Bouck arrived to conduct a 1000-inch machine gun range. The day before, another officer had conducted the same range very badly. Soon, several high-ranking visitors arrived to observe the training. Among them was MAJ Kriz. He watched Bouck issue instructions to his men about how the range would operate that day. Bouck had experience with this type of range at Fort Benning and was very familiar with the assignment. Kriz approached Bouck and questioned him about his range instructions. Bouck explained. Impressed by the young officer's competence and self-confidence, Kriz asked Bouck to command the new I&R Platoon. Bouck accepted.

Kriz and Bouck became very good friends. They worked closely as they interviewed over 90 soldiers before settling on the required 32 necessary to fill the table of organization. They chose the strongest, most physically fit soldiers as well as the best marksman. Many of the men were extremely intelligent. Some came from the Army's ASTP (Army Specialized Training Program), a program designed to send college hopefuls to school and then to OCS. However, the personnel demands of the war dissolved this program. Instead, the ASTP candidates ended up as line soldiers in combat units.

The I&R Platoon became a well-oiled machine and functioned smoothly in the field. The rough but caring T/SGT Bill Slape provided the necessary discipline. The platoon even managed to acquire more weapons, equipment, and ammunition than normally authorized. By the time the German counteroffensive struck in December, Bouck was down to only 24 men. Six were performing duties away from the platoon. All Bouck had to fight with on that hill northwest of Lanzerath were 18 men, but they were 18 good men.

Bouck and his men returned to their foxholes and worked to improve them. They checked for possible damage inflicted by the German artillery. Down the hill to the east, 500 meters away, lay the small village of Lanzerath. Historically, the town belonged to Germany, but after World War I and the Treaty of Versailles, it became part of Belgium. The town had 10 to 15 small, wooden houses, useless as protection against weapons fire of any sort.[3] The real significance of the hamlet lay in its one, solitary road. This north-south road led to either Losheimergraben in the north or, at a fork, to Honsfeld in the west. Any force that commanded this north-south road could easily outflank the vital crossroads to the north and open a rapid avenue to the west. The road was well-packed and could support armored vehicles. The Germans recognized its value.

Since Lanzerath lay outside the V Corps and just inside the VIII Corps boundary, it marked the northern limit of the Losheim Gap. This nine-kilometer north-south gap was covered by Task Force X of the 14th Cavalry Group. Task Force X's capabilities only allowed them to occupy this large front with small strongpoints or outposts. Four towed 3-inch gun crews from the 2nd Platoon of Company A, 820th Tank Destroyer Battalion, occupied one of these posts. A same-size element from the 612th Tank Destroyer Battalion had occupied Lanzerath until relieved by Company A of the 820th on 10 December, the same day the I&R Platoon moved into position. The 2nd Reconnaissance Platoon from the 820th reinforced Company A. A total of 55 soldiers manned the outpost at Lanzerath.[4] The 820th men parked their anti-tank guns and half-tracks behind the houses in the village. The GIs then occupied one of the homes where they ate and slept. LT Bouck contacted the 820th Tank Destroyer men on 10 December, the same day the I&R Platoon occupied their position on the hill overlooking the town. Since Company A already had an observation post in town, Bouck saw no need to establish one himself. He asked if the tank destroyer unit would offer him advance warning of any enemy attacks. The men agreed, and Bouck's radio operator ran a land line to their position. This arrangement couldn't have worked out better for Bouck. He was already down to nearly half of his authorized strength of 32.

The men of Company A, 820th Tank Destroyer Battalion, occupied a house belonging to the Schur family, people who appreciated the American presence and what the Allies were doing for them. The Schur's fed the young GIs and, in return, the soldiers offered them hard-to-find items such as coffee, chocolate, and cigarettes. Suzanne (Sany) Schur, their pretty 25-year-old daughter, waited on the soldiers constantly. At night she slept between her mother and father for fear the men might molest her. Her young first cousin, 16-year-old Adolf, who lived in the northern part of Lanzerath, helped her to wait on the men. He worshipped the GIs. The men joked and laughed with young Adolf. The GIs offered him more attention than he could imagine in his wildest dreams. Since Adolf could only speak German, he tried to learn English from the soldiers. They taught him words he didn't understand. The men laughed every time he repeated them. Adolf knew they were probably teaching him to swear in English, but he didn't care. The attention and admiration he received from his new friends was worth it.[5]

Back on the hill above Lanzerath, LT Lyle Bouck stood outside his foxhole, his binoculars scanning the south. He thought the Germans might try a ground assault. He didn't believe the Germans had used so much artillery for no reason. At 0830, Bouck heard rifle fire and loud explosions to the north. SGT Slape approached him from behind.
"What's all that noise?" asked Slape.
"Don't know," answered Bouck. "Sounds like it's coming from Losheimergraben."
Bouck turned left and focused his binoculars north. As he did, he heard vehicle engines roar in Lanzerath. Through his binoculars, he saw four half-tracks with anti-tank guns in tow rapidly moving north and taking a left onto the western road to Honsfeld. The men of the 820th Tank Destroyer Battalion had suddenly left without notifying Bouck; they had not bothered to call him on the land line he had run to them.
"Gee," said PVT Tsakanikas, "if they can't sign off on the phone, they might at least wave good-bye as they leave."[6]
"Why the hell did they do that?" Bouck asked Slape.
"I don't know, sir," answered Slape, "but something is wrong. You'd better call Regiment and see what's going on. Somebody's out there shootin' for some reason."
Bouck went to his foxhole and picked up his radio handset. PVT Tsakanikas had told him earlier that the artillery knocked out the wire lines to regimental headquarters. Bouck soon heard the voice of Major Kriz, the regimental S-2, crackling over the handset.

"The tank destroyer unit has departed with no explanation," said Bouck into the radio. "I heard firing to the north near the 1st Battalion as well. What should I do? Over."

"Get down into that town and set up an observation post," came the reply. "The 1st Battalion is being hit very hard north of you. If something big is happening, we'll need to see south of your position. Out."

Bouck dropped the handset and told SGT Slape he wanted a two-man observation post in the town to replace the one abandoned by the tank destroyer men. Bouck instructed Slape to find two volunteers. Bouck would accompany the men into the town and position them in a house to observe the area south of Lanzerath. Slape returned minutes later with PVT William Tsakanikas and PVT John Creger. Tsakanikas was only one year younger than Bouck, and he was highly motivated. Bouck chose him to be his radio operator and driver. Both Bouck and Tsakanikas shared the same foxhole.

"I need you up here," Bouck told Tsakanikas.

"Oh, come on, sir," replied the young soldier, "lemme help."

Bouck realized that arguing with Tsakanikas would get him nowhere. He told Tsakanikas and Creger to secure a field phone and a spool of wire to run a land line. They would leave in five minutes.

"I'm gonna come, too," insisted Slape. "If something happens, I'll need to know where they are."

Soon, all four men made their way down the hill left of the platoon position. They went straight for the northern part of town. To avoid exposing themselves unnecessarily, they moved in the contour of a small ravine that bordered the hill. They still weren't certain what was going on. Somebody nearby was shooting. Shooting meant trouble, and Bouck wanted to be ready.

Young Adolf Schur, Sany Schur's 16-year-old cousin, was heartbroken to see his new friends depart so suddenly. He saw one of them talking into a radio. Then they hurriedly packed up their equipment, hooked up the anti-tank guns, and headed north. They didn't even pause long enough to offer a good-bye. Saddened, he returned to the cellar where his cousin Sany and the rest of the Schur family had been hiding since the artillery began.[7]

Suddenly, Adolf looked behind him and saw some Americans. The men were looking south from the second floor window of a house on the east side of the road. They spoke in hushed tones and appeared to be operating radios and other equipment. A jeep was parked outside behind the house. He couldn't remember seeing these Americans before. He didn't know who they were, but he decided to leave them alone. One heartbreak for today was all he could handle.

Inside that house, LT Warren Springer of Battery C, 371st Field Artillery, looked south from the upstairs window.[8] Springer and his three-man observation team had been there since yesterday. Springer's team had moved from the northern ridge overlooking Losheim the day before, where they supported the 3rd Battalion at Buchholz Station.[9] Springer had decided to move farther south

Lanzerath: "Hold at All Costs!"

to a better vantage point, and Lanzerath seemed to him to be the best place. The town offered clear observation to the south. Springer informed the men of the 820th Tank Destroyer Battalion of his new position the day before; the tank destroyers made him feel more secure.

Many suspicious-looking civilians milled about the area. Springer thought these civilians took an unusual interest in the activities of the observation team and the anti-tank men. Springer was certain some were spies. Springer stopped a man the day before coming into Lanzerath from the south on a bicycle. The man claimed to be picking up some shoes he had left with a cousin to repair. Somehow his story didn't seem quite right to Springer. The artillery officer turned him over to the tank destroyer men who promised to send him to their battalion S-2. Despite his suspicions, LT Springer felt Lanzerath was his best choice for an OP. If any Germans attacked the flank of the 3rd Battalion, he would know about it first.

The other three men with Springer were SGT Peter Gacki, T/4 Willard Wibben, and T/5 Billy S. Queen. T/5 Queen was a pudgy man with round, wire-rimmed glasses. Queen didn't seem like much of a soldier, but he was an expert artillery observer. These three men checked their antenna and the radio remote, a device with a speaker and handset used to maintain communication by running field wire to the radio on the jeep outside. The jeep radio was far more powerful than any hand-held device; this radio was the observation team's only link to the supporting artillery batteries.

"What do you see out there?" asked SGT Gacki.

"Nothing," replied Springer. "It's too misty. We'll have to wait till this damned fog clears before we can see."

"The radio's working fine, anyhow," said Gacki. "You know, those tank destroyer guys pulled out pretty fast. I wonder why?"

There was no response from Springer. He pressed his binoculars to his face, leaning forward through the window and squinting hard against the eyepieces.

"Sir, did you hear me...?" asked Gacki.

Springer raised his right arm to indicate silence. The men crowded closer to the window.

"What is it?" asked T/5 Queen.

"Holy Christ!" yelled Springer. "Germans! Lots of them! Heading straight for us!"

"Call for fire!" screamed Wibben.

"Wait a second," said Springer. "I wanna see if there are any of those tank destroyer guys left."

Springer ran downstairs and out of the house. The lieutenant spotted a half-track, the last to leave, as it pulled out onto the road leading north. The men in the vehicle told him a German column was coming up the road. Then, the half-track quickly sped off to the north. Frustrated at the prospect of being abandoned, Springer ran back into the house.

"Okay," he said, "let's bring the artillery in."

Springer called for artillery to fall 200 meters south of the town. That would put the rounds on top of the approaching column. But a frantic voice responded on the other end. The voice said the guns couldn't fire; the Germans were apparently attacking the rear firing batteries with small-arms fire.[10] Springer saw no other option but to retreat. They didn't stand a chance alone.

"Let's go," said Springer. "We'll make it to a nearby hill and call for fire from there."

The men scrambled outside and piled into the jeep. Another jeep carrying three men (perhaps from a withdrawing forward observation post established by the tank destroyer men) drove by heading north. The unknown GIs yelled for the OP party to follow. The three men claimed they could show Springer's observation team where to find a prepared defensive position overlooking Lanzerath. Springer agreed to go, and all four artillerymen clambered into their vehicle and followed the jeep. Adolf Schur saw the two jeeps roar off to the north. Shaking his head, he watched the men disappear into the waning morning fog. Standing in the road, he turned and faced south. In the distance he saw a large column of men moving straight up the road toward Lanzerath.

Just before the artillerymen's jeep roared away, LT Bouck and his men entered a two-story house in the northern part of Lanzerath. The men looked around and decided the house would serve as a good observation post. They prepared to run a new land line from the house back to the platoon.

"I'm gonna check upstairs," said Tsakanikas.

Bouck followed the man. He was eager to make sure that the upstairs provided the best observation south of the town. Tsakanikas and Bouck entered the first room. They surprised an old man speaking on a phone in German. Tsakanikas rushed forward and slapped the phone out of the startled man's hand.

"A spy!" he yelled. "I should blast you right here!"

"Hold it, Tsak," said Bouck. "Can't you see he's terrified?"

"If nothing's wrong, why's he so nervous?" asked Tsakanikas.

The angry soldier leveled his rifle, complete with fixed bayonet. The frightened man shook uncontrollably. He slowly raised his hands in the air and mumbled something under his breath.

"I think you're right, Tsak," said Bouck, "He's up to no good. But let him go. This isn't how we do things. We don't have room for prisoners. He can't cause any more trouble now."

The terrified man seemed to understand Bouck's words. As soon as Tsakanikas lowered his rifle, the man flew from the room, down the stairs, and out of the house. As the frightened man ran by SGT Slape, the platoon sergeant moved to the bottom of the stairs and looked up.

"What was that all about?" Slape asked.

"Nothing, just a spy," answered Bouck.

"A spy?" asked Slape. "Are you kidding me?"

Lanzerath: "Hold at All Costs!"

"Come upstairs," said Bouck. "You and Creger can put your OP up here on the second floor. I want to leave you with the OP because I think you and Creger may have to leave quickly. If you do, I know that with you here, you'll both make it back to the platoon safely."

Slape agreed. He and Creger went upstairs and unraveled some wire for the field phone. Tsakanikas kept watch near the window.

"I thought I just heard a jeep," Tsakanikas mumbled as he looked outside.

His entire body tensed. Tsakanikas looked south of the town, squinting through the diminishing morning mist. He barely made out the forms of several men moving into Lanzerath from the south.

"Hey, sir," he called to Bouck, "look at this."

Bouck approached the window and froze. He could clearly see German soldiers in two columns moving north along either side of the Lanzerath-Losheimergraben road. The helmets had a distinctive shape to them. Bouck remembered seeing one in a photo in an Army manual on the German order of battle. These helmets lacked the normal flare of a standard German helmet. These men were paratroopers, reputedly Germany's toughest and most elite fighters. Bouck was, in fact, seeing the 1st Battalion, 9th Fallschirmjaeger Regiment of the 3rd Fallschirmjaeger Division. This sudden revelation terrified Bouck. He almost couldn't speak.

"Germans!" he yelled. "Paratroopers coming right up the road!"

"Damn it!" cried Slape. "Get out of here, sir! Go back to the platoon!"

Bouck agreed, directing SGT Slape and PVT Creger to send reports until the Germans got too close for comfort. Then the sergeant and the private were to return to the platoon. The Germans moved cautiously, slowly. Slape and Creger would probably have time to get back if they were not discovered by the Germans. Bouck and Tsakanikas grabbed the end of the communications wire and ran from the front door. They bolted for the ravine that led to the I&R Platoon's position, unraveling the wire as they went. Within minutes, they were in their foxhole. Bouck quickly informed his men to prepare to fire—but only on command.

The Germans of the 9th Fallschirmjaeger Regiment, 3rd Fallschirmjaeger Division, moved slowly up the road leading into Lanzerath. Oberst Helmut von Hofmann, the regimental commander, was inexperienced and overly cautious. He slowed his 1st Battalion's main body so that his advance guard could approach Lanzerath in a broad movement from the east. The commander didn't want any surprises! He simply wanted to survive. Hofmann yearned for his previous assignment: a Luftwaffe desk job in Germany. Officers like von Hofmann, pulled up from the rear echelons, were the German military's last hope of achieving victory.

The Germans moved stealthily toward the center of Lanzerath. LT Bouck called regimental headquarters, and an unknown officer answered the call. Bouck told the officer there was at least one German battalion in Lanzerath and he needed artillery fast. The officer didn't believe Bouck. Bouck yelled into the handset that he wasn't joking. The officer responded with an order to "Hold at all costs." Disillusioned and irritated, Bouck threw aside the radio. He watched the Germans with his binoculars. Bouck wanted them directly in front of his platoon before he fired. The Germans were 300 meters from that point now.

Bouck heard the roar of a vehicle echoing behind him. He turned and saw a jeep carrying four men approach from a side trail that ran behind the platoon's defenses. LT Warren Springer jumped from the passenger side and moved from foxhole to foxhole, asking for the platoon leader. Bouck called to him softly. Springer approached at a low crouch.

"I'm Warren Springer from the 371st," he told Bouck. "I've got a jeep and a radio. I'm ready to give you fire support."

"Thank goodness," responded Bouck. "I just called my regiment for artillery. I don't know if I'll get any support."

"Well, let me know when you want artillery," said Springer. "My team and I will work back here."

"If you don't hear from me, bring in the artillery when you hear us fire," said Bouck.

Springer agreed and sprinted to his jeep. Bouck's field phone rang. Bouck lifted the handset and heard the familiar voice of SGT Slape.

Inside the house that served as the OP, SGT Slape and PVT Creger watched the Germans approach from the south. PVT Creger called to Slape from the other window. Germans were already outside the house. Part of the German advance guard had approached from the east. Slape and Creger heard the Germans enter the house below. The paratroopers were searching for booty.

"Be quiet," whispered Slape.

Creger nodded as Slape carefully picked up the field phone's receiver. Slape cranked the handle several times. He soon heard LT Bouck's voice at the other end.

"Sir," he whispered into the receiver, "the krauts are in the house downstairs. I don't know how they got there. What should we do?"[11]

"Get out of there!" came the reply. "I'm sending someone to get you out!"

"Well, we're not waiting for 'em," said Slape.

Slape and Creger grabbed their rifles and made for the top of the stairs. The two men paused to listen for movement below. The Germans had gone back outside. Slape couldn't see them from the window anymore. Slape and Creger moved quietly down the stairs. Slape leveled his M1 carbine. Both men approached the back door and looked out. No Germans were in sight. Slape noticed a barn next to the house. He told Creger to follow, and the two men made a dash for the entrance. Once inside the barn, Slape and Creger crouched behind a few cows in a stall and waited. With luck, they would find an opportunity to slip away and return to the platoon.

Lanzerath: "Hold at All Costs!" 93

As soon as LT Bouck hung up the field phone, he crawled to a foxhole on his left. CPL Aubrey McGehee, PVT James Silvola, and PVT Jordan Robinson shared the three-man position. Robinson was 37 years old; everyone in the platoon referred to him as "Pop." Bouck instructed the three men to help SGT Slape and PVT Creger return safely to the platoon's defensive position. The three men listened carefully to their platoon leader. When Bouck finished, McGehee, Silvola, and Robinson prepared to go. Bouck told them the OP was in the house farthest to the north and to avoid enemy contact. The men nodded and made their way off the hill and into the small ravine.

Back inside the barn in Lanzerath, Slape and Creger had heard nothing outside the house for several minutes. Both men decided to make a run for the woodline to the north. Slape and Creger left the barn and scrambled into the forest. They crunched through the snow as fast as possible. Once inside the forest, Slape and Creger crossed the main road and headed back to the platoon position. They approached the edge of the road. Slape looked south to see if any Germans were around. All seemed quiet. They made a sudden dash across the road. Several German paratroopers from the advance guard rounded the corner of the barn. They saw Slape and Creger cross the road. One German, who carried an MG42 belt-fed machine gun, fired from his hip. The other German joined in with an MP40 sub-machine gun.

Creger managed to get safely into the woods. But a round from the MG42 hit Slape in the left heel of the boot, knocking the heel completely off.[12] The force of the impact caused Slape to fall forward onto the road, face first. He hit hard. The impact broke a rib and his chest bone. The Germans kept firing. They missed as Slape got up and plunged into the forest. Creger and Slape could hear the Germans yelling. Both men sprinted through the forest to the west, toward the hill and the platoon's defenses. To their amazement, they ran into LT Bouck who, with CPL Risto Milosevich, had come to look for them.

"What the hell are you doing here?" Slape asked Bouck.

"I got impatient waiting for you," answered Bouck. "I sent Silvola, Pop, and McGehee to find you. Where are they?"

"I haven't seen 'em," said Slape, "but we gotta get outta here. The krauts'll be here any minute."

"We can ambush 'em from here," offered Milosevich. "I've got some grenades."

"No!" said Slape. "We'll get killed. C'mon, let's go."

Bouck agreed, and the men started toward the platoon's position on the hill. They moved up the ravine and through the underbrush. Strangely enough, as Slape and Creger moved west through the forest with LT Bouck and Milosevich, they completely missed, by a distance of only several meters, the three men sent to rescue them.[13]

CPL McGehee and his men trudged east. The sounds of machine gun fire rang out nearby. McGehee feared that Slape and Creger were in trouble and needed help. McGehee, Silvola, and Robinson emerged from the ravine west of the road and saw Germans moving everywhere. The three men made a sudden dash across the road and toward the barn where Slape and Creger had hid only minutes before. McGehee, Silvola, and Robinson approached the barn entrance. The same German machine gunner who engaged Slape and Creger fired at them. The gunner's steady fire pinned them down in a gully outside the barn. This time, the German had set up his MG42 in the forest next to the barn. Now he could fire north and south of the road. His partner unpacked more ammunition.

"Damn!" said McGehee. "We're cut off. That kraut has us pinned here."

"What are we gonna do?" asked Pop.

"Try to get to those woods behind that machine gun," answered McGehee. "If that kraut's not gonna let us go back to the platoon, then maybe we can find the 1st Battalion."

Silvola poked his head above the gully. The Germans fired another burst at him, barely missing his head. The Germans showed no sign of moving. From the gully, all three GIs heard the sound of more German soldiers moving nearby. The GIs were surrounded. Their options seemed limited.

"Well," said Pop, "let 'em come. I'll put a world of hurt on 'em before they get me."

The German column had just moved in front of Bouck's defensive positions when the machine gun fire north of the town caused the paratroopers to pause. Although a few houses obscured some of the Germans, Bouck's men could still take the German column under fire. Bouck, having quickly returned to his foxhole, was certain he heard singing coming from the column but quickly dismissed the notion. From his position, he could see a three-man German command group pause in the middle of the road. The German officers seemed to be consulting a map. The three men were between the lead German paratrooper element and the rest of the main body. The German officers talked and pointed to the north. Obviously, one of the German officers was the battalion commander. He seemed to be giving instructions to his lead company commander.

PVT Tsakanikas aimed his M1 rifle at the three men. He had one of them in his sights. Bouck prepared to give the order to open fire. Suddenly, a small, blonde, 13-year-old girl ran into the street and approached the three German officers. Her name was Tine Scholzen. Her family owned the Cafe Scholzen beside which the Germans now stood. Bouck held on for a moment. He was concerned for the young girl's safety.[14] Suddenly, she pointed to the hill where Bouck and his platoon were. The German officers shouted and ran for cover. Little Tine followed them. Several Germans from the lead company opened fire at the hilltop position. The wild rounds merely hit the trees overhead. Bouck shouted to his men above the roar of the German small-arms fire.

"Fire!" he yelled. "Springer, get me some artillery!"

Suddenly, the entire hilltop erupted in a thunderous cascade of small-arms

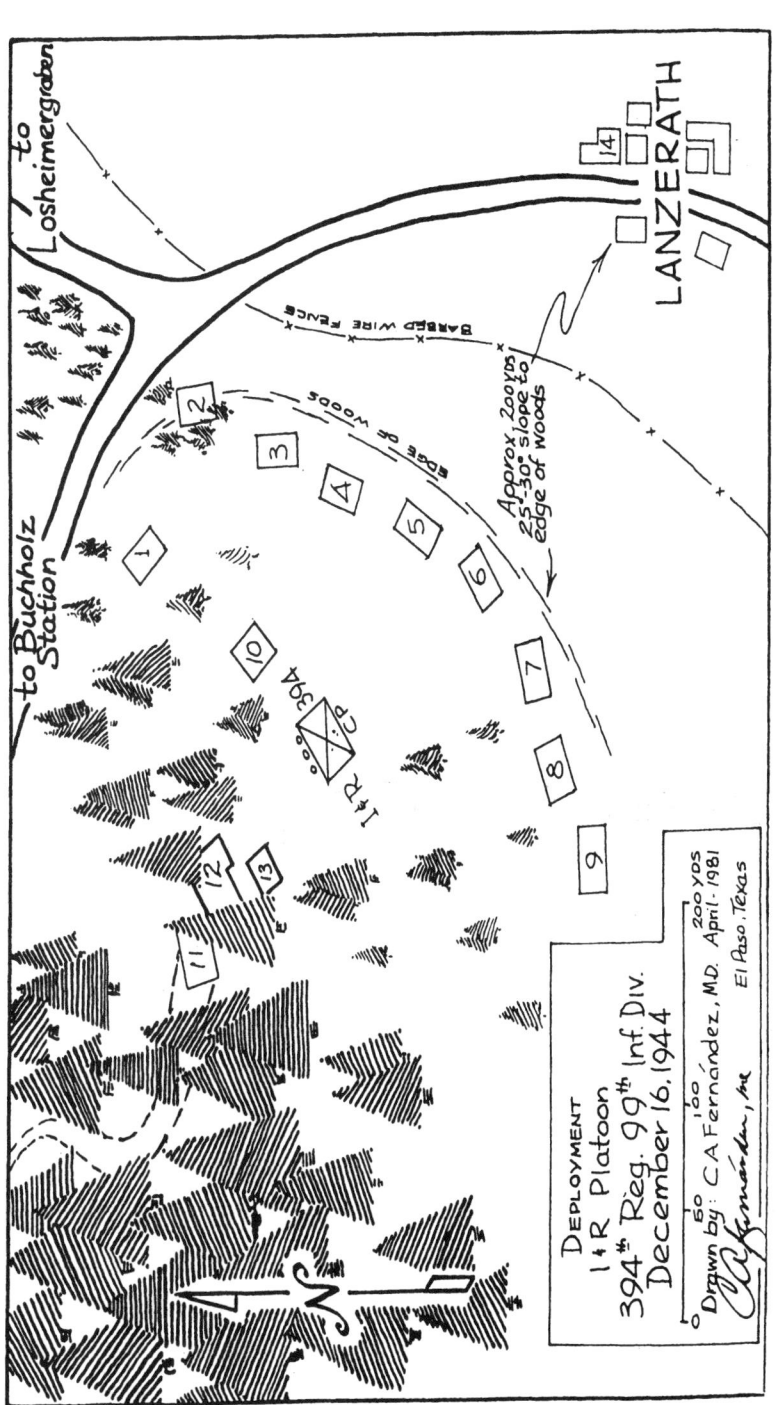

Hand-drawn map of the I&R Platoon position at Lanzerath by platoon member Dr. C. A. Fernandez. The platoon members were in the following foxholes: 1. Redmond and Kalil; 2. Robinson, Silvola, and McGehee (Bazooka/BAR); 3. Slape and Milosevich (.30 cal. MG); 4. Bouck and Tsakanikas; 5. Fansher and artilleryman Queen; 6. Baasch and Fort; 7. Creger and Adams; 8. Dustman and McConnell; 9. Jenkins and Preston; 10. Jeep-mounted .50 cal. MG fired by Tsakanikas and Slape; 11. Radio jeep and sometimes Fort; 12. Log hut. Springer and FO party may have used this hut; 13. Entrenchment adjacent to cabin (Bouck, Fort, and Tsakanikas were here on and off); 14. Slape and Creger's OP in Lanzerath. Courtesy Dr. C. A. Fernandez.

fire. The murderous volume rained down upon the exposed Germans on the road below. Several Germans made sickening gestures as M1 rounds tore into their flesh, killing them instantly. The Germans ran for cover and returned fire.

"Keep firing!" yelled Bouck.

Just then, Bouck saw an amazing sight. The Germans were attacking straight up the hill from the town. They ran and crawled along the open fields to the front of the hill. These attackers had nowhere to hide from the I&R Platoon's murderous fire. Only a thin, barbed-wire fence, bisecting the fields from north to south, separated the two forces. Bouck felt sorry for the Germans. They were valiantly attempting the impossible. Despite severe losses, they continued to attack.

To Bouck's left, CPL Risto Milosevich fired a .30 caliber machine gun with deadly accuracy. In his own foxhole, PVT Tsakanikas fired his M1 with amazing results. He averaged one German for every three rounds fired. LT Warren Springer, in the jeep behind Bouck's position, called for artillery but with no results. He demanded priority of fires, but the guns were either committed to other missions or still under German attack. Suddenly, Springer received a transmission on his radio. There were rounds on the way. Within seconds, four to five artillery rounds landed among the attacking Germans. The bursts tore up the snow-covered fields with amazing force. The men of the I&R Platoon could hear the moans and screams of wounded Germans. Just then, the artillery ended. LT Springer, angered at receiving so few rounds, called for more.

The Germans kept attacking, however. They crawled to within 150 meters of the platoon's positions. Several GIs picked them off as they tried to climb over the barbed-wire fence. A shrill whistle suddenly rang through the air, rising above the rifle and machine gun fire. The Germans withdrew from the hill, leaving behind scores of wounded and dead comrades. Bouck understood what this retreat meant. The Germans wanted to regroup and develop a better plan of action.

"No more frontal assaults, I bet," he said to himself.

The I&R Platoon went silent. German medics ran forward and administered first aid to the wounded closest to the road. They dared not come any closer for fear of being shot by Bouck's men.

"Hold your fire!" shouted Bouck. "We'll get our chance again soon enough."

It was now 0930, two full hours since the German barrage had ended that morning.

CPL McGehee and his two men lay low in the gully by the barn. The battle between the paratroopers and the I&R Platoon was deafening. The sound of small-arms fire echoed in the forest behind them. As soon as the firing started, the German machine gun team that had pinned the three men down was strangely silent. In fact, the three men neither heard nor saw evidence of German paratroopers near them. CPL McGehee stuck his head above the gully for a quick look.

"Hey," he said, "the krauts are gone. They must have gone toward the fighting."

"Well, let's get outta here!" exclaimed Silvola.

"We can't go back to the platoon now," said Pop. "We're gonna have to try for the 1st Battalion."

The men agreed. After a quick look around, they ran for the nearby forest. The men quickly entered the woods and ran north. The hard snow crunched under their footsteps.

"Okay, hold it," said McGehee, "We're safe for now. Let's move a little slower. We're making too much noise."

McGehee, Silvola, and Robinson continued north, paralleling the Lanzerath-Losheimergraben road. The three men could also hear rifle and machine gun fire from the vicinity of the crossroads ahead. They moved more cautiously for fear of more Germans in the woods around them. Within minutes, the men reached the east-west railroad cut leading to Buchholz Station. The tracks were 25 feet below, with steep slopes on both sides. Several meters to their left, the men could see where the bridge over these tracks had been blown. Now, only remnants of the bridge existed, scattered about the tracks below. The Germans themselves had destroyed the bridge several weeks before as they withdrew, under pressure from the Allies, across the Siegfried Line. The Germans would now have to build a new bridge if they wanted to use this road for the current offensive. McGehee, Pop, and Silvola stood on the south side of the embankment and looked at the tracks below.

"If we're gonna cross," said McGehee, "then we've gotta go down and up."

"That's not gonna to be easy with all this snow," muttered Silvola.

"But we gotta do it," said Pop, "so let's go."

Suddenly, Pop leapt forward and slid down the steep slope to the tracks below. The other men watched him go down. His clumsy manner amused them. McGehee and Silvola looked at each other, shrugged, and went down themselves. Once at the bottom, the men struggled up the other side. Silvola's weapon was a Browning Automatic Rifle. He had carried the BAR ever since they had left the platoon. McGehee saw him struggling with the BAR and suggested they switch off carrying it up the hill. The men finally came up on the other side, wet and exhausted from the climb. They heard movement in the woods to their front. Silvola stopped and took a knee.

"Hey, get down!" he whispered. "Somebody's up ahead."

All three men crept behind the trees, just in time to see several German infantrymen approaching. The German soldiers were clad in their trademark white camouflage jackets. From the way the Germans were looking, McGehee, Silvola, and Robinson realized the fusiliers had seen them.

These German soldiers were from Oberstleutnant Heinz-Georg Lemm's 1st Battalion, 27th Fusilier Regiment. The fusiliers had entered the forest from the rail line in an attempt to outflank the 394th's 1st Battalion at the Losheimergraben Crossroads. McGehee, Silvola, and Robinson had just missed running into the 27th's 3rd Battalion. The 3rd Battalion had moved west along the railroad tracks to Buchholz Station. These particular Germans, members of the 1st Battalion, were preparing to assault the American positions when they saw the three GIs emerge from the railroad cutting. The fusiliers now approached cautiously, attempting to determine where the men were hiding.

CPL McGehee saw the fusiliers. McGehee realized they had no choice but to take the Germans on. There were several Germans, at least a platoon. The three men would be sitting ducks if they tried to go back down the embankment.

"Aw, geez...," muttered Pop as he stood and fired his M1 into the ranks of the approaching Germans.

Several Germans screamed and fell. The rest rushed to the safety of nearby trees. Silvola opened fire with the BAR. He hit one or two Germans. The Germans returned fire with their StG 44s and MP40s. Since it was such a close battle, the men from both sides had nowhere to hide except where they fell when the firing began. PVT Silvola was in the open. A German round wounded him badly in the shoulder, but he continued to fire his weapon. Silvola quickly expended all of his BAR ammunition. He looked over at Pop. Pop lay beside a tree, severely wounded in the calf of his right leg. McGehee realized they were out of ammunition. He saw Silvola drop his BAR and grimace in pain. The Germans understood what happened and slowly rose to their feet. McGehee propped himself up on his knees and raised his hands above his head.[15]

"Christ," he muttered, "we got nabbed."

The Germans forced McGehee to his feet while their medics treated both the wounded GIs and German soldiers. They marched McGehee through the woods to the east and into captivity.

As soon as the Germans withdrew back to Lanzerath, LT Bouck ordered all ammunition redistributed throughout the position. They had expended a lot of small-arms rounds. If the Germans came back, and Bouck knew they would, each man would need his fair share. Bouck was now down to 15 men in his position. This number didn't include LT Springer's four-man artillery observation party. Springer's men had trouble getting an artillery battery to fire for the platoon. The firing batteries were supposedly still under German attack and couldn't help. Springer's men occupied some foxholes and dugouts in an effort to contribute to the battle. Gacki and Wibben stayed in the rear dugout while T/5 Queen went forward and found a foxhole to fight from in the platoon's main defensive line.

Bouck reported his situation to Regiment. The headquarters simply acknowledged his transmissions and told him to "hang on." The I&R Platoon remained silent for about an hour and a half. Suddenly, at 1100, Bouck heard voices and movement to his front. To his amazement, the Germans began rushing across the field to his front again, this time in strength. The Germans were trying another frontal attack. Bouck was puzzled. He was certain the

Germans would try to flank him. The I&R Platoon again erupted in a loud cacophony of small-arms fire. Several Germans in the front ranks fell. The air again filled with the mixed and confused sounds of rifle fire, screams, grenade explosions, and machine gun bursts. The Germans made progress by the sheer weight of their numbers and again approached the barbed-wire fence that bisected the field to the front of the I&R Platoon's position. Many were mowed down as they tried to climb over the fence.

PVT Tsakanikas had left the foxhole he shared with Bouck. Manning the .50 caliber machine gun in the jeep behind Bouck's position, he fired mercilessly into the ranks of the Germans who tried to climb the barbed-wire fence. The powerful .50 caliber rounds went through several paratroopers. The impact propelled their bodies backward with tremendous force. The scene was horrible. Bouck winced every time he saw the mangled form of a German spin and hit the blood-covered snow of the pasture. SGT Slape jumped into the jeep with Tsakanikas. Each man took a turn firing the weapon while the other fed ammunition. As before, no Germans advanced beyond the barbed-wire fence. Each German fell before ever crossing over the fence, but not before one paratrooper fired a rifle grenade. The grenade traveled straight into PVT Lou Kalil's hole and hit him in the face. The round was a dud and didn't go off, but the grenade had done damage. The dud grenade broke Kalil's jaw in four places and drove five teeth up into the roof of his mouth. Kalil slumped over, dizzy from the intense pain of his wound. His partner in the foxhole, SGT George Redmond, grabbed him by the collar and shook him.

"Hey," he said to the injured man, "snap out of it."

"My jaw hurts...," mumbled Kalil.

Redmond realized the extent of his partner's injury, but he needed him to keep fighting. He grabbed some snow from outside the foxhole and rubbed it on the man's face. He then made Kalil swallow a couple of 'sulfa' pills.

"There," he said, "you're all better. I don't want any freeloaders here."

"I'll cover you if you want to get away...," mumbled Kalil.

"No way," said Redmond. "We're in this together. Now get up here and start firin'."[16]

Both the snow and words of encouragement seemed to help Kalil. He struggled to his feet and grabbed his rifle.

"Thanks, Sarge," he mumbled.

"Any time," muttered the sympathetic Redmond under his breath.

Soon, the entire field to the front of the platoon was littered with dead or dying German paratroopers. Their second attack had failed miserably. Many of the Germans stopped firing and ran back to the bottom of the hill in disorder. Some stayed in the field. Many knelt beside wounded comrades to comfort them. They seemed completely oblivious to the danger around them. German medics ran from one body to the next. The German medics did what they could for their wounded soldiers. Bouck became aware that his men had stopped firing. Now the GIs stared from their foxholes at the carnage before them. The scene was horrible; it looked like some medieval battlefield on which scores of bodies littered the ground after a tremendous battle between archaic phalanx formations. Bouck told his men to stop firing, but there really was no need to at this point.

At 1145, a German medic waving a white flag walked onto the field from the town below. In broken English, he requested some time to remove the wounded Germans from the battlefield. Bouck agreed and shouted his response to the man. The I&R Platoon watched as the German medics slowly and cautiously walked onto the casualty-strewn pasture. The medics assembled litter teams who carried the wounded Germans into town. The removal of the wounded took over an hour. During this time, Bouck again had his men redistribute ammunition. SGT Slape crawled from foxhole to foxhole. He talked to the men and encouraged them. He spoke to the wounded PVT Kalil, who insisted he was well enough to fight. LT Bouck called Regiment again. He insisted on more artillery support and reinforcements. No one at Regiment seemed to know what was going on. In frustration, Bouck threw the radio handset down. LT Springer tried to get more artillery, but he couldn't seem to get priority of fires. Most of the division's artillery was being used to the north, where the Germans were apparently trying to penetrate the front lines in force. Springer tried to explain that he was facing a large enemy force as well but to no avail. Like Bouck, he too tossed aside his handset in frustration.

At 1400, the third attack by the German paratroopers began. Bouck was bewildered. Once again, the Germans made a frontal assault. Bouck began to doubt the rumors he heard about German paratroopers. The paratroopers definitely weren't short on guts, but they were supposed to be tactical experts who could quickly defeat an enemy by moving rapidly to his flanks and enveloping him. But these Germans were not veteran paratroopers. Most were not even parachute qualified. The 9th Fallschirmjaeger Regiment was a new regiment of raw recruits taken from Luftwaffe ground-crew support units. Many had only rudimentary infantry training. Only a few were actually veteran paratroopers. Most of the veterans were NCOs. The NCOs were the only ones who wore the distinctive helmet of a German fallschirmtruppe (paratrooper).

The attack began as the Germans had proceeded twice before. Two German companies moved straight up the hill at the I&R Platoon. The platoon crackled with fire again. Massive casualties appeared in the German ranks. Many Germans tried a new tactic: crawling forward and only rising to fire every few feet. This tactic protected many of them for some time. Some even came fairly close to the hilltop.

PVT Kalil was firing again with SGT Redmond. Both men took deliberate, well-aimed shots with their M1s. They scored a hit nearly every time.

Alone, CPL Risto Milosevich continued to fire his .30 caliber machine gun from his hole. The corporal kept a steady rate of grazing fire to the platoon's front, which forced the Germans to crawl forward instead of rushing. To his left, Milosevich saw a German who had crawled to within five meters of his position. The German produced a stick grenade and prepared to pull the pin. Milosevich quickly swung the machine gun to his right. Terror-stricken, he fired at the nearby German. He was so startled by the man's presence that he didn't stop firing until he was certain the German was cut in half. Suddenly, his machine gun jammed. Milosevich pulled back repeatedly on the machine gun's charging handle to clear the breech.[17]

From his position in the jeep, SGT Slape noticed Milosevich struggling with the gun. Just then, several StG 44 rounds hit the breech of the .50 caliber machine gun. The ensuing damage rendered it inoperative. Slape dove for cover and grabbed his M1 rifle. He sprinted for Milosevich's position. Two Germans took him under fire from about 50 meters away. SGT Slape returned fire furiously until his rifle overheated and jammed. He killed only one German; the other continued to fire at him. Slape's rifle was so hot he could barely hold it. In desperation, Slape threw the rifle at the German. Amazingly, he hit the man in the head and knocked him backward.[18] He crawled to Milosevich's foxhole. Milosevich helped clear the weapon and feed Slape ammunition. Milosevich had been unable to clear the machine gun by himself. Slape fired the weapon at a steady rate. He killed scores of German soldiers to his front.

"This is like shooting clay ducks at an amusement park, ain't it, Sarge?" asked Milosevich.

"Yeah, but I wouldn't call this fun!" exclaimed SGT Slape.

Just then, Milosevich noticed what he thought was a German medic bending over a wounded soldier on the field. The man appeared to be speaking, either to himself or to the wounded man. The German looked up in quick glances. He tried to act preoccupied with giving first aid to the downed soldier.[19]

Suddenly, German mortar rounds burst around the platoon position. The effects forced several of the I&R men down into their foxholes. SGT Slape dove for cover, but Milosevich's eyes remained fixed on the German crouching in the field. The German appeared to be speaking into something hidden in his jacket. As the German moved slightly, he revealed a holstered pistol in his waist. By then, Slape was back on the machine gun. He fired it until the weapon glowed with heat.

"Sarge, get my rifle behind you," said Milosevich.

"What for?" asked Slape.

"I'm gonna get that kraut out there about 30 yards away on the left," he answered.

"Forget him!" said Slape. "There are still too many comin' up the front."

"He's the one calling in the mortars," said Milosevich quietly. "He's got a radio and he's pretending to be a medic."

"Why, that son of a...," said Slape.

The platoon sergeant grabbed Milosevich's rifle. He aimed the M1 carefully and fired. The German with the pistol lurched backward, arms flailing.

"That's that!" exclaimed Slape.

Slape and Milosevich continued to fire the red-hot weapon at the attacking Germans. They cleared the weapon by opening the feed tray on top. Even after Slape released the trigger, short bursts erupted from the red-hot barrel. These cook-offs continued as the men kept firing. Milosevich took over again as Slape slumped down inside the foxhole for a break. As the platoon sergeant rested for a moment, he noticed two very distinct bullet holes in his field jacket.

"Well, I'll be..." he muttered to himself.

LT Bouck was firing himself. He killed several Germans as they charged up the field to his front. He picked up the handset to his radio and tried to call Regiment for more assistance. Suddenly, a loud snap near his head made his ears ring. He ducked down inside his foxhole. A German bullet had shot the handset from his hands. It lay shattered on the foxhole floor. He no longer had contact with anyone.

He looked from his foxhole to see what was happening. Several Germans were close to the platoon's foxholes. One German got up and rushed straight at PVT Joe McConnell's position on the right. McConnell shot the German squarely in the chest. The man pitched forward onto the snow. As he fell, the German's StG 44 discharged straight at McConnell. Several rounds struck him in the left shoulder. Severely wounded, McConnell slid down inside his foxhole and quietly lost consciousness.[20]

Behind the I&R Platoon, LT Springer and his men sought refuge in a log hut. A mortar round struck their jeep, rendering the radio inoperable. All they could do to help now was fire their rifles when necessary. T/5 Billy Queen, the pudgy artilleryman who occupied a forward position with other members of the platoon, was struck in the stomach by several German sub-machine gun rounds. SGT Gacki didn't see Queen get shot, but he heard from several of the platoon members that Queen was dead. He was the only man to die in the position that day. SGT Gacki felt helpless; he had no way to check on the fate of his fellow artilleryman.[21] He did not know that Queen had panicked. When Queen emerged from his hole to run to the rear, he lost his life.[22]

LT Bouck desperately wanted to resume communications with Regiment. But the Germans kept up the pressure despite heavy losses. The GIs would soon need a resupply of ammunition. In the foxhole to his right, CPL Sam Jenkins and PFC Robert Preston fired vigorously at the oncoming Germans. Bouck called to the two men.

"Hey, I want you two to run back to the 3rd Battalion or Regiment and tell them what's going on," yelled Bouck above the din. "The radio's been destroyed, and we need more men and reinforcements."

Jenkins and Preston understood. Both men clambered from their holes and bolted into the woods to the west. They headed straight for Buchholz Station and the 3rd Battalion. They would never make it to Buchholz Station or to the regimental CP; the Germans would force them into hiding in a barn in Hunningen for three days before capturing them.

As Bouck watched the men depart, he felt he had done his best to get help for the platoon. He was down to only 12 men, including himself. The .30 caliber machine gun fired by Slape and Milosevich stopped firing. He could see both men arguing about the barrel, which was now bent because the heat had

Lanzerath: "Hold at All Costs!"

melted it. Loss of the machine gun was a severe setback to the platoon's firepower.

Fortunately, Bouck noticed fewer Germans to his front. The attack had stopped. He could only hear a few of his men taking well-aimed shots at Germans who remained on the field. Bouck stuck his head up long enough to see that the Germans had once again given up. The German paratroopers quickly retreated to the safety of the town below. It was now 1500. The gray afternoon darkened as day turned to evening. LT Bouck realized, after a quick inventory of ammunition, that the platoon had to pull out. The men had few if any bullets left. The .50 caliber machine gun was inoperable. Nearly everyone was wounded. The platoon would not be able to withstand another German attack.

In the town of Lanzerath, young Adolf Schur watched from a window as the German paratrooper officers argued among themselves. Adolf understood that many of the paratroopers were opposed to the frontal assaults that had taken place. Wounded lined the streets. The Germans were taking over several houses to serve as aid stations.

Suddenly, a German sergeant in a camouflage smock, Feldwebel Vince Kuhlbach, approached the group of men. He wore the distinctive paratrooper helmet and appeared to be a seasoned veteran. He complained to the officers about the stupid tactics they had been using. He demanded that they follow him in a flanking movement up the draw leading north to the hilltop. The officers shrugged and agreed. The feldwebel turned his back on them and stormed off.[23]

LT Bouck passed the word that the platoon would withdraw on a signal of three short whistle blasts. Everyone was supposed to leave his foxhole and move back to the west. They would rendezvous at a specific point on the dirt road to their rear. SGT Slape made certain everyone understood. The men prepared themselves.

PVT Tsakanikas returned, and both he and Bouck moved to their alternate position in the rear. Tsakanikas had just finished removing the distributor caps from the jeeps and, as he clambered into the new dugout, studied the tormented look on his platoon leader's face.

"What's wrong, sir," he asked.

"I can't leave," came the reply. "I'm responsible for holding this hill and I'm going to stay. When I blow the whistle, you go with the others. Tell them any volunteers are welcome to come back to their foxholes and stay with me."

"Like hell!" shouted Tsakanikas. "You're coming with us or we all stay!"

Bouck saw a stubborn determination in Tsakanikas's eyes. The man meant business. Bouck submitted.

"Okay, you win," he said. "I'll go."

Suddenly, both men heard shooting to their left rear. Someone shouted that the Germans were coming up on their left flank. Another yelled that they were on the right flank as well. Before Bouck could say anything, the German paratroopers were on top of their positions. They fired directly into the foxholes.

Bouck fired his last magazine of ammunition, satisfied that he had killed two Germans with his last rounds.

"Where is the commandant?" shouted a German speaking excellent English. "What are you going to do?"

Before Bouck could answer, two Germans pulled the overhead cover from his foxhole.

"How many of you?" demanded a voice in broken English.

"Zwei, zwei!" yelled Bouck in the only German he knew.

Tsakanikas raised his rifle at them. The German fired his MP40 at point blank range. The rounds impacted on the right side of Tsakanikas's face and ripped it open, exposing raw flesh. The rounds also wounded Bouck in the fleshy part of his legs. The wounds caused him to stumble as he tried to stand up. Bouck felt Tsakanikas fall against him. He grabbed Tsakanikas and tried to support him. The German soldier with the MP40 reached down and pulled the wounded GI upright. Suddenly, Bouck caught a glimpse of Tsakanikas's face. His right eyeball hung onto his cheek, connected by only loose muscle tissue. The entire right side of his face was gone. It looked like a large, bloody mass of raw meat. The German soldier looked away.

"Mein Gott!" he exclaimed.

A German feldwebel approached Bouck and asked if he was the commandant. Bouck nodded in affirmation. The feldwebel was probably the same man who called to him before. Sporadic rifle fire could still be heard on the hilltop.

"Why are your men still firing?" asked the German.

"They aren't," he answered. "They must be yours because we're out of ammunition."

The feldwebel nodded and walked away. Ironically, the feldwebel suddenly fell to the ground, wounded in the legs by some unknown rifle fire. The German soldiers helped Bouck out of the hole. The paratroopers propped the severely wounded figure of PVT Tsakanikas against him. Bouck was surprised that the Germans didn't shoot him. As the Germans escorted Bouck down the hill, Bouck saw up close the carnage he and his men had caused. There were German soldiers scattered all over the pasture. The sight was appalling and heart rending. Bouck saw German soldiers kneeling next to their fallen comrades and crying.

"Ach!" exclaimed one. "Meine kameraden!"[24]

Another German soldier approached Bouck with a wild and hostile look in his eye. He demanded to know, in English, if Bouck had fought at St. Lô. The 3rd Fallschirmjaeger Division had suffered heavy losses in that particular area several months before. Bouck shook his head, and the German put his fist in Bouck's face. He proclaimed that the Americans who bombed his comrades at St. Lô last summer were "pigs." The man circled behind Bouck, put a rifle into his back, and pulled the trigger. A loud click caused the officer to flinch. Bouck didn't know if it was a misfire or if the weapon was empty. A German sergeant yelled "Raus! Raus!" at the man, and he went away as quickly as he came.

Although severely wounded, PVT Tsakanikas could see certain things in a dreamlike state. As LT Bouck helped him down the hill, he could see the form of a young, blond German lying face down on the snow. The man's eyes were wide open. There was no apparent sign of physical violence. The wounded man thought this image to be strange. He also thought he saw the image of a young boy watching him. Tears streamed down the boy's youthful face. It was young Adolf Schur. Tsakanikas soon felt himself being placed against a wall. He listened as several people speaking German bandaged his head. Then Tsakanikas passed out.[25]

The Germans occupied the Cafe Scholzen, using the cafe for their regimental command post. The Germans brought Bouck and Tsakanikas to the cafe and sat the two men on a bench. The paratroopers soon took the wounded man away and then returned him with a paper bandage on his head. Bouck was thoroughly exhausted and emotionally drained. He watched quietly as the Germans milled about the cafe. They spoke rapidly in German and occasionally pointed at him. They seemed irritated that they had found only a handful of men on the hill. The Germans must have thought they were fighting a battalion or something larger. The cafe seemed a strange combination of a command post and an aid station. Wounded men were scattered everywhere.

Bouck looked up as the Germans brought in more of his men. SGT Redmond carried in PVT Kalil, who also had his face bandaged. All Bouck could see was Kalil's nose and one eye. SGT Slape followed behind them. Two Germans brought in McConnell after that. McConnell's jacket had been cut away so they could bandage his severely wounded arm. McConnell looked as though he were in a complete daze. The German medics set him down next to some wounded Germans who sat against the cafe wall. Slape quietly eased over to Bouck and whispered in his ear.

"We can get out of here, sir," he said. "The security is lax, and the back door is wide open."

"No," said Bouck, I'm staying. These men are mine, and I want to make sure they get medical treatment."

Slape agreed to stay as well. The platoon sergeant watched carefully as Bouck shifted his weight slightly to allow Tsakanikas to rest easily on his right shoulder. The wounds in his legs caused him a lot of discomfort. He also noticed a tear in his field jacket. He had been grazed in the shoulder as well. A small amount of blood seeped out.

"We did our best, didn't we, Sergeant?" Bouck asked Slape.

Slape looked over at Bouck carefully. The man paused a moment before answering. He was grimacing slightly under the pain of his broken ribs.

"Yes, sir," he said quietly. "We damn sure did."

"Good...," muttered Bouck as he stared at the cafe floor.

Aerial photo of the Losheimergraben Crossroads taken several months after the battle. The customs houses are on the lower right. On the road near the houses, an arrow points to the wreckage of the assault gun destroyed by Weidner and Kirkbride. Courtesy National Archives/Hatlem Collection.

Wartime photo of the Losheimergraben Crossroads taken prior to the battle. Courtesy John Hilliard.

Wilhelm Osterhold. Courtesy Wilhelm Osterhold.

Heinz-Georg Lemm. Courtesy Heinz-Georg Lemm.

Siegfried Moldenhauer. Courtesy Siegfried Moldenhauer.

Gerhard Kruse. Courtesy Bundesarchiv, photo number 695/413/12.

Kurt Steinhofel. Courtesy Kurt Steinhofel.

Joachim Peiper. Courtesy West Point Archives.

Ben Legare. Courtesy Richard Byers.

Norman Moore. Courtesy Richard Byers.

Wesley J. Simmons. Courtesy Wesley J. Simmons.

Robert Newbrough. Courtesy Robert Newbrough.

Arthur Mings. Courtesy Arthur Mings.

Charles C. Kent. Courtesy Charles C. Kent.

William Sears. Courtesy William Sears.

Mel Weidner. Courtesy Mel Weidner.

Richard Byers. Courtesy Richard Byers.

George Bodnar. Courtesy George Bodnar.

Buchholz Station today, looking southwest. The railroad tracks are in the left foreground. Courtesy Wilhelm Osterhold.

Aerial photograph of Lanzerath looking north. This photo was taken several months after the battle. The I&R Platoon's position was in the triangle-shaped woodline on the upper left. Courtesy National Archives/Hatlem Collection.

Lyle J. Bouck, Jr. Courtesy Lyle J. Bouck, Jr.

Warren Springer. Courtesy Warren Springer.

William James Tsakanikas, John S. D. Eisenhower, and Lyle J. Bouck, Jr. during Eisenhower's research of the battle in the late 1960s. Courtesy Lyle J. Bouck, Jr.

The Cafe Scholzen in Lanzerath as it looks today. Photo by author.

CHAPTER 9

Desperate Stand

MAJ Norman Moore, commander of the 3rd Battalion, 394th Infantry, continued to hold his reserve position at Buchholz Station. The Germans had not attacked since their last assault failed at 1145 that morning. It was 1430, and MAJ Moore still had no contact with the regimental command post. Companies K and L remained in place east and southeast of the station house. Both companies improved their defensive positions. Moore was still uncertain about the events and situation around him. He knew that the 1st Battalion at the crossroads had held during the initial German assault, but some Germans had penetrated the line. Moore expected to encounter these Germans at his position, but it never happened.

After consulting MAJ Clayton, the battalion executive officer, and CPT Charles P. Roland, the battalion S-3, Moore decided they were in an untenable and dangerous position. The battalion was not at full strength due to the company and a half attached to the 393rd for the Roer River Dam offensive. He felt he was holding too much ground with too few forces. A greater German effort might easily dislodge the battalion in the future. Such a situation would threaten the entire division's southern flank and, more immediately, the flank of the 1st Battalion. All three officers decided it would be best to shorten the ground the battalion covered by withdrawing to a defensive position in the north, south of and astride the east-west arterial highway leading from Losheimergraben to Bullingen in the west.[1] This position would afford greater protection to the division's flank and provide a more cohesive and integrated defense for his two rifle companies. From this position, they could better support one another and concentrate fires in key areas much faster and with greater effect. These new positions would be close to the battalion's original assembly areas. The two companies could take advantage of the prepared positions already there.

MAJ Moore sent a runner to summon CPT Simmons and 1LT Brown to the CP. Both men soon arrived. Moore briefed them on the proposed plan. He wanted Company L to withdraw from their positions first. One platoon from Company K would temporarily replace them at the railway station on the tracks. Once Company L was set in the new defensive position, Company K would follow and set up on their left. The final position would have both companies astride the highway facing south, with Company L to the west and Company K to the east. Moore told them to move at 1500 hours, 15 minutes from the time he briefed them.

At 1445, Moore moved the battalion CP to the vicinity of Company K's old assembly area. At the same time, 1LT Brown withdrew his company from the station house and railroad tracks. The GIs assembled on the road near the intersection. CPT Simmons, working closely with 1LT Brown, moved his 2nd Platoon, under LT Thibadeaux's command, left of the 1st Platoon and into Company L's old position. CPT Simmons also withdrew the 3rd Platoon, under LT Schlemmer, to a company reserve position behind the 1st Platoon. Simmons knew he had to give Brown time to get set in the new position. He decided that as soon as darkness set in, he would send a squad-sized patrol down the road to Lanzerath to see what the situation to the front looked like.[2]

Company L moved north to the new position and set up a hasty defense just south of the battalion's new CP location. At the CP, MAJ Moore and MAJ Clayton worked to establish contact with Regiment but with no luck. 1LT Brown told his men to dig in quickly, so Company K could join them. Moore sent a messenger to LTC Douglas, the commander of the 1st Battalion. The message informed Douglas of the 3rd Battalion's move. Moore told Douglas that as soon as Company K moved into position, Moore would have Simmons establish contact with either Company A or B on the 3rd Battalion's left. Douglas agreed and told Moore he would keep him informed of all events in his area. Soon after, a messenger from Company K arrived. The messenger carried CPT Simmons's request to send out a patrol at dusk. Moore agreed and sent the messenger back with permission.

Back at Buchholz Station, Company K waited patiently for word to move. They were tired and hungry; their first day of combat had been exhausting, but they felt a deep sense of satisfaction at having thwarted such a large German attack. The company was unable to feed hot chow that day because of the battle's fluidity; the company kitchen couldn't begin cooking because an unexpected clash with the Germans might force them to move. CPT Simmons looked up at the darkening sky. He waited for the right moment to send out the patrol. He instructed LT Schlemmer to send him the 3rd Squad, 3rd Platoon, for the patrol. These men, commanded by a young sergeant, patiently sat outside the station house, the company's new CP, and waited for CPT Simmons to brief them.

At 1630, CPT Simmons appeared and told them to leave in 15 minutes. He produced a map and briefed the young squad leader.

"All I want your patrol to do is head straight down the road to Lanzerath for 500 yards. Stay off of the road. Don't allow yourself to be detected. All I need to know is where the German positions are. Listen for sounds such as talking and vehicle engines. If you hear but don't see anyone, take your best guess as to what's out there. Determine their strength if you can. I know this is a tall order, but I'm depending on you. You can use this map."

Simmons handed the young squad leader the map. After a brief salute, the soldier turned to brief his own men. The squad left at 1645, just as dusk set in. The snow was soft, so the sound of their footsteps was not easy to detect. Simmons watched them move southeast along the road to Lanzerath until he no longer saw them in the waning daylight. He worried about his troops. The troops were going into an unknown and dangerous situation. As far as he was concerned, at that moment those troops were the bravest men on earth.

While CPT Simmons waited for his patrol to return, MAJ Moore regained contact with the regimental command post and COL Riley. COL Riley was aware of the 1st Battalion's situation but not of the 3rd Battalion's. He was glad to hear from Moore that the 3rd Battalion had fared well. Moore informed him of the battalion's new position, moved only on Moore's own initiative, and Riley agreed. Riley then told Moore to stay in radio contact as he would soon issue further instructions. Moore learned little from Riley about the big picture except that a large attacking German force had hit the entire division. Both regiments in the line had held, but no one knew how long the regiments would last in the face of repeated German assaults. This information didn't really shed much light on things for Moore. Moore informed Riley of the von Rundstedt message captured by Company L; but, like Moore, the regimental commander could only speculate on its significance. In any case, Riley said he would send the German message to MG Lauer immediately. In the meantime, Moore had to keep his ear to the radio for a change in mission or disposition.

Back at Buchholz Station, CPT Simmons waited patiently for the patrol to return. At 1800, he heard movement outside the station house. Soldiers were whispering the current challenge and password. The patrol had returned, much to Simmons's relief, without incident. The squad leader told Simmons that they had gone down the road undetected for 500 yards and had seen nothing. However, from the lowest point they reached on the road, they heard tank and vehicle movement on the Losheimergraben-Lanzerath road. Simmons sent this information to Moore as the squad, thanked for a job well done, returned to the 3rd Platoon.

At the battalion CP, MAJ Moore received the report from CPT Simmons and sent it to Regiment. He was about to instruct Company K to move to the new defensive position when COL Riley called with new instructions. He told Moore to leave two of Company K's platoons at Buchholz Station as a security force. The rest of Company K had to move to a new position. Company K would receive two platoons from Company L and then move to a backup position behind the 1st Battalion. Once in this backup position, Company K was attached to the 1st Battalion as a reinforcement company.

The orders struck Moore as ridiculous. Why fragment the entire battalion and endanger an already firmly established unit integrity? Moore argued the point with Riley but to no avail.[3] They would have to comply as soon as humanly possible. Frustrated, MAJ Moore ended the conversation and grimly accepted the orders of his commander. He would have to split up Company L to augment Company K to support the 1st Battalion, leaving two platoons to their fate at Buchholz. This new mission did not sit well with Moore, but he had to do it. The true origin and reasoning behind Riley's order remains a mystery. Lauer may have instructed Riley not to abandon the station area because of the threat posed to the division's open right flank. In any case, Riley firmly insisted on compliance. Moore contacted CPT Simmons and 1LT Brown and told them what had to happen. Both men protested as well, but they were "preaching to the choir." Moore knew how they felt. CPT Simmons called his officers together inside the station house and briefed them.

"We have to withdraw and support the 1st Battalion. They're taking the brunt of the fighting at the crossroads. We have to establish a fallback position to their rear. Unfortunately, we can't abandon this position, which is why two platoons, the 1st and 2nd, will remain in position as a security force. LT Rose will be in command."

Simmons could see the concern on his officers' faces. LT Rose looked at him. Deep consternation was apparent in Rose's voice.

"Sir, that means we'll be sitting ducks if those armored vehicles our patrol heard come roaring through here," he said in a slow, deliberate tone.

"I can't lie to you, Joe. I don't like leaving you here, especially since I have to take the support elements with me," responded Simmons.

"Will we have artillery support?" asked Rose.

"Yes, if you can call for it yourself. I'll be on the other battalion's frequency by then," said Simmons.

"Well, then I have a request, sir," said Rose. "Please leave the radioman, SGT Rausch, here. He's the best and at least we'll have a fighting chance with some artillery."[4]

Simmons agreed. He knew full well that he was giving up one of his best assets, the expert radioman SGT Alvin Rausch. But he knew Rose would need a good radio-telephone operator (RTO). He instructed the radioman to stay behind with the rest of the men at Buchholz Station.

Outside the station house, Simmons gathered his weapons platoon and 3rd Platoon and moved to the battalion's new location. The darkness made for slow movement. They arrived at the 3rd Battalion CP at 1945, just as MAJ Moore was receiving a report from the 1st Battalion. Moore quickly turned from the radio and faced Simmons.

"Jerry, you'll have to move quickly. The 1st Battalion took a lot of casualties this morning and their defense is extremely weak now. The Germans could renew their attack tonight. Anyway, it's probably a sure thing they'll hit again by morning. If they do, the 1st Battalion will have no choice but to give."[5]

Desperate Stand 111

"But where am I to go and where can I find the two Company L platoons that belong to me now?" asked Simmons.

"They're about 100 feet from here," answered Moore. "Position yourself 600 yards northwest of the crossroads. You'll be on the north side of the Losheimergraben-Bullingen arterial highway, but don't straddle it. You'll serve as a base from which to help the 1st Battalion fall back should the going get rough. Right now, that's all I know. CPT Roland will give you the 1st Battalion's frequency, callsigns, and password. You can get Douglas to clarify things for you when you get set. Take care of yourself."

Simmons thanked MAJ Moore and then linked up with the two platoons from Company L. Simmons and his new charges quickly moved through the snowy darkness to their new position, across the main east-west road and northwest of the crossroads. After placing the three rifle platoons in position, Simmons switched his radio, an SCR-300, to the 1st Battalion frequency. He kept his other radio on the Company K frequency out of concern for LT Rose and the others still at Buchholz Station. Perhaps, if LT Rose called for help, Simmons might be able to do something. It was 2100. He decided to get some sleep. The next day would be difficult, and his role would be significant.

In Lanzerath, all was quiet except for the distant rumbling of armored vehicles in the east. Occasionally, American artillery shells impacted nearby or in the town. Inside the Cafe Scholzen, 1LT Lyle Bouck sat on a bench under a grandfather clock. He still held the horribly wounded face of PVT Tsakanikas in his hands. Bouck's field jacket was soaked through with the young soldier's blood. The atmosphere in the cafe was strange; most of the German paratroopers, many not even dressed like paratroopers, sat around the open cafe. They slept or were half asleep in chairs or sitting against the wall. Many appeared to be officers. It was close to midnight, and Bouck found himself exhausted as well. The Germans hadn't grilled him for information as badly as he expected. In the dim lantern light that covered the sleeping forms in a soft glow, Bouck thought he could make out the rest of his men. They were also taken prisoner and brought inside the cafe. The commander of the 9th Fallschirmjaeger Regiment, Oberst Helmut von Hofmann, sat in a chair and dozed. Bouck was amazed to see this level of inactivity, especially since Bouck knew there were no American units to prevent the Germans from advancing further. Why were the Germans just sitting here?

Tsakanikas's wounded form jerked irregularly. The sudden movements brought Bouck out of a slight doze. Tsak's breathing sounded okay, but he needed medical attention quickly. Just then, Bouck heard voices shouting outside, followed by the loud roar of armored vehicles. The sleeping paratroopers inside the cafe stirred. Von Hofmann rose from his chair. The sound of armored vehicles was close now. One seemed to stop right outside the door of the cafe. Shouts and orders in German could be heard. The door to the cafe swung open. A form, all in black, stood in the shadows. The figure stepped forward into the dim light and shouted in German. Bouck understood nothing, but the body language said it all.[6]

"Who is in command here?" demanded the man in black.

"I am," answered von Hofmann, somewhat meekly.

The man slowly approached von Hofmann. He wore black leather pants and a jacket. This leather garb covered his field gray uniform underneath. On his head sat an SS-style visor cap, of the "crusher" variety, piped in pink and with a white metal skull and eagle on it. Around his neck he wore one of Germany's highest decorations for valor and leadership, the Knight's Cross of the Iron Cross with Oakleaves. He stood right in von Hofmann's face. The mysterious man fully intended to intimidate the paratrooper commander, even though his SS rank insignia indicated he was a lieutenant colonel, one full grade lower than von Hofmann.

"I'm SS-Obersturmbannfuehrer Peiper," said the man. "Why have you stopped? What's wrong?"

Obviously flustered by the confrontation, von Hofmann nervously groped for a map in his leather map case.

"The resistance ahead is too strong," he replied. "I want to wait until daylight. I think there is at least a full American battalion in front of us. They've mined the road."

Peiper looked the man up and down. This nervous, uncertain oberst was not the type of field commander Peiper was used to dealing with. As commander of the 1st SS Panzer Regiment, now designated "Kampfgruppe Peiper," he had waited all day for the paratroopers to clear a path so he could use either Route C or D. The rest of his division was still behind him. They wasted precious fuel by sitting idle in traffic congestion miles long. The commander of the 1st SS Panzer Division Leibstandarte-SS "Adolf Hitler," SS-Oberfuehrer Wilhelm Mohnke, depended on Peiper moving early. Several railway bridges on the Losheim-Losheimergraben-Lanzerath road network were destroyed in autumn by the German forces that withdrew behind the Siegfried Line. Now, the only available roads were unimproved trails. Most of these trails were congested with horse-drawn trains from the 12th Volksgrenadier Division. The missing railway bridge in front of Peiper had forced him to bring his own bridging equipment forward. His efforts—and his efforts alone—got him to Lanzerath where he now stood.

Peiper spent the day idle and in frustration. He wanted to get moving. He spent several hours in the morning at Generalmajor Engel's 12th Volksgrenadier Division CP. Peiper tried to get a feel for the situation. He wanted to assess the infantry's progress so that he could select the right moment to launch his battle group. But progress was slow, and, at 1400, Peiper left the command post in disappointment. He would have to wait until the roads were clear. The success of the entire counteroffensive depended on rapid penetration and exploitation. Commanders like von Hofmann, dredged up from the rear echelons, lacked the drive and experience to understand this concept. Von Hofmann's uniform only indicated one rear-echelon award, the War Merit Service Cross

2nd Class with Swords. Peiper's uniform, by contrast, reflected awards earned over years of relentless, successful combat on the Eastern front. Relentlessness truly characterized Peiper. He was determined to move at all costs.

Von Hofmann took out the map and set it on the table, next to a dimly lit lantern. He indicated where he thought the strong enemy positions were. He told Peiper they had defeated one of the enemy platoons, but with heavy casualties.

"Did you send out patrols to confirm this?" asked Peiper.

"No," said von Hofmann in a nervous tone," it was too dark by then."

Peiper looked at the map again. He squinted through the dim light but couldn't make out where von Hofmann claimed the Americans were located. Out of nervous frustration, Peiper pulled two knives from his belt and, quite dramatically, stabbed the map onto the cafe wall to see it under better light. Bouck sat and watched this amazing scene unfold before him. He was fully aware that this German officer meant business. It was clear to Bouck that Peiper was definitely of a different breed than von Hofmann.

Von Hofmann tried once again to indicate the alleged American positions on the map. Peiper instead turned on him and barked in a loud voice.

"There's nothing out there!" he yelled. "You've been sitting here for nothing. You didn't conduct a reconnaissance or anything! I want you to give me one of your parachute battalions immediately. I will attack at 0400 hours. If there are truly American mines in the road, then I'll just plow right through them!"[7]

He turned sharply on his heels and walked out the door. All von Hofmann could do was nod meekly in compliance. He wasn't very impressed with the Waffen-SS, but right now officers like Peiper were forcing their hand to get things moving. A quick call to the I SS Panzer Corps headquarters confirmed the detachment of von Hofmann's 1st Battalion. [No matter what, Kampfgruppe Peiper would be off in a few hours and into the American rear. On his way, he would stop at a crossroads called Baugnez, near Malmedy. At that location, his men would participate in a prisoner massacre that would forever make Peiper infamous. American soldiers everywhere would remember it as the Malmedy Massacre.]

Von Hofmann watched the door slam as Peiper walked out. The grandfather clock behind Bouck sounded midnight. It was now 17 December, Lyle Bouck's 21st birthday. He had an aunt, a palm reader, who once told him that if he could make it to his 21st birthday, he would live a long and healthy life. Bouck remembered the comment now. He somehow felt that just then, when things were at their worst, he would make it just fine. All things considered, he was now a man.[8]

Several hours before this incident at the Cafe Scholzen, SGT Dick Byers arrived by jeep at Buchholz Station. With him was 1LT Harold Mayer and SGT Curtis Fletcher, all from Battery C, 371st Field Artillery. They arrived to replace LT Springer's forward observation team. Springer's men were now prisoners, along with the I&R Platoon, at Lanzerath. Battery C, according to the division's task organization, routinely provided direct support artillery fires to the 3rd Battalion. LT Springer habitually provided this support. But when he took his team forward to Lanzerath and was captured, their loss left the 3rd Battalion without a trained forward observation (FO) team. Because no one had heard from Springer since earlier that day, Byers and his crew were sent to fill in. They arrived at 2130.

Byers backed his jeep into a small barn connected to the farmhouse across the road from the train station. LT Mayer and SGT Fletcher got out and walked around to see who they could find in charge. LT Rose had kept the station as his CP. He now commanded from there with SGT Rausch on the radio. LT Mayer learned of the CP location from one of Company K's soldiers. He crossed the road and informed LT Rose of the forward observer party's presence.[9]

Byers and Fletcher secured their gear from the jeep and brought the bags into the farmhouse basement. Both men could see that the basement served as the Company K aid station. Several medics were there. Some wounded GIs lay, covered with blankets, against the wall. Byers and Fletcher found a place to spread their bedrolls. In the dimly lit but warm cellar, they tried to get some sleep.

At 2400, Byers awoke and went outside on the front porch of the house to help stand watch for one shift. He found a soldier from Company K out there. The sentry shifted his weight from either foot to keep warm in the bitter cold.

"Cigarette?" asked Byers.

"Don't mind if I do," replied the soldier. "Thanks a lot, Sarge,"

"Don't mention it, bud," said Byers.

Both men took turns ducking inside the doorway to warm up and take a few puffs of their cigarette. Suddenly, the dull but obvious roar of revving engines echoed in the near distance. Every now and then, a voice could be heard. The sounds created an eerie and haunting echo throughout the dense, pine forest.

"What's all that noise about?" asked Byers. "It sounds like quartermaster troops on maneuvers in Louisiana."

"That's the Jerries," replied the soldier glumly. "They've been out there all night. Once in a while you can hear their tank engines. They must be bringin' up the big stuff, though. They didn't use tanks on us yesterday."

Byers looked at the soldier's dimly lit face in the faint light of his cigarette. The man was remarkably calm considering what might soon transpire at Buchholz Station. Byers took one last puff of his cigarette, crushed it out with his boot, and returned to the cellar to get some more rest. He would need it, he thought.

It was now 0100 and Peiper had scheduled his attack for 0400.

Back at the Cafe Scholzen in Lanzerath, Kampfgruppe Peiper sprang to life. It was 0400; SS soldiers roused the German paratroopers. The 1st Battalion, 9th Fallschirmjaeger Regiment's paratroopers, now supporting Peiper's kampfgruppe, were placed on the outsides of the tanks. Seated on the panzers, they could move as quickly as the tanks and then dismount rapidly for combat. Peiper himself drove to the front of the column in his panzergrenadier battalion commander's command car, a half-track-type vehicle called a SdKfz 251/3 Ausf. D.[10] The commander of the 1st Battalion, SS Panzergrenadier Regiment 2, SS-Sturmbannfuehrer Josef Diefenthal, rode with him. As far as Peiper could tell, all was ready. This young, 29-year-old regimental commander, one of the youngest in the Waffen-SS, was about to ride into infamy. The first Panther tank lurched forward into the darkness, heading straight for Company K's small security outpost at Buchholz Station.

At Buchholz Station, LT Rose began receiving reports from the two platoon leaders, LT Spencer and LT Thibadeaux. Enemy vehicles could be heard moving toward their location. Rose ordered both men not to fire until he gave the word. He didn't want to unnecessarily risk the lives of the men under his command. If the force were too large, they had the option to withdraw. The two platoon leaders spread the word.

Suddenly, the sound of German voices became audible over the dull roar of the tank engines. It was the sound of the German paratroopers ground-guiding the big, heavy tanks around the bend in the road east of the station. They used white handkerchiefs as a visual signal for the panzer drivers to follow.[11] The two platoons held their fire while Rose instructed SGT Rausch to report what was happening to MAJ Moore.

Dick Byers, asleep in the farmhouse basement, awoke slightly to a commotion in the rest of the cellar. He couldn't see what was happening. Fletcher, sleeping next to him, hadn't budged, so it must be nothing. Byers laid his head back down and snored. Soldiers bustled around everywhere. They hurriedly evacuated the aid station. Suddenly, LT Mayer called Byers's and Fletcher's name. He got no response but heard loud snoring in a corner of the cellar. One of the wounded soldiers lying on the floor yelled. The man pointed toward Byers and Fletcher. The lieutenant ran over and discovered the two sleeping forms.

"Get up, you two!" he shouted. "There are Germans outside!"

Mayer followed this request with a swift kick to both men. Byers and Fletcher jumped up. Both were now aware of the situation.

"Let's go, you two!" shouted the lieutenant. "I'll wait for you outside."

Byers and Fletcher pulled on their overboots and ran up the stairs and outside. Byers heard a small tinkling sound and turned to Fletcher.

"What's that sound?" he whispered to Fletcher.

"My overboots," said Fletcher. "I didn't finish buckling them."

The two men now stood outside in the courtyard behind the barn. They could see dark figures moving everywhere. LT Mayer moved right up behind them.

"Where are they comin' from?" Byers asked.

"They're coming right up the road, but the bend seems to be slowing 'em down," answered the lieutenant.

"We need to get to the radio on the jeep," said Byers. "We can call fires down on 'em at the bend."

All three men agreed and moved toward the barn that housed their jeep. Suddenly, the sound of German voices broke the silence nearby. Silhouetted against the snow were two German paratroopers, distinctive in their soup-bowl helmets without the traditional German flared rim. It appeared to Byers that both men were carrying MP40 sub-machine guns. All three artillerymen froze in place. The Germans couldn't see them because the GIs were up against the dark, stone courtyard wall. Byers clutched his .45 caliber pistol until his knuckles turned white. All three men stood in silence for what seemed an eternity.

"If there are Germans all over the place," he thought to himself, "then why doesn't Company K open fire?"

LT Rose in fact had continued to hold his fire. He wanted to get as many Germans into his engagement area as possible. However, he was unaware of the paratroopers coming up the treeline south of the road. Most of these German soldiers were already at the road intersection behind the station. Two of these Germans were now within five feet of Byers and his OP party.

Byers, Fletcher, and LT Mayer held still. The Germans soon turned and walked off, mumbling to themselves. The three men chose to abandon the jeep and radio and make a run for it. They ran through a side gate, into the woods, and headed due west through the deep snow. The going was rough. Each man had to lift his legs above the five or six inches of snow to keep moving. Byers still clung to his .45. He hoped he wouldn't be forced to use it in the dark forest. The snow became too much for SGT Fletcher and his unbuckled overboots. He lagged behind. Each step through the snow became a struggle. The tinkling sound made by his unbuckled boots quickly attracted some German paratroopers. They moved in the direction of the fleeing GIs. Fletcher stopped to buckle his boots. He didn't realize the Germans were coming toward him. They found Fletcher on one knee, frantically trying to fasten his overshoes. Fletcher sensed their presence and looked up. Two MP40 "Schmeisser" sub-machine gun muzzles were two inches from his head.

"Hands up," said a voice in German.

Fletcher rose slowly and raised his hands above his head. The war was now over for him—because of a pair of rubber overboots he couldn't get buckled in time.

Byers and LT Mayer ran through the dark forest. They changed direction to the north. Byers periodically looked back at Fletcher, to make sure that his fellow artilleryman was still there. He saw Fletcher begin to lag. Now, as he turned once again, Fletcher was nowhere to be seen. In the darkness nearby, Byers clearly heard transmissions coming from one of Company K's platoon SCR-300s. A voice, obviously German, was using a captured SCR-300 to try

Desperate Stand   117

and make the GIs compromise their positions. The voice spoke all-too-perfect English. The German constantly repeated, "Come in, come in, come in. Danger, danger, danger. We are launching a strong attack. Come in, come in, anyone on this channel." He was met with silence.

Byers soon realized that Rose's order for Company K to hold their fire was unnerving and frustrating both the veteran and inexperienced paratroopers. The Germans couldn't locate Company K's positions in the dark. The roar of the tanks made any noise infractions by the Americans meaningless. Strangely enough, Byers didn't feel as afraid of the Germans now as he had been before. Now he knew where they were; they were no longer part of an unknown, mystical force hiding in the woods. They were flesh and blood. He felt he could "deal" with them if the need arose. Byers and LT Mayer chose to keep moving northwest, back to their gun positions in Hunningen where they could be of some use.

Inside LT Rose's CP, all was tense. He knew that German infantry soldiers were on the road and in the woods around him. The SS panzers were having difficulty moving around the bend in the road from Lanzerath. But Rose knew that his anti-tank weapons were not accurate in the dark. The tanks would have to come closer, so he chose to wait. He sent a runner to find Mayer's OP party. The man returned with the news that he couldn't cross the road to the farmhouse because of the paratroopers. Rose would have no artillery support from the FO party for the coming fight. This fact unnerved him. He could wreak havoc on the Germans with just a few well-placed artillery rounds on the road bend. SGT Rausch called for fire support through battalion headquarters, but nothing fell on the bend in the road.

Suddenly, Rose heard a loud revving sound as the first German tank cleared the bend. The panzer rolled slowly past the station. Other tanks behind the first one tried to catch up. SGT Rausch reported the strength, as far as he could see it, of Kampfgruppe Peiper to battalion. Rose told Rausch to request reinforcements from battalion; he knew the time to fire, to make a stand, had come. He couldn't let the Germans roll through without a fight. He told Rausch to call the two platoons and have them open fire.

Both platoon leaders received the word. The order quickly spread to the men. The patient soldiers of Company K suddenly unleashed a tremendous barrage of small-arms and bazooka fire on the German tank column. The lead tank halted and turned its turret toward the station house. German paratroopers, still clinging to the exterior of the tanks, dismounted rapidly. Some screamed as M1 rounds tore into their flesh. Company K maintained a steady rate of fire. The volume kept the dismounted Germans on the ground and unable to move. The flash of tracer rounds and explosions created an eerie sight at the station. These flashes briefly silhouetted running German soldiers and panzers turning their turrets.

Suddenly, a German 20mm quad flak gun, called a "Wirbelwind," moved around the bend. The flak gun fired into Company K's positions near the road.

The fire was devastating. The rounds penetrated the overhead cover on the fighting positions and killed or wounded many American soldiers. The 20mm flak gun gave the German infantry time to get up from the ground and rush the newly revealed American positions. Combat turned to hand-to-hand. The Germans and Americans struggled one last time for control of Buchholz Station and a gateway to the west. A German tank in the column fired point blank into the station house. LT Rose and SGT Rausch dove for cover. Rausch quickly grabbed his SCR-300. He informed the battalion CP of the situation. The German tanks alternated machine gun fire with main gun rounds. This murderous fire caused much of Company K's defensive position to disintegrate. The battle raged on in the early morning darkness. Both sides fought valiantly for possession of the station.

In the same farmhouse that SGT Byers and LT Mayer had just left, PFC Nolan Williams of Company K abruptly awoke from his slumber on the first floor of the structure. Williams and several other men tried to get some much-needed rest after a night patrol. Flying glass from a window, perhaps caused by a German rifle grenade, fell on the prostrate form of PFC Williams. The glass snapped him back to reality. He heard a voice next to him suggest they wait out the "bombardment" in the safety of the cellar.

Williams little realized the deadly situation outside. He slung his rifle across his chest, stuffed a box of K rations into his shirt, and carefully picked up his brand new, precious rubber overshoes, issued to him only the day before. He moved down the dark hall and through the door that led to the basement. He paused when he heard a voice speaking German in the cellar below. Williams assumed it was only one of the company's interpreters. He continued down the stairs until he bumped into a dark form to his front. Then he heard several more voices speaking German below. Frightened, he placed his hand on the head of the figure in front of him, pulled it close, and whispered into the man's ear.

"There are Jerries in this basement."

Suddenly, he realized the helmet he was holding did not have the standard American camouflage netting on it. In fact, it was of a completely different shape. The German soldier slowly turned his head to face Williams. The man's eyes were as big as "saucers." At that same moment, a German officer shined a flashlight up at the two men and spoke in perfect English.

"Hands up, boys," he said. "The war is over."

"Like hell it is!" shouted Williams.

He pushed the astounded German soldier down the stairs, directly on top of the officer with the flashlight. Williams ran back up the stairs, through the hallway, and out into the courtyard. He still kept a firm hold on his overshoes. As he ran for the barn where SGT Byers had parked the FO Party's jeep, he could see the silhouetted form of a German paratrooper, MP40 at the ready, blocking his way. Without thinking twice, Williams smacked the man in the head with his overshoes. The blow forced the German backward. Williams then literally ran over him from "toe to head like a freight train" and then straight into the barn.

Frightened and out of breath, Williams dropped his overshoes and took his rifle off his back. He leveled the rifle, butt stock first, in preparation for another encounter. A dark form suddenly appeared in front of him. Williams raised the rifle up, prepared to butt stroke the unsuspecting figure. As the man approached, Williams was relieved to see the familiar face of one of his sergeants. Both men quickly decided to leave the area in search of help.

They moved from the barn, into the forest, and up to the road. They then noticed Kampfgruppe Peiper, in its entirety, slowly moving along the road headed west. Traffic was bumper to bumper. Tanks, half-tracks, and other vehicles struggled to move forward in the darkness. Both men prepared to dash across the road during a break in the column. Williams hesitated for a moment and looked back.

"What's wrong," whispered the sergeant.

"I wanna go back and get my overshoes," replied Williams.

"Like hell!" exclaimed the sergeant.[12]

Dick Byers and LT Mayer moved northwest and away from Buchholz Station. They passed through the last of Company K's foxholes, positioned to provide rear security for Buchholz Station. The officer had to stop repeatedly in front of these foxholes to give the challenge and password. He would approach a fighting position and hear a loud "Halt!"

"Don't shoot," he yelled. "I'm an officer from Battery C, 371st Artillery. I'm trying to get through with my sergeant here."

"All right, stay put," said the voice from the foxhole. Then the voice said, "Shining."

The lieutenant quickly responded with the countersign, Knight. The soldier let both men pass, but not before Byers heard tank firing behind him at Buchholz Station. He knew those men were in for it, and his heart sank.

"Nobody can withstand a tank attack like that," he mumbled to himself. He turned his large, 6' 6" frame and followed his lieutenant north, toward the gun positions in Hunningen.

At the 3rd Battalion CP, MAJ Moore listened as SGT Rausch anxiously reported the desperate fight on the radio. Rausch had already reported the presence of 30 tanks and 28 half-tracks.[13] It was nerve-wracking to hear. Everyone in the command post was silent. They listened intently to LT Rose's valiant stand at Buchholz Station. Moore heard Rose's request for reinforcements, but he could offer him nothing. All he had were two platoons from Company L. These platoons were now defending the division's southern flank. He called Regiment and asked for permission to withdraw the platoons. COL Riley denied the request. Suddenly, SGT Rausch's voice crackled over the radio again.

"Enemy soldiers inside the station house. Positions are overrun by tanks. Request artillery on this position immediately. Commanding officer taken prisoner. This is my last transmission. I am now destroying the radio. Out."[14]

There was a strange, almost eerie calm in SGT Rausch's voice as this final message came over the radio. Everyone in the battalion CP was struck to the core by it. Some even fought tears. It was over. The two platoons from Company K were gone, overrun by the most powerful battle group in the area, Kampfgruppe Peiper. All MAJ Moore could do now was wait. He knew they would have to move as soon as the sun rose. The Germans had just made a significant penetration at Buchholz Station; they had compromised the entire regimental and division position. The Losheimergraben road intersection was in extreme jeopardy. Moore called COL Riley and told him of the last transmission from Buchholz. It was 0530. Soon the fighting would begin again on a much larger scale.

CPT Simmons, at his position northwest of the Losheimergraben Crossroads, also heard SGT Rausch's last transmission.[15] He felt the pit of his stomach burn as he thought about his men. The Germans had overrun and destroyed over half of his original company. In one way, their sacrifice was a waste; in another, it was a costly delay for Peiper, who wanted to get as far behind American lines as he could before daybreak. Simmons looked around in the dim light of the new day. Soon, he too would have to put up a fight just like LT Rose at Buchholz. All he and his men could do was wait for the inevitable and hope their luck hadn't run out.

CHAPTER 10

The Final Push

As LT Rose's men fired their last bullet at Buchholz Station, LTC Robert Douglas, commander of the 1st Battalion, sat impatiently in his command post. Although his CP was south of the east-west Losheimergraben-Bullingen road and 1,000 meters west of the crossroads, Douglas could hear the noise made by Kampfgruppe Peiper as the unit moved past Buchholz toward Honsfeld in the west. Throughout the night, Douglas also heard the kampfgruppe's preparations in Lanzerath. The engine noises prompted him to send out several patrols from Companies A and B. Some patrols that went due east did not return. One of the last was led by T/SGT Wesley Kibler from Company B. Kibler left in the early morning darkness. His patrol went just south of Company B's position and along the railroad tracks used the previous day by Lemm's regiment. He encountered nothing there, but, like Douglas, he heard the sounds of the battle that raged at Buchholz Station. He returned and reported his findings to his company commander, who relayed them to Douglas.

Douglas knew something was going to happen. Since the last assault on his position the previous afternoon, there had been little or no enemy activity on his front. He heard the sounds of Kampfgruppe Peiper, but that was all. His battalion was down to roughly 50 percent of its original strength. He shifted most of his forces to concentrate on defending the crossroads. It was obvious to him that the 48th Grenadier Regiment wanted to control the critical junction. Company A still held positions south of the crossroads, oriented along parts of the railroad line. North of Company A, Company B held the area of the crossroads, with scattered positions remaining on either side of the east-west road to Bullingen. To the north, a small element of CPT Jim Graham's Company C covered the battalion's left flank. Douglas instructed Graham to send a platoon each to reinforce Companies A and B. The platoon that went to Company B met a lot of resistance in the forest as they moved to that part of the sector.

They managed to position themselves on the company's northern flank, but, because Company B was so fragmented, they ultimately returned to Graham's control. Company C's 1st Platoon, led by LT Plankers, occupied, with the 1st Battalion's mix of men, the customs houses. Plankers also had two squads from the 2nd Platoon, led by 2LT Charles N. Dean and SSG Mel Weidner, the platoon guide. These two squads arrived at noon the day before and spent a relatively quiet night there. The 3rd Platoon, originally slated to help Company B, arrived as reinforcements during the night. Led by LT Matthew Reid and T/SGT John Trent, the 3rd Platoon occupied a house near LT Plankers's platoon position. SSG John Hilliard, one of the 3rd Platoon's squad leaders, assisted Reid and Trent.[1]

Douglas planned to move his own CP forward to a house at the crossroads. From there, he could better see the battlefield and make more timely decisions. These customs houses, which sat just east of the crossroads, housed a whole potpourri of soldiers from the regimental AT Company and Companies A, B, and C. Douglas sent a truck to the houses to deliver mortar and anti-tank rounds during the night. He knew this brave, trustworthy mix of men would do their best against another attack from Osterhold's grenadiers. Yet it was only a matter of time before they gave way and either withdrew, surrendered, or died.

LTC Douglas was still unaware of Major Kruse's 2nd Battalion hiding in the woods north of his own CP location. Kruse kept a low profile and waited patiently for the rest of the regiment to catch up with him. He only captured American soldiers who blundered into his position. Many of these GIs were withdrawing or moving from one unit to another. As Osterhold had directed, Kruse continued to wait.

LTC Douglas knew COL Riley intended to send reinforcements, but he had not heard from anyone about the matter. If the 1st Battalion withdrew under pressure, there would be no unit in place to anchor the withdrawal. Regiment insisted such a force was in place, but Douglas couldn't verify this fact. He didn't want to risk sending a messenger into the darkness to find them. An excursion into the night could result in an unnecessary and tragic incident of fratricide if the messenger stumbled upon friendly positions and was mistaken for a German. Douglas chose to wait. It was 0545. Daylight would soon replace the newly breaking dawn.

CPT Wesley Simmons waited in his backup position behind the 1st Battalion. He hadn't heard from anyone since he occupied the position the night before. Prior to midnight, he picked up occasional transmissions on his SCR-300; however, after midnight, he heard only silence. He tried several times to reach Douglas by radio. His efforts were met with silence. The only thing he heard on the radio that night were the final transmissions of LT Rose's force at Buchholz. At 0600, MAJ Moore radioed Simmons on the company's frequency. Moore informed him that Regiment had released the two Company L platoons back to the 3rd Battalion for a particular mission. Simmons grudgingly informed the two Company L platoon leaders to return to their company south of the east-west highway. Both platoons quickly left the position. Simmons wondered how effective he could be with only a rifle and a weapons platoon. He quickly restructured his position. The machine guns now anchored the platoon's flanks while the 60mm mortars occupied a defilade position behind the platoon. He was at least ready to fight with what he had. Still, he had doubts about how long he could hold if the enemy hit him hard. It was 0630. The sun now created a soft glow behind the dull, gray December clouds.[2]

During the night, Oberstleutnant Osterhold, commander of Grenadier Regiment 48, and Oberstleutnant Lemm, commander of Fusilier Regiment 27, met with the 12th Volksgrenadier Division commander, Generalmajor Engel, in the woods east of the crossroads. All three men devised a plan that would finally take the crossroads in the morning. Engel received a lot of pressure from the commander of the I SS Panzer Corps, SS-Gruppenfuehrer Hermann Priess. Priess insisted that the infantry take the crossroads immediately at dawn. He needed to get the SS panzers moving. Tank columns were backed up for miles, protected from Allied air attacks only by the bad flying weather. The meeting began when the commander of the sturmgeschutze battalion, Major Holz, arrived.

"We must seize the crossroads at dawn," insisted Engel. "The timetable for the panzer attack is 24 hours behind schedule. Priess insists the counteroffensive will fail if we don't open up the crossroads."

"We understand, Herr Generalmajor," replied Osterhold. "However, our experienced leadership resources are limited. Some of our best officers became casualties yesterday. Lemm and I both lost seasoned battalion commanders. These new recruits need frontline leadership."

"Exactly," replied Lemm. "We can still take the crossroads in the morning, but we have to be careful. Right now, my regiment is in an assembly area south of the intersection and railroad tracks. My patrols have located a gap between the American units defending the crossroads and Buchholz Station. If this is the case, Osterhold and I can envelop them quickly in the morning."

"Precisely," responded Osterhold. "I have the remnants of one battalion in the forest northeast of the crossroads. My 2nd Battalion found a gap in the lines. They're now behind the enemy positions with three companies. Oberleutnant Steinhofel deserves recognition for this feat. We can take the crossroads as Lemm says, but it must be a coordinated effort. We'll need sturmgeschutze and artillery support."

Engel turned and looked at Major Holz, the commander of the assault gun battalion. Holz was no stranger to combat, himself a veteran of the Eastern front and holder of the Knight's Cross of the Iron Cross. Everyone at the meeting seemed aggravated at this man, due in part to the weak assault gun support received the previous day. It was not really Holz's fault that only three or four assault guns made it into the battle. The bridge over the railroad cutting on the Losheim-Losheimergraben road had only just been repaired.

"Will we get the required sturmgeschutze support, Major Holz?" asked Engel.[3]

"Yes, Herr Generalmajor," replied the veteran officer. "The bridge is now repaired. I can offer you several sturmgeschutzen for the attack. The reason you saw so few yesterday is because only a handful found their way through the firebreaks in the forest. The rest were waiting to cross the bridge once the engineers repaired it. But remember, the anti-tank threat at the crossroads is great. If I start to lose sturmgeschutzen to American panzerfausts, then I'll withdraw until the area is clear. I hope you realize my situation."

All three men agreed with Holz's comments. They set the attack for 0630. Osterhold would attempt to reach his 2nd Battalion by attacking directly across the international north-south highway. Lemm, with his regiment in the south, would exploit the gap between the 1st and 3rd Battalions of the 394th. They would preface the attack with an artillery preparation of known American positions. There was also a possibility that the Luftwaffe might provide limited air support. All four men returned to their headquarters. Each hoped the next day would offer them success.

At 0640, ten minutes later than scheduled, the German attack began.[4] Oberstleutnant Osterhold led his depleted 1st Battalion in an attack on the remaining elements of Companies B and C. The Americans fought back with determination. They quickly stalled Osterhold's men with withering small-arms fire. German artillery rounds impacted on the American positions, but the young GIs continued to fight. A lone ME109 from the Luftwaffe appeared briefly overhead. The plane came in low and dropped one or two bombs near the defending GIs. The bombs did no damage. They only succeeded in scaring some of the younger American soldiers.[5] PFC Carl Combs of the 1st Platoon, Company B, furiously fired his .30 caliber machine gun at the plane from his new position inside one of the customs houses. He was frightened by the plane's tracer rounds and thought they were coming straight for him. He never even knew when his belt of ammunition ran out. Suddenly, he felt a slap on his back and heard a voice say "good job." He turned to see LTC Douglas, who had come forward in his jeep, turn and exit the building.[6]

The battle soon turned into a close-quarter exchange of gunfire. Some of Company B's men withdrew across the international highway. Osterhold directed his 1st Battalion to maintain the pressure. He then moved to the treeline north of the east-west highway. Osterhold looked for Holz's sturmgeschutzen to come down the road. He didn't see any, and the artillery had also stopped. Osterhold moved back east through the forest with his radio operator, toward his regimental headquarters. Osterhold was experiencing a small measure of success at the crossroads, but he needed artillery and sturmgeschutze support. Osterhold finally arrived at his command post. He ordered his staff to discover why the artillery had stopped and what happened to the sturmgeschutze support. He chose to wait at the CP until he got an answer; his staff might need some command assistance in getting the required results. Once again, unforeseen and unexplainable problems with support elements stalled potential success.

South of Osterhold's main attack axis, Oberstleutnant Lemm ordered his two battalions to move quickly north. The Germans moved down the railroad embankment and up the other side. They hoped to quickly exploit this weak flank in the American position. Lemm's fusiliers trudged through the early morning snow, moving with as much stealth as conditions would allow. Lemm's lead battalion moved quickly into the gap between the two American battalions. The fusiliers pressed forward without enemy contact. A scar-faced, battle-hardened feldwebel led the way, determined to find success in this battle. Lemm remained behind his lead battalion, the 1st. He kept his men moving so that the attack wouldn't stall unnecessarily. The scar-faced feldwebel led the 1st Battalion quickly through the forest and north toward the crossroads. Suddenly, the feldwebel stopped. He went down on one knee and pointed with his other hand. In the early morning haze, the Germans could make out American soldiers in log huts. The GIs were waving at them. The feldwebel turned and, with a raised eyebrow, looked back at his men. The waving GIs confused him. A young gefreiter came up next to him and whispered.

"They think you're an American comrade," said the soldier.

"You're right," replied the feldwebel. "Listen, everyone stay behind me and don't shoot until I shoot."

The German soldiers nodded and watched the feldwebel straighten up. He walked toward the American soldiers like they were his friends. He waved back at them as he came. Suddenly, as the feldwebel approached, the Americans realized who he was. They scrambled for their weapons. The feldwebel opened fire. He killed several young GIs. The Germans, having missed much of Company A, were now behind Company B. They fired into the positions and log huts. Members of the Anti-Tank (AT) Company also had positions there. The AT men covered the road intersection with their 57mm anti-tank guns. The AT men returned fire as well. Many emerged from their foxholes to fire to their rear. The attack raged on. Both sides racked up severe casualties. The scar-faced feldwebel was at the forefront, running and firing. Somehow he avoided getting shot himself. The feldwebel and his men paused for a moment outside one of the American log huts. Inside they found a jackpot of American chocolate, cigarettes, and other goodies. They quickly confiscated these items and hid them in the bread bags on their belts.[7]

Lemm's fusiliers reached the Company B command post, which had been moved closer to the customs houses because of the previous day's fighting. The Germans had only hit a few of Company A's positions, which they almost totally bypassed. They did most of their damage to the remnants of Company B. The Company B commander, CPT Sidney Gooch, ran from his CP, .45 caliber pistol blazing away. The Germans scrambled for cover while American soldiers inside the CP's log hut emerged and opened fire. The Germans quickly killed or captured them. The commander, CPT Gooch, ran off into the woods to the west.[8] Unfortunately for Lemm, the attack temporarily stalled when his men hit a line of foxholes several meters south of the intersection. His now exhausted men went to ground. They occasionally fired at the American positions. For the most part, the attack was successful; Lemm was only a few short meters from the road junction.

Several men from Company B avoided capture or death at the hands of the 27th Fusilier Regiment. PFC Ralph Gamber of the 4th Platoon followed as his section leader, SGT Lilly, took their 60mm mortar squad and moved away from the fighting. The flank attack took Gamber and the mortar men by surprise. They quickly picked up their mortars and went in the direction of the customs houses. A fellow soldier in the squad, nicknamed "Pap," helped Gamber move the mortars and ammunition. Three or four other members of the section helped as well. "Pap" was a 48-year-old private. The men in the 4th Platoon mortar section affectionately gave him this nickname. He was a hard worker, and he proved it by carrying one mortar tube with base plate by himself. SGT Lilly, Gamber, SGT Bail, SGT Ball, a man called "Big Moose," and the other men arrived at the customs houses and went into the building farthest from the road. Once inside, they took inventory of their equipment. They had two 60mm mortars and one bazooka with eight rounds.

"Who knows how to work this bazooka?" asked Gamber.

"If we need to, I can give it a go when the time comes," answered "Pap." "I remember firin' one of them things on a range once or twice."

The men gathered their mortars and ammunition and took them outside. They set the mortars up in a small depression behind the house. "Big Moose" did most of the ammunition stacking and heavy work.

"Okay," said SGT Lilly. "Let's see what's next. I hope to hell we're not surrounded."

His men glumly agreed. They stacked the remaining ammunition next to the guns.[9]

PVT William Kirkbride, of the Anti-Tank Company, was still in his recaptured gun position forward of Company A's reserve platoon. His 57mm anti-tank guns covered the crossroads from the woodline south of the road. The guns also covered the main approach from Lanzerath to his rear. When Lemm's men attacked, Kirkbride and the other men in the platoon turned around and occupied hasty defensive positions facing their rear. The sounds of battle from behind caught Kirkbride off guard. He fully expected to employ his 57mm anti-tank guns at the crossroads. He thought the Germans would preface their next attack with a tank assault there. He had no idea where his platoon leader, LT Gifford Benson, had gone just before the fighting started. One of the platoon's NCOs, T/SGT Piar, was missing as well. The staff sergeant in charge of the section was back. He had gone in search of LT Benson's CP to get more orders or information. The platoon's field phone wasn't working. Kirkbride wasn't sure what to do except hold in place. He and the other men waited for the fighting to reach them. Suddenly, a young captain brandishing a .45 caliber pistol burst out of the underbrush. Exhausted and panting, the man identified himself as CPT Gooch, the Company B commander.

"What's going on, sir?" asked Kirkbride.

"My CP's been overrun," he gasped. "There's nothing left of my company. My men are either fighting by themselves, or they've been killed or captured."

Suddenly, Osterhold's attack on Company B's left flank reached their vicinity. Kirkbride and the officer could see some American soldiers rushing back across the international highway. The GIs turned to fire as they moved.

"That's the rest of my company," said Gooch. "The Germans are behind us and in front of us. The only place I know we're still holding is those customs houses straight over there."

Kirkbride looked east down the road at the houses. He saw little activity there.

"If you want my advice," said the officer, "go there and help those guys out. I'm goin' back to the battalion CP and tell the colonel what happened."

Suddenly, the man was gone. He dove into the underbrush and headed west. Kirkbride didn't know what else to do. He rallied the men. Kirkbride told them to load up the truck and hook up one 57mm anti-tank gun to it. Kirkbride got behind the wheel of the Dodge 6x6 and drove straight to the houses. He parked the vehicle between the nearest two. Suddenly, German small arms fire erupted from across the road. The anti-tank men quickly unloaded their equipment. They dodged the German bullets and positioned the anti-tank gun behind the house closest to the road and facing toward Losheim.

Kirkbride and the men heard voices in the cellars of the houses. Inside, they discovered LT Plankers's platoon and other 1st Battalion soldiers. Kirkbride asked the lieutenant what was happening and what they should do.

"This is the front line," said Plankers. "Much of the 1st Battalion seems to have withdrawn to about the same line we're on now. We're still ready to fight. We received an ammo resupply last night."

"Well, we have a 57mm anti-tank gun outside if we need it," replied Kirkbride. "Who are those Germans shooting at us from across the road?"

"They've been there since we arrived yesterday," broke in SSG Weidner. "They take potshots at us every now and then. They must be a security company or something. It's too dangerous to try and cross the road to get them, though."

Kirkbride chose to settle in and wait in the cellars with the rest of this mixed group of soldiers. As he entered the cellar, he found a young second lieutenant lying face down on the ground. Everyone ignored the man. Kirkbride went to him and spoke gently into the man's ear.

"Are you okay, sir?" he asked.

The man looked at him with a blank stare. He seemed scared, but he wasn't hysterical, crying, or shaking. He didn't seem shell-shocked. Kirkbride realized this man was in no shape to lead. He just left him there, face first on the dirt floor of the cellar. Some men just couldn't handle the stress of the situation.[10]

Kirkbride and his fellow platoon members took turns running outside to get equipment from the truck. They dashed between the houses, dodging rifle fire from the German company across the road. Kirkbride made a final run to the truck. A German StG 44 round caught him in the fleshy part of his leg, just above the ankle. PVT Dan Rodman, one of Kirkbride's friends, rushed to help him. Limping, he and Rodman carried the equipment inside the cellar of the first house. A fellow soldier administered first aid to the wound. The pain made it difficult for Kirkbride to walk. But this setback would not keep him from fighting should a battle erupt at the customs houses.[11]

LTC Robert Douglas sat in his new battalion CP, which he moved forward to one of the customs houses. He waited for reports from his companies. The attack came suddenly but not unexpectedly. He knew the Germans must have hit his men hard. The initial sounds of German artillery had been deafening. Small-arms fire echoed throughout the snow-covered forest. He received a report from Company C indicating the company, or part of it, was still in place on the left but had no contact with Company B. Company C also reported moving some of their positions back to the international highway, as did some elements from Company B. There was no contact with Company B. There were only occasional transmissions from Company A.

LTC Douglas knew the 1st Battalion was on its last leg, no matter how well they did in the recent battle. He called COL Riley and requested to withdraw to form a more cohesive defense in the west. Douglas told Riley he had positive radio contact with only Company A and parts of Companies B and C. The main part of Company C now appeared cut off from the rest of the battalion. Douglas proposed that Riley attach Company C to the 2nd Battalion, to ensure they wouldn't be left without command guidance.

He waited several minutes for a response. COL Riley called back and instructed Douglas to withdraw his battalion to the high ground east of Murringen at 1300 hours.[12] They had to complete the withdrawal by 1530 to take advantage of the early darkness. Riley also agreed to attach Company C to the 2nd Battalion. The 2nd Battalion would soon be withdrawing as well.[13] That news sounded great to Douglas. He wanted to get his men out of the immediate area. The remnants of the 1st Battalion could then reorganize into something he could effectively command. Right now, only his soldiers' initiative prevented complete success for the 12th Volksgrenadier Division.

Douglas instructed his radio operators to inform everyone in the battalion of the withdrawal plan. This plan called for a systematic thinning of the lines. Douglas didn't want to risk picking up the entire battalion at once and moving rearward; such a move would put the battalion at a tactical disadvantage and give the Germans an opportunity to rout his force. The radio operators reported that Company A received the message. Some of B and C Company's remaining elements acknowledged as well. Although risky, LTC Douglas decided to walk

The Final Push 129

to the forward houses to make certain everyone knew what had to happen. It was now 0900. The withdrawal would begin in a few short hours.

North of the 1st Battalion, Captain Legare's 2nd Battalion spent a relatively quiet night, marred only by occasional German artillery fire which did little or no damage. At 0630 that morning, in concert with the German attack to the south, the 990th Grenadier Regiment of the 277th Volksgrenadier Division attacked the 2nd Battalion. CPT Patterson's Company E again received the brunt of the attack, which comprised large numbers of infantry in camouflage overwhites supported by three assault guns. Patterson's company sat in front of the only road leading through the battalion's defensive position, the Weisser Stein Trail. The assault guns went straight for his men. The attack originated from the small hamlets of Udenbreth and Neuhof in the east. The German plan quickly fell into difficulty as Patterson called down massive amounts of pre-planned artillery fire on the assaulting German infantry. The German soldiers dove for cover. Many withdrew to the safety of the forest once again.

The sturmgeschutzen kept coming, however. They went directly for the Weisser Stein Trail. Company E's bazooka team sat squarely astride this road, their weapons oriented east. The GIs engaged the first assault gun. A bazooka scored a direct hit on the vehicle. It burst into flames. The second vehicle tried to move around the first. Its 75mm gun roared as it came. The bazooka men fired again. They hit the assault gun in the left front hull. The vehicle lurched to a halt. The sound of grinding gears reached the ears of the Americans in the foxholes. Suddenly, smoke poured from the hatches. Two crew members tried to escape from the top of the vehicle. Riflemen from the foxholes cut them down. The other sturmgeschutze tried to back away. The crew realized that they too would suffer a similar fate if they moved forward. One of the bazooka gunners emerged from his position. He took cover behind a burning assault gun. As the withdrawing assault gun turned around, the soldier moved into the open and fired his bazooka. He hit the vehicle in the rear. A tremendous gasoline explosion followed. The three vehicles sat and burned on the road. CPT Patterson called CPT Legare and told him what happened.

At the battalion command post, CPT Legare acknowledged the report. He sent his congratulations to the men of Company E. The battalion had fared well in the fighting to date. He was proud of his men and his battalion—except for one person. The actual battalion commander remained a useless, blithering hulk. He still cowered in a corner of the log hut. Legare had almost forgotten about him. This man's behavior was a disgrace. As the battalion executive officer, Legare felt guilty that he hadn't tried harder to have this man relieved. But loyalty and soldierly duty stood in Legare's way. He simply could not bring himself to turn against his own commanding officer. It would have been a poor example to the other officers and soldiers in the battalion. Now, with his commander a useless mass of flesh stretched out pitifully on the floor of the CP, Legare's fears had taken shape. He approached the broken man and spoke to him in a harsh tone.

"Sir, get up," he said. "You've been there since yesterday. Go outside and take a piss."

The man looked up at Legare with helpless eyes. Legare wasn't certain if he was reaching him.

"Sir," he said again in a louder voice, "get up and take a piss!"

The man slowly rose to his feet. He swayed slightly from side to side. A private came over, took him by the arm, and escorted the man outside to urinate. Legare shook his head in disgust. The battalion commander, no longer able to function as an officer in any capacity, would ultimately return home in disgrace.

The rest of the morning and early afternoon remained quiet for the 2nd Battalion. Legare received the order attaching the rest of Company C to his battalion at 1100. He quickly sent a runner to establish contact with the company commander, CPT Jim Graham. The Germans had not tried to attack again since that morning. CPT Legare saw that as a good sign.

"Good," he muttered to himself," they think we're a tough nut to crack. That should keep 'em off our backs for a little while."[14]

CPT Wesley Simmons maintained his position 600 meters northwest of the crossroads. He had yet to receive any transmissions from the 1st Battalion. The 1st Battalion had changed passwords and frequencies at midnight but neglected to pass the changes on to Simmons. The 1st Battalion was never certain if Simmons was really in place behind them. Simmons now sat and waited, trapped in an unknown and confusing situation.

At 1030, Simmons heard movement in the forest to his left and right. He ordered his men to hold their fire. LT Ralston, the weapons platoon leader, moved forward to his position.

"Sir, those are our men moving to the rear," he whispered. "They're all around us."

Simmons looked left and right. He watched the ghostlike forms of the 1st Battalion's men withdraw to the west. They were part of the earliest forces to fall back, before the main body withdrew that afternoon. Many soldiers had simply withdrawn on their own, under pressure from the attacking German grenadiers.

"You're right," said Simmons, "they're from the 1st Battalion."

"Maybe we ought to go, too," said Ralston.

"No," answered Simmons," we haven't received instructions from Colonel Douglas. He may be relying on our presence here."

Simmons tried again to radio the 1st Battalion. There was no response. He watched for several minutes as a continuous stream of soldiers, many carrying wounded, moved west.

"No," he told Ralston, "we'll stay here until we hear otherwise."

Somehow this plan didn't sit well with Simmons. But he just couldn't pick his men up and abandon the 1st Battalion when they might be depending on

The Final Push   131

him. He chose to wait, to stick to his original orders and maintain a fallback position until the commander of the 1st Battalion changed his mission.

LTC Douglas emerged from the building that housed his forward command post. He approached the western side of the customs houses. Spotting a nearby building, he moved quickly to a side door and cautiously entered. Inside, PFC Carl Combs sat, resting against a wall. Combs and other members of the 1st Platoon, Company B, had refused to surrender with LT Lubick. T/SGT Kibler led Combs, PVT Youngblood, and others to the customs houses where they now waited for either more instructions or a German attack. As soon as he heard Douglas open the door, Combs grabbed his rifle and yelled.

"Halt!" he shouted. "Oh, it's you, sir. Sorry."

"That's okay, "said Douglas. "Who's in here anyway?"

"Well, sir," replied Combs, "I'm an assistant squad leader from the 1st Platoon of Company B. I'm here with some of my men. There are others next door."

Just then, PVT Jim Cotter, also from Company B, entered the building carrying a bazooka. Another soldier followed.

"What's goin' on, sir?" he asked Douglas.

"Well, men," answered Douglas, "we're going to withdraw. I need some soldiers to stay here and cover the withdrawal by denying this road to the Germans. Can you men guard this road for me with that bazooka?"

"Yes, sir," answered Cotter. "But where are we going? How long do we have to stay here?"

"Stay here until I tell you to leave," answered Douglas. "We should be moving by dark. We're going to Murringen to set up a new defense. Don't forget to pass the word to the men in the rest of these houses. You can leave as a group. I'll be with you along with my headquarters. Keep safe and don't get nabbed by the krauts."

The men grinned nervously as they watched Douglas depart. PFC Combs observed Douglas through a window as the officer returned to his CP. Douglas turned and waved at the men. He accidentally dropped his .45 caliber pistol at his feet. Combs watched nervously as Douglas, completely exposed to enemy fire, slowly bent down to retrieve the weapon. He then calmly walked on. Douglas exuded nothing but composure and calm, an inspiration to battle-weary men like Carl Combs.

Combs and Cotter spread the word, but the information failed to reach the others in the customs houses to the east. The GIs in the customs houses would find out the hard way.[15]

LTC Douglas arrived back at his CP. He ordered his staff to burn all maps. He told one of his men to get a thermite grenade to destroy the building. He didn't want the Germans using his CP for anything. Douglas then emerged from the house for the last time. Suddenly, some random German artillery rounds impacted near the CP. Douglas and his staff dove for cover. His command jeep took a direct hit. The artillery stopped. Douglas rose to survey the damage. There were no casualties, except for his musette bag which was sitting on the jeep when it was hit. Douglas looked on the ground and saw his toothbrush, shaving cream, and other toiletries scattered about.

"Damn," he muttered. He bent down to pick up whatever he could salvage from the musette bag.[16]

Back at the 48th Grenadier Regiment's CP, Oberstleutnant Osterhold just finished talking to Lemm on the radio. Both agreed to resume the attack at 1300. By then they would have the much-needed support of Holz's sturmgeschutzen, which failed to arrive earlier in the morning due to a traffic jam involving tanks from the 1st and 12th SS Panzer Divisions. Holz now assured both commanders that the assault guns would attack at 1300. He would move straight up to the crossroads and help break the stalemate there. Neither Osterhold nor Lemm was aware that the 1st Battalion was withdrawing. Osterhold's 1st Battalion still reported a presence at the customs houses. The American presence indicated to the veteran officer that the GIs still wanted to defend the intersection. But the group at the customs houses never received the withdrawal order. In effect, they were being left behind.

At 1300, the depleted 1st Battalion, 48th Grenadier Regiment, resumed its attack on the 1st Battalion, 394th Infantry. The Germans quickly realized there was little or no resistance. The Americans had disappeared. The 1st Battalion moved quickly across the international highway. They ran directly into Major Kruse's 2nd Battalion. Kruse told a young officer with the 1st Battalion that the Americans were withdrawing. With his radios working sporadically, Kruse had no way of notifying the regiment earlier. He told the officer he would now move west. Kruse also told the man to send someone to recover his 5th Company, which he left at the crossroads. Kruse wanted them to catch up before the main body moved too far. This company was the same one that wounded SSG Kirkbride at the customs houses. The 2nd Battalion came to life and pressed forward. The grenadiers took shots at individual American soldiers who made their way west. The Germans followed the east-west road, staying in the woodline to its north. Unknown to Kruse, they were heading directly for CPT Simmons and Company K's position.

CPT Simmons heard a lot of activity in front of his position, including sporadic firing. He told his two platoon leaders to stay alert. Something might happen very soon. Members of the 1st Battalion were still moving to the west, usually in pairs or singles now. Suddenly, Simmons saw a large group of figures moving toward his position. He couldn't quite make out who they were or what they were doing. He signaled his men to get ready. The figures moved closer. Simmons and his men quickly recognized the camouflaged overwhites and flared-rim helmets of the Germans. They belonged to Kruse's 2nd Battalion. The Germans were gaining ground rapidly.

The Final Push

Simmons ordered his men to fire. The crackle of small arms fire broke the silence of the gray, early afternoon. LT Schlemmer's 3rd Platoon brought withering fire down upon the German formation. The grenadiers dove for cover. The Germans quickly returned fire with StG 44s and MP40s. An MG42 went into action on Company K's left. Many of Schlemmer's men stopped firing and sought cover. Simmons was aware that the Germans were present in force. They outnumbered him by at least three to one. He called back to LT Ralston and told him to start firing the mortars on the final protective line in front of the position, planned the night before.

Within seconds, 60mm mortar rounds impacted among the Germans. Casualties were severe. The German attack lost momentum, but Simmons knew their tactics. He saw some of the grenadiers disengage from his front and move to the low ground to his left. Just like the battle at Buchholz Station, these Germans were attempting to flank his small position. They were masters of this maneuver. Simmons knew Company K couldn't hold the position for very long. Obviously, Simmons wasn't going to get any further orders from what appeared to be a now nonexistent 1st Battalion, 394th Infantry. He decided to withdraw west, in search of the rest of the regiment.

Simmons moved over to LT Schlemmer's position. He told Schlemmer to move his men quickly to another position about 300 meters to the west. He ordered Schlemmer to leave one squad in place. This plan would allow the GIs to leap-frog backward without exposing themselves unnecessarily to German fire. Simmons then told LT Ralston to do the same with his mortars. The GIs would only displace one gun at a time to the rear. Everyone understood what had to happen. They quickly began the move. Ralston kept the Germans occupied with mortar fire while Schlemmer's squad pinned them down with rifle fire. Simmons moved back with the first element. He helped establish the first fallback position to the west. The Germans quickly realized what was happening. The grenadiers kept up the pressure and moved forward in pairs by rushing from one tree to the next. When the rifle squad and mortar team made it back to the first fallback position, the Germans were dead on their heels. The GIs performed this maneuver one more time. Simmons realized that his men's ammunition supply was low. The mortar tubes and ammunition were slowing his men down. He looked on his map. They were only a few hundred meters east of Murringen. Simmons and his men would have a better chance of fighting from there. Simmons told Ralston to fire his remaining ammunition to cover this final withdrawal. The mortar men complied. The rounds rained destruction on the still attacking Germans, and as they sought cover, Company K gained enough time to move into the dense underbrush and off to Murringen, or wherever they could find other American troops. Ralston's men abandoned the mortar tubes and followed the rest of the company. They damaged the tubes enough to make the mortars unusable for the Germans. The GIs quickly made their way out of the forest. Simmons felt satisfied that he had done the best he could with what he had. His men had fought bravely and had not panicked, even though it was clear that the Germans outnumbered them significantly.

Simmons checked the map one more time and then followed his soldiers as they moved northwest.[17]

Back in the north, CPT Legare received a visit from the assistant regimental S-3. The officer carried with him withdrawal orders that were to take effect immediately. The officer also informed Legare that control of Company C was to revert back to the 1st Battalion immediately. Legare acknowledged the instructions, and the man left his CP. Legare told his S-3, CPT Robert McGee, to call in representatives from each company to receive the withdrawal order. The CP had only recently reestablished field phone contact with all of the companies in the line. Soon, lieutenants from each company arrived. Each officer represented his respective commander. Legare explained the situation.

"Okay, listen up, men," he began. "We're going to withdraw from this position in one hour, at 1500. The 1st Battalion to the south is long gone. They've already moved back to the high ground east of Murringen, where the regiment's establishing a new defense. We'll tie in to the right of the 3rd Battalion and defend the same way we're deployed now."

He pulled out a map and drew two withdrawal routes on it. The men listened intently as Legare continued.

"We'll use two withdrawal routes. CPT McGee will be in charge of the movement from this location. He'll assign the routes to each company when I'm finished. Notice that they go straight through the forest to the west. They'll end at the foot of the high ground east of Murringen. I'll remain behind with a covering force, which will stay in place until 1630. This covering force will include two 81mm mortars I'm leaving here from the battalion. For this covering force, I want each company to leave one squad behind per platoon, one 60mm mortar per company, and one machine gun per section. I'll command this force from here. We'll assemble at the CP at 1630 for our own withdrawal. It's essential that you move quickly. We don't want to bump into each other on the withdrawal routes. Any questions?"

The group remained silent. They absorbed every word, every detail. Legare had had this plan on his mind for many days. He was frustrated at not having had the time to plan and rehearse it prior to the German offensive. He was a man who tried to keep all bases covered. It was an excellent, thorough plan, which comforted the officers of the battalion. The officers quickly returned to their respective companies to inform their commanders of the situation.

Legare walked over to the shaking battalion commander. He was still lying on the floor of the log hut. CPT McGee came over as well.

"Bob," he said, "take the colonel with you. Assign two enlisted men to carry him out of here."

"All right, Ben," he replied.

Both men walked away in silence. They soon turned their attention to the withdrawal, which would begin within the hour.[18]

At the same time CPT Simmons and Company K came in contact with Osterhold's 2nd Battalion, Major Holz's sturmgeschutze assault finally began. Four assault guns made their way west along the Losheim-Losheimergraben road. The assault guns moved quickly as they rounded the slight bend. The GIs inside the customs houses spotted them and scrambled for their weapons.

SSG Weidner called out when he saw an assault gun coming straight for the house nearest the road, the one they occupied. SSG Kirkbride rushed to the cellar window and looked out. The lead assault gun fired its main gun. The round punched a hole in the house next door and killed a soldier named Onderdonk. The assault gun moved right, ahead of the others. The assault gun entered the woodline and came parallel to the buildings and then emerged from the forest and onto the road. The assault gun aimed its main gun directly at Weidner and Kirkbride's house.

"Dammit!" yelled Kirkbride. "Somebody get on the 57mm gun outside and hurry," he called to his platoon members in the cellar.

Several volunteers scrambled. The volunteers grabbed their weapons and helmets. One soldier emerged from the cellar. Small-arms fire from the German company across the road forced him back.

"Hey," the soldier called to Kirkbride, "those krauts are takin' potshots at us. We can't get close to the gun."

Kirkbride turned around and swore. He looked out the window next to Weidner and wondered aloud what they would do.

"We've got a bazooka here," yelled Weidner as he grabbed for the weapon from a corner of the cellar. "Can you help me with it?" he asked Kirkbride.

"You bet, Sarge," answered Kirkbride.

Kirkbride quickly loaded the bazooka. Weidner aimed the weapon at the advancing sturmgeschutze. Suddenly, they saw a German officer signal the assault gun from across the road. He was pointing to the houses. The assault gun moved toward the German. The vehicle aimed its main gun tube at the first house. Just then, other soldiers in the cellar fired from the window that faced the road. Several rounds hit the German officer. He fell into the ditch next to where the assault gun had stopped to turn. The GIs had just critically wounded Kruse's 5th Company commander. The sturmgeschutze lacked a turret, so it pivoted on its tracks to take aim at the house.

"It's gonna shoot!" yelled Kirkbride.

"Oh, yeah," said Weidner, "let's see what it says about this."

Weidner fired the bazooka. A huge rushing sound filled the cellar as the back blast caused soldiers to seek cover. The projectile hit the left front track of the assault gun. The assault gun stopped its pivoting motion. The broken track unraveled from the road wheels. The vehicle tried to move. Kirkbride quickly reloaded the weapon. He slapped Weidner on the back.

"Okay, fire!" he yelled.

The second round ricocheted off the front hull. The vehicle lurched slightly to the rear. A German sergeant, the vehicle commander, tried to jump from the hatch. Small-arms fire crackled from the men at the other cellar window. The

German ducked back inside. SSG Hilliard, in the house next to Weidner's, hastily fired a bazooka round at the assault gun as well. But when the smoke cleared, he wasn't certain if he hit it. It didn't matter, though. The assault gun just sat there, silent and immobile.[19]

Suddenly, an explosion farther down the road broke the silence once more. The second assault gun, now moving quickly again, fired at the house. A round hit one of the upper floors. Kirkbride and Weidner could hear wood splinters and glass tinkling on the floors above. Luckily, the blast injured no one in the house. Another round impacted on the other house nearby. SSG Hilliard and LT Reid of Company C's 3rd Platoon dove for cover. Because the vehicles were next to the bend in the road toward Losheim, Weidner, Kirkbride, and Hilliard were unable to spot them. The lead vehicle fired again, this time at the other house to their rear. The round struck one of the upper floors of the house occupied by PFC Gamber and SGT Lilly's 4th Platoon, Company B mortar section. Lilly's men were in a better position to observe the advancing sturmgeschutzen.

"What was that?" cried one of Lilly's men.

"Tanks!" yelled another. "They're comin' up the road. Those guys in the other house got the first one."

"Quick," yelled Gamber, "get me the bazooka. Maybe we can get the others from here."

The assault gun moved slowly up the road. It fired its 75mm main gun as it came. The rounds impacted near the houses but caused no American casualties.

"'Pap,'" called Gamber," you said you knew how to work this thing. Give me a hand."

The 48-year-old private calmly came forward. He took the bazooka from Gamber.

"I'll fire, you load," he said quietly.

Gamber quickly loaded the bazooka from the rear. He slapped "Pap" on the back and told him to fire.

"I can't reach the button," said "Pap." "Push it for me, will ya?"

Gamber pushed the button. The first round missed. He quickly reloaded the weapon and tapped "Pap" on the back.

"Don't miss, 'Pap,'" he said, "we only have seven rounds left."

"Okay," replied the man.

Gamber pushed the button again. The projectile roared as a loud rushing sound came from the rear of the bazooka. This time "Pap" scored a direct hit. The assault gun burst into flames.

"You got it!" exclaimed Gamber. "Let's get the others."

The sturmgeschutze directly behind the burning vehicle kept moving. The assault gun tried to push the smoking hulk out of the way. This maneuver made it easier for "Pap" to sight in on the vehicle. Gamber reloaded and "Pap" took aim. The projectile scored a direct hit on the second assault gun as well. It, too, burst into flames.

"Okay, 'Pap,'" said Gamber, "you got it! Now we have just one more."

"I think there are more than just those," said another soldier looking out the window. "Listen, I hear more down the road."

It was true. They could all hear the sound of many more vehicles in the distance, muffled by the bend in the road 600 meters from their house. Their thoughts quickly returned to the third assault gun as it fired. The assault gun's projectile barely missed the house. The sturmgeschutze tried to move around the left side of the other burning vehicles, vainly attempting to push them aside. "Pap" fired again. He hit the vehicle just above the left front bumper. The assault gun stopped for a moment, then kept going.

"Quick," said "Pap," "reload me. It's still coming."

"Pap" fired again. This time he hit the assault gun just above the left bumper. The track broke off. Flames poured from the inside compartment as the vehicle lost control. The assault gun pivoted helplessly to the left and into the ditch beside the road. The main gun bored itself straight into the ground. The men of the mortar section cheered, but not for long. They could see German soldiers at the far bend in the road. The Germans emerged from the woods to see what had happened. These men were still part of the 48th Grenadier Regiment. The Germans tried to determine where the enemy fire came from. SGT Lilly, the mortar section leader, quickly yelled for the men to get outside on the mortars. "Pap," Gamber, and the others rushed outside. They fired 60mm rounds at the scattered German troops. The Germans withdrew into the forest as the rounds impacted nearby. More than likely, these Germans were part of Osterhold's logistical support troops that followed the attacking 1st Battalion, which by now had already moved across the international highway northwest of the customs houses.[20]

Back inside the first house, which contained SSG Weidner and PVT Kirkbride, the men were aware that fighting was going on outside. They couldn't see what was happening from their vantage point. Several men who occupied the other customs houses, including Gamber, SGT Bail, and the others, chose to leave the position by moving west through the forest. PFC Charles Kent, "Mudcat," and other men from Company B, who occupied a house close to the forest, chose to withdraw west also. Weidner learned that the 1st Platoon leader, LT Plankers, was gone, as were several other men from his platoon. Plankers had maintained a separate foxhole line in the forest south of the customs houses. The grenadiers pushing through the tree line forced him back. Plankers and 20 other men managed to escape to the west. Plankers and his men were distressed at leaving the other GIs behind in the customs houses.[21] The fact that these GIs had escaped did not encourage the men inside the customs houses, but they soon accepted the idea that the Germans probably had them surrounded and that the 1st Battalion had withdrawn to the west.

Although exhausted and low on ammunition, the men prepared to fight. No one officially took charge, but that wasn't important. The men would fight individually if necessary and then make a run for it if the opportunity presented itself. The GIs at the customs houses had done well, however. These Americans continued to frustrate the German plans to seize the crossroads. But the GIs knew it was only a matter of time before the grenadiers succeeded in flushing them out. The second German attack of the day was now an hour and a half old. Afternoon had arrived. But the Germans still couldn't make use of the Losheimergraben road leading west.

CHAPTER 11

The Customs Houses

At mid-afternoon on 17 December, Oberstleutnant Wilhelm Osterhold came forward again to the Losheimergraben Crossroads to inspect the progress of his soldiers. Wearing a greatcoat and visored field cap, he approached the customs houses from the east. He was a thin, wiry man of medium height with a firm and confident bearing. At 30 years of age, he was one of the youngest regimental commanders in the German Army. Osterhold had tried since the day before to get more artillery support, but communications problems prevented any contact. Even now, he had just reestablished contact with the supporting batteries at his regimental CP. As far as the Oberstleutnant knew, Kruse's 2nd Battalion was still behind the 1st Battalion, 394th Infantry. The 2nd Battalion occupied a hasty defense 1,000 meters west behind the crossroads. Kruse had one company, the 5th, east of the international north-south highway. Osterhold could see the 5th's men north of the customs houses. The 5th Company had positioned two 20mm guns in the woodline, facing south. The grenadiers occasionally fired these guns into the windows of the customs houses.

For Osterhold, this objective had been difficult to take. It was perhaps his most difficult in the war to date. Once again, he had to overcome tremendous adversity to get the job done.[1]

Wilhelm Osterhold had joined the German Wehrmacht out of necessity, not tradition. In the early 1930s, the infancy of the Third Reich, Osterhold's father, an anti-Nazi Reichstag representative, spoke out repeatedly against the regime and Hitler's dictatorship.[2] Because the Gestapo saw to it that all walls had ears, including the use of children as spies against their own parents, the elder Osterhold's views found ears in the hierarchy. The Nazis linked a series of anti-Nazi literature to him as well. These anti-Nazi railings resulted in the elder Osterhold spending time in a concentration camp, which at that time was thought to house only political prisoners or enemies of the people. Wilhelm shared his father's beliefs and knew the Nazis would eventually come after the entire family. His family could ill afford to suffer even the slightest perception of disillusionment with the government. To appease and show solidarity with the existing government (and perhaps to seek leniency for his father), Osterhold joined Infantry Regiment 27 in the 12th Infantry Division prior to the outbreak of the Second World War.

Young Osterhold distinguished himself in the early Polish and French campaigns of 1939–1940. He served as an infantry platoon leader and machine gun company commander. On 22 June 1941, Osterhold participated in Operation Barbarossa, the invasion of Russia, with the 12th Infantry Division. In Russia, he distinguished himself as a gutsy, highly competent, compassionate leader. He led by example and was always up front with his soldiers. The 12th Infantry Division met with success as it drove east with Army Group Center. Osterhold, already the bearer of both the Iron Cross first and second class, received the German Cross in Gold for his leadership as the commander of the 12th Company, Infantry Regiment 27. He endured encirclement with his men at Demyansk, but he truly distinguished himself in February 1944, when, as a major and battalion commander, he held off an incredible Russian onslaught for days. His bravery won him the Wehrmacht's highest award for valor and leadership, the Knight's Cross of the Iron Cross.

Despite initial successes experienced by the German Army in the East, 1943 and 1944 saw a reversal of roles as the Russians became the hunters and the Germans the hunted. In heavy fighting in early summer 1944, the 12th Infantry Division became combat ineffective, nearly depleted of all equipment and personnel. In essence, the division ceased to exist. Major Osterhold and several remaining officers from the division personally went to Hitler's Wolfschanze in East Prussia to ask the Fuehrer to reconstitute the division. Unfortunately, the date was 20 July 1944, and Oberst Graf von Stauffenberg would attempt to kill Adolf Hitler with a bomb that very afternoon. When the bomb went off, Osterhold, in astonishment, thrust his head from a window and asked a passing SS guard what had happened.

"Someone tried to kill the Fuehrer!" yelled the man.

Hitler's guards detained Osterhold and his friend, Major Heinz-Georg Lemm, while the situation cooled down. Since it was an attempted coup by Army officers, no one in army uniform escaped suspicion. Eventually, Osterhold and Lemm were found innocent of any knowledge of the conspiracy. Osterhold and Lemm saw Hitler and secured his permission to reorganize the division. The two officers also successfully requested, through General Guderian, the OKW (Oberkommando der Wehrmacht, or German Armed Forces High Command) chief of staff, a new division commander: Hitler's own adjutant, Generalmajor Gerhard Engel. Lemm and Osterhold made it clear that they chose him and not the other way around. Engel was competent and a good man, but he also had influence with key personnel. Specifically, his relationship with Minister of Armaments Albert Speer made him desirable to Lemm

The Customs Houses   141

and Osterhold. Both officers knew that to get the best weapons and equipment from the Nazi regime, you had to know people in high places. Lemm and Osterhold knew the war was over, but they still felt they had to attempt to frustrate the "unconditional surrender" terms of the Allies. In July 1944, in East Prussia, the new 12th Infantry Division, commanded by Generalmajor Engel, took shape. Hitler redesignated the 12th a Volksgrenadier Division, an honorarium indicating that the soldiers were "elite" and part of the "people's army." Only a few veteran soldiers in the division really merited that honor.

The three regiments, 27th, 48th, and 89th, retained their numerical designations but with a great influx of new and inexperienced officers and men. Osterhold took command of the 48th, Lemm of the 27th, and Gerhard Lemcke the 89th. All men held, or would earn, the Knight's Cross of the Iron Cross. This decoration distinguished them as a unique and highly experienced regimental command group. Due to changes in organization, each regiment had only two battalions; the 48th and 89th were designated Grenadier Regiments and the 27th a Fusilier Regiment. The titles "fusilier" and "grenadier" had no impact on the organization of the regiments; each regiment was the same.

As soon as the 12th Volksgrenadier Division received its equipment, the division departed for the Western front and spent the fall of 1944 in action around Aachen and Dueren. The division distinguished itself and earned the distinction of "the best infantry in the area." By December, new replacements arrived, and everyone became aware that something "big" was up. In mid-December, the 48th Grenadier Regiment, with the rest of the division, occupied assembly areas near Frauenkron.

Osterhold, an Oberstleutnant since October, briefed his two battalion commanders on the upcoming offensive. The attack began on 16 December and now, mid-morning on 17 December, the Losheimergraben Crossroads were surrounded but not cleared.

Since the Losheimergraben Crossroads delineated the border between Belgium and Germany, a series of customs houses existed on the east side of the crossroads. They were 500 meters due east of the actual intersection. These houses, made of paneled wood and painted white, normally housed customs officials and the like. Now these houses were abandoned and damaged from the war. Many of the customs houses had smashed windows and bullet-pocked walls. Some buildings were two stories tall and offered a defender or observer an excellent view down the road to Germany. An assortment of soldiers from the 394th's AT Company and Companies A, B, and C now occupied these houses. They were accidentally left behind after the withdrawal of the 1st Battalion to Murringen. Two squads from the 2nd Platoon, Company C, under LT Dean and SSG Weidner, arrived the day before to help reinforce Company A's hold on the crossroads. The entire 1st Platoon, led by LT Plankers, accompanied them. During the night, LT Reid's 3rd Platoon came in as well. These units spent a relatively quiet night there.

Just across the road from the customs houses, Osterhold saw one of the 75mm sturmgeschutzen supporting his regiment. The assault gun was immobile and occasionally fired its machine gun at the customs houses. Osterhold noticed that the left track had been blown off with a bazooka, courtesy of SSG Weidner and PFC Kirkbride. Farther east, behind the disabled assault gun, were three other sturmgeschutzen. They, too, had been part of this assault. The vehicles had paused when the lead assault gun was damaged by Weidner and Kirkbride's bazooka attack earlier that morning. Now, thanks to PFC Gamber and "Pap," these vehicles no longer threatened the Americans. The assault guns sat in the middle of the road facing different directions. Smoke slowly escaped from their damaged hulls.

The scene infuriated Osterhold. This détente went against his own principle of rapid and decisive assault. It was a stalemate between a disabled assault gun and a bunch of young American soldiers hiding in the cellars of the customs houses.

"Where's the commander of this company and of the assault gun section?" yelled Osterhold.

A head soon popped from the top hatch of the disabled assault gun. The head belonged to the Unteroffizier in charge of the vehicle.

"Sir," he began, "the 5th Company commander is in the ditch next to my vehicle. He's badly wounded. A medic is tending the commander."

Osterhold bolted across the road and into the ditch. Before Osterhold lay the bleeding body of the 5th Company commander, an oberleutnant. A medic worked furiously to relieve the wounded man's pain. Osterhold knew he couldn't rely on this unfortunate soul for leadership. He called for some of the 5th Company's men to assist their commander.

Osterhold looked around the side of the assault gun at the customs houses. He knew that if he could get close enough to one of the buildings, he could flush the defenders out. But how?

Osterhold moved back down the road to his captured American jeep.

"Get me some tear-off time fuses and some captured American mines," he told one of his feldwebels. He called to the men of Kruse's rear company, still across the road from the customs houses, for volunteers to help him flush out the buildings' defenders. Two feldwebels came over to assist. Osterhold briefed them.

"All right, now listen. We're going to put our German tear-off time fuses on these captured American mines. We'll throw the mines into the windows and cellars of the buildings. Your company across the street will cover us. This attack should convince the enemy to surrender."

The two sergeants agreed and gathered the mines. They moved with Osterhold to the rear of the sturmgeschutze and waited for an opportune time to move. Just then, the anti-tank men in the customs houses wheeled a 57mm anti-tank gun around the corner of one of the buildings. They fired two rounds at the assault gun. The loud reports broke the silence. The rounds ricocheted off the front hull of the assault gun. The impacting rounds convinced the Unteroffizier to get the hell out. He jumped from the hatch and into the ditch next to Osterhold.

"Herr Oberstleutnant, we need to help the driver, who is still inside the vehicle. He's wounded."

Osterhold saw this event as a good opportunity to move. All three men sprinted across the street and up against the closest house.

"Get ready," instructed Osterhold.

As he prepared to pull the fuse and throw the mine, Osterhold stopped. Osterhold realized the mine would create a terrific explosion within the enclosed space of the house. The young men inside would suffer a horrible, senseless death. Osterhold already owned the crossroads. Their deaths were really unnecessary and excessive at this point. Osterhold instructed his two men to hold fast; he pondered what to do. Somewhat fluent in English, Osterhold mustered every word he knew in that language and called to the Americans in the houses.

"Hello there! Can you hear me?"

He heard some faint responses like 'go to hell, kraut' and a couple of other comments. Osterhold was now aware they could hear him. He called again.

"I am the commander of this infantry unit. We've already encircled you. There's no reason to continue this struggle. You have fought honorably and we recognize this. We're not SS soldiers and we will not harm you. If you surrender, I'll personally guarantee that your clothing, cigarettes, and other personal possessions remain with you. If you don't, I will be forced to throw some quick-fuse mines into the houses and kill all of you."

Osterhold heard some grumbling inside but no response. PFC Kirkbride of the AT Company stuck an improvised white flag out of the window of the second house. Osterhold saw it and stepped into the open. Kirkbride, astonished at seeing the German officer emerge from behind the building, went outside to greet him.[3] He limped from the wound in his ankle. Someone in the 5th Company had fired an StG 44 at Kirkbride earlier that morning. Kirkbride had played cat and mouse with the German rifle fire while moving around outside buildings.

"Do you understand the conditions of the surrender?" asked Osterhold.

"Yeah, I guess so," answered Kirkbride. Kirkbride was struck by the clean appearance of Osterhold and his calm demeanor. He felt he could trust this man, especially since Osterhold claimed not to be SS. That sense of trust meant a lot to the soldiers. Osterhold understood their feelings. The reputation of the Waffen-SS preceded them, whether or not the reputation was unfounded. Rumors of prisoner executions by the SS terrified Americans throughout the theater of operations.

"I'll have to go back inside and ask the rest of the guys," said Kirkbride. "I'm not the one in charge."

"How do we know he's not setting us up?" called a voice from the cellar of the house.

Osterhold answered back immediately. "I'll inform my men not to fire on you. But I'll have to do this in German. Any of you who can speak the language may verify that I am telling the truth."

Osterhold called to his men not to fire. These instructions, though in a foreign language, seemed to satisfy the GIs in the buildings. Osterhold followed Kirkbride into the cellar of the building. He saw, in the dim light, many tired, disheveled, and dirty soldiers. There were roughly 40 in the entire group. But the GIs straightened when Osterhold came in, proud in spite of their situation.

"These enemy soldiers are no pushovers," thought Osterhold, remembering intelligence reports that belittled the ability of the 99th's "green" soldiers. "These men are serious and mean business. They put up a tremendous fight."

Osterhold negotiated the surrender terms in the presence of PVT Kirkbride, SSG Weidner, PFC Dan Rodman, and others. Osterhold looked around the room and realized that something was wrong.

"What's the matter?" Osterhold asked.

Several young soldiers produced hand grenades from behind their backs and showed them to Osterhold.

"We can't find the pins," said one of them.

Another recommended tossing the grenades out the window and letting them explode.

"No!" cried Osterhold. "I have no way of telling my men outside what is happening. This act might revive the battle. My soldiers might think you ambushed me."

Osterhold produced a flashlight and everyone, including Osterhold, got down on his hands and knees to look for the pins. One by one they found the pins and placed them back inside the grenades. Osterhold and the Americans emerged from the basement and into the waiting arms of the German grenadiers. Osterhold instructed the GIs to leave their weapons behind and to gather only personal belongings. Osterhold was astounded to see that the prisoners from all the houses numbered nearly one hundred.[4] He then spied Kirkbride's Dodge 6x6 truck with trailer behind one of the buildings.[5]

"Does that work?" he asked.

Kirkbride told him it did. Osterhold asked him to start the truck. Kirkbride turned the engine over and got out of the vehicle. Osterhold instructed the captured men to unload their gear from the truck so that they wouldn't be without it as they walked east into Germany, into imprisonment. Some of the men even smiled at Osterhold. He seemed sincere and was treating them well, as were all of Osterhold's soldiers. Osterhold's behavior was chivalric, which was relatively uncharacteristic in the Second World War. Later, Osterhold would even chastise some of his men for taking cigarettes from the soldiers. Osterhold scolded his grenadiers for their "dirty habit" and for disobeying his orders. Osterhold's men even had to return the cigarettes.

The young Americans marched off to the east under guard of men from the 48th Grenadier Regiment. Osterhold stood in the street facing west. The crossroads were finally his, but Osterhold was over 36 hours behind schedule. The

The Customs Houses 145

1st SS Panzer Regiment, commanded by SS-Obersturmbannfuehrer Peiper, was well on its way to the west and a last stand at La Gleize. The 12th SS Panzer Division "Hitlerjugend" needed the crossroads to forge ahead. These German units, including Osterhold's, still had other objectives to take, other battles to fight. Osterhold knew the war was over. Germany had lost, but he still couldn't stand the notion of "unconditional surrender." The war had to end on a better note than that. He hated the Nazis and Hitler's manipulation of the military, but the German people, the innocent ones, would have to suffer the pains of "unconditional surrender." Osterhold could not reconcile such a demand within himself.

The time was 1500 on 17 December 1944. Osterhold would have to move west again with his division and regiment. Hitler would later award Osterhold the Oakleaves to his Knight's Cross for taking the crossroads, but, at that moment, such an honor didn't seem to matter. Oberstleutnant Wilhelm Osterhold turned and solemnly walked back to his jeep.

CHAPTER 12

Completing the Record

Sunset on 17 December marked the close of the first phase of the great German counteroffensive on the northern shoulder. The 99th Infantry Division's resistance cost the 6th SS Panzer Army precious time. The Germans were nearly 36 hours behind schedule, a substantial success for the newly blooded GIs of the 99th. The Germans managed some minor successes but at a very high cost. Inexperienced recruits and a lack of veteran leadership still plagued them. Despite this fact, the German infantry pressed on to their next objectives. For them, the offensive was far from over. Many German units had already shot their bolt.

The 394th Infantry Regiment successfully withdrew to the safety of the small hamlets of Hunningen and Murringen in the west. Waiting to help were the men of LTC John Hightower's 1st Battalion, 23rd Infantry, from the 2nd Infantry Division. Rerouted south after the German attack began the day before, Hightower's men occupied the small town of Hunningen. They covered the withdrawal of the 394th. While the exhausted "Checkerboard" men moved north to the twin villages of Krinkelt-Rocherath, the "Indianhead" soldiers blocked further German advances. However, the 394th's job was far from over. A great battle ensued at the twin villages. The struggle ultimately resulted in the withdrawal and reorganization of the 99th Division on Elsenborn Ridge located to the northwest. It was on this piece of high ground that the 99th, along with the 1st and 2nd Infantry Divisions, drew a line in the sand that the Germans on the northern shoulder would never cross. Despite the repeated attacks of the 277th Volksgrenadier, the 12th Volksgrenadier, and the 12th SS Panzer Division "Hitlerjugend," the 6th SS Panzer Army would fail to move farther west. Only one battle group managed to squeeze through, Kampfgruppe Peiper. Peiper and his men later became notorious for the prisoner massacre at the Baugnez Crossroads near Malmedy in the west. But they eventually lost their impetus at a small town named La Gleize where, out of gas and low on ammunition, Peiper infiltrated back to his own lines at night and on foot with all that remained of his battered kampfgruppe. This stalwart defense in the north marked a major success for the American forces in that sector. From that point on, the GIs experienced only victory. The Allies erased the "bulge" by late January 1945 and pursued the remnants of the once-proud German Wehrmacht over the Siegfried Line and into Germany itself.

Unfortunately, many members of the 394th Infantry, taken prisoner during the battle, never experienced this victory. These were the men captured at the Losheimergraben Crossroads, Buchholz Station, and Lanzerath. Most endured long foot marches to prison camps in the heart of Germany, forced to wait five months before their comrades liberated them. Men like SSG Mel Weidner and PFC William Kirkbride suffered long treks to the German rear and a frightening and uncertain fate at the hands of their captors. Severely wounded by shrapnel in his right leg, SSG Bill Sears marched with little or no medical attention. While in captivity, gangrene set in and only a timely operation by his liberators in April 1945 saved his leg.[1]

Many of these men found that the frontline German infantryman who captured them usually treated the GIs well. A mutual respect existed between fellow soldiers at the front, but the farther into Germany the prisoners got, the worse the treatment. Most of this harsh treatment was at the hands of rear-echelon personnel who had endured Allied bombing raids in their cities. They had a bone to pick with the "Amis." Such was the experience of LT Warren Springer, captured with LT Lyle Bouck and the rest of the 394th's I&R Platoon. While being transported by train from the Hammelburg stalag to a camp in Nuremberg, Allied aircraft strafed a railroad marshaling yard where the train had stopped. As the air raid siren sounded, the German guards ran to the air raid shelter. The guards clearly indicated to the prisoners that they remain in the boxcars or be shot. When the first bombs landed, the prisoners poured from the freight cars despite the guards' threats and ran straight for the shelter. When Springer got inside, a fellow prisoner thought the bombs had wounded the artilleryman. Blood and bone covered Springer's trench coat. But the blood wasn't Springer's; bomb shrapnel apparently struck some poor soul running beside Springer, splattering blood, bone, and brains from the unfortunate man's head all over Springer's overcoat. For Warren Springer, this gruesome event became a bitter memory of his captivity.[2]

But what happened to some of the men who fought in the battle for Losheimergraben? While others spent the rest of the war in prisoner of war camps, many managed harrowing escapes. Both the Germans and Americans experienced high casualty rates. Many of the wounds allowed the soldiers to return home to the States or back into Germany. For those who returned to the Fatherland, it was only a matter of time before the war once again reached them. The tide of events had turned against Germany and the Wehrmacht. Soon the war would be over.

Completing the Record

The 1st Battalion, 394th Infantry, was one of those units that experienced a high casualty rate. The 1st Battalion took the full brunt of the major attacks at Losheimergraben and still held for almost 36 hours. The 1st Battalion continuously defied the 48th Grenadier Regiment's efforts to dislodge them, thanks largely to the brave, stalwart leadership of LTC Douglas, who succeeded in getting the remnants of his battalion to Elsenborn Ridge. Once there, the battalion was reconstituted and placed back into the fight. Only 260 officers and men from the original unit made it out of Losheimergraben.[3] LTC Douglas still commanded the battalion and would do so until the final victory in Germany.

Men like PFC Bob Newbrough and his fellow soldiers from the Company D mortars were able to take part in the final, victorious push to Germany. It was their reward for escaping the clutches of the advancing Germans. Others like SSG George Ballinger and his men spent the rest of the war in prison stalags in Germany. Many of these GIs, because of their capture, felt as though they had failed, that they hadn't done their part. However, this belief was far from the case. The men of the 1st Battalion later received the Presidential Unit Citation for their valiant stand at Losheimergraben. This citation gave the 1st Battalion's men the recognition and credit they deserved.[4] Despite this award, men like Ballinger still couldn't shake the ghosts of fallen friends left in the forest near Losheimergraben. Ballinger was never able to check if PFC Alphonse Sito had indeed died that day. He wouldn't know the truth until nearly 44 years later.

In 1988, two young Belgian "Bulge" enthusiasts, Jean-Louis Seel and Jean-Philippe Speder, were near Losheimergraben looking for souvenirs from the battle. Once they neared the original positions of Company B, their metal detector registered something beneath the ground. They dug into the soft earth and uncovered an American mess kit. They dug deeper and found a winter overboot with a sock and some small foot bones. They then unearthed a wallet, rosary, Bible, some religious crosses, and two dog tags. Finally, after excavating the entire position, Seel and Speder found the still-clothed, seated skeleton of a GI. A bullet hole in the helmet explained the man's sudden death. The skull was shattered in twelve separate pieces. Seel and Speder took a close look at the dog tags. They clearly made out the name of Alphonse Sito, the machine gunner from Baltimore who perished the first day of the offensive. After 44 years in the Ardennes, Sito finally came home.[5]

CPT Legare's 2nd Battalion withdrew from the Losheimergraben area nearly intact. His men executed his withdrawal plan superbly. Most made it back to Murringen and then on to Elsenborn Ridge. However, one unfortunate incident did occur. On 18 December, CPT Bob McGee, the battalion S-3, while leading one of the first elements out of the forest east of Hunningen and Murringen, suddenly came under small-arms fire. He had picked up some stragglers from the 393rd Regiment and, after a night of difficulty, made for Murringen. His group emerged from the forest along the lower withdrawal route, a trail near a small Belgian farm complete with grist mill. Before the 2nd Battalion GIs could climb the high ground into Murringen, they were met with a withering hail of German small-arms fire that forced the GIs to move northwest. With casualties from the small-arms fire, the 2nd Battalion moved toward the farm. Just then, artillery rounds fell around the GIs. Casualties were enormous. The 2nd Battalion men ran for cover. They dove into the ditches alongside the dirt trail. The artillery stopped as quickly as it began. McGee and the other 2nd Battalion men ran back into the forest and moved north toward friendly lines. Thanks to the leadership of several officers and NCOs, the 2nd Battalion avoided a near panic. The men were split into small groups to make the movement easier. Many GIs carried their own wounded with them.

But who fired the artillery rounds on them? An artillery liaison officer from the 1st Battalion, 393rd Infantry, located somewhere far to the north, heard on his radio that the nearest American troops were already well north of Krinkelt. Based on this information, he decided to fire a concentration on Murringen. Little did he know that his rounds would have a fratricidal effect on fellow soldiers from his own division. The incident was an ironic twist to what could have been a tremendously successful withdrawal under enemy pressure.[6]

Like the 2nd Battalion, MAJ Moore got his 3rd Battalion out of the Losheimergraben area and back with the rest of the regiment. Company K, commanded by CPT Simmons, linked up with the battalion on Elsenborn Ridge and participated in the defense of that key piece of terrain. Company K was later recognized for their part in establishing a defense west of the crossroads. Like the 1st Battalion, they received, by name, the Presidential Unit Citation. CPT Simmons went on to have a distinguished and diverse military career before retiring as a full colonel in 1972. After the war, he was assigned to the 26th Infantry, 1st Infantry Division, in Nuremberg. He returned to the states in January 1946. After making the Regular Army, he spent three years in GHQ, Tokyo, Japan, followed by the Officer Advanced Course at Fort Benning, Georgia, as well as a brief stint there as a tactics instructor. After attending the Command and General Staff College, he became the S-3 of the 35th Infantry Regiment, 2nd Infantry Division, in Korea followed by an assignment as professor of military science at Lehigh University from 1955 to 1959. He returned to Germany and served as the executive officer and then commanding officer of the 30th Infantry, 3rd Infantry Division, in Schweinfurt. He then commanded the 7th Army NCO Academy from 1962 to 1963, spent four years in operations at the Pentagon, and one year in operations with the Eighth Army in Korea. His last assignment before retirement was as the commander of the Personnel Center at Fort Dix, New Jersey. Upon retirement on 15 June 1972, Wesley Simmons became a Math teacher in senior high school until 1984, when he moved to West Virginia where he now resides with his family.

CPT Simmons never learned what happened to his men at Buchholz Station until April 1945, when the 99th Division overran the Moosburg prisoner of war camp. Now the 3rd Battalion's executive officer, Simmons was reunited with his former company executive officer, LT Rose, SGT Al Rausch, and LT Spencer, his 1st Platoon leader. Simmons learned that when Kampfgruppe Peiper overran the men at Buchholz Station, Rose called for fire on his own positions before SGT Rausch destroyed the radio. Peiper's men quickly captured the GIs. Their capture marked the beginning of a long and strange odyssey as Kriegsgefangener (POWs) in Germany. The Germans transported the men eastward into Germany by train and foot. The GIs endured the fury of their own American Air Force. The prisoners feared for their lives as the planes strafed the boxcars they huddled in during their move to the German interior. They moved from one camp to another, beginning with Limburg, Hammelburg, Nuremberg, and finally ending in Moosburg. After this last encounter with LT Rose, Simmons only managed to locate him again after the war in 1991. Simmons still maintains contact with Al Rausch, who resides in Indiana; both men exchange a letter or two per year.[7]

SGT Dick Byers, who escaped the carnage at Buchholz Station, made it back to friendly lines. He was wounded before the final push into Germany. Byers wasn't able to participate with the division in their final victory in Germany, but he was certainly there in heart and spirit. He ultimately ended the war as an artillery lieutenant. Today, Dick Byers is active in the division's association. He is a routine contributor to the association's excellent newsletter, *The Checkerboard.* He is also a very active member of the Archives Committee. He assembled artifacts and relics from the war that pertain specifically to actions involving the 99th Division. Byers has set up superb displays in the Ohio Military History Museum and at the annual 99th reunions, which take place all over the country. He has painstakingly assembled photographs, maps, and other documents, which he makes available to all members of the division association. He routinely encourages his fellow "Checkerboard" members to tell their stories and, frankly, without his help much of this book wouldn't have been possible. Dick Byers's most prominent and personal crusade has been to get recognition for the four men from his artillery forward observer section who participated with the I&R Platoon in their action at Lanzerath. Many postwar histories of the battle omitted the forward observer section's contributions, and he strove to see this error corrected. He firmly believes that LT Springer and his men made a difference that day.[8] He especially did not want to see the death of T/5 Billy Queen, the pudgy bookworm who died a tragic and controversial death that day, go unnoticed. It didn't; all four men received the Silver Star for their actions in Lanzerath, medals awarded long before Lyle Bouck and his men ever received their decorations.

LT Lyle Bouck, the platoon leader of the I&R Platoon, began his own trek into captivity on 17 December, the day after his capture. He moved east by foot from Lanzerath into Germany and finally ended up in the officer camp at Hammelburg, Stalag XIII D. But Bouck's adventures were far from over. He soon became involved in one of the most controversial American actions of the war, the raid on Hammelburg. At first, the Hammelburg camp appeared slovenly to Bouck. The officers showed little or no military bearing or discipline. Morale was low, partly due to the weak and vacillating leadership of COL Charles Cavender. Cavender commanded the 423rd Infantry Regiment of the ill-fated 106th Infantry Division. At the beginning of the Ardennes Offensive, the 423rd and 424th Regiments were surrounded on the Schnee Eifel and forced to surrender. Many of Cavender's men resented this decision. This resentment somehow affected his own view of himself, and this attitude carried over into Hammelburg where, as the senior Allied officer, he was placed in charge.

Things changed when COL Paul R. Goode, an officer from the 29th Infantry Division, arrived at the camp. Goode quickly whipped things into shape, and military bearing and discipline again became an issue. His stern manner irritated many of the captured officers.[9] Despite their grumbling, they knew it was for their own good. Among the group at Hammelburg was a very special individual, LTC John Waters, at least to a particular Army general. LTC Waters, captured by the German Afrikakorps while with the 1st Armored Division in 1943, was the son-in-law of LTG George S. Patton, Jr. When Patton learned of his presence at Hammelburg, the flamboyant general ordered the 4th Armored Division to create a task force to rescue the officers at the camp. Since the 3rd Army was only west of Frankfurt am Main at this time, the raiding force would have to traverse 50 or 60 kilometers of enemy-held territory. Patton never mentioned the presence of his son-in-law at the camp. He even refused to speak of the raid at the war's end. However, many people knew or suspected the truth. The intrigue involved surrounded the entire event with a blanket of controversy.

CPT Abe Baum was placed in charge of the 4th Division's task force and sometime in March 1945 moved out to the east. Despite incredible odds, Task Force Baum, after inflicting severe damage on several German units and having a bridge blown up in its face, made it to Hammelburg.[10] Baum rolled through the gates of Stalag XIII D to the delight of Bouck and other prisoners. However, the camp had more men than Baum had room to take. LTC Waters was wounded during the skirmish to take the camp and so couldn't make the trip out. Tearfully, Baum informed the overjoyed prisoners that he could only take a small group of them. He recommended that the others make it out on foot. Bouck and a fellow lieutenant from Company C of the 394th captured at Losheimergraben, Matthew Reid, hopped on one of Baum's tanks, determined to get out with the raiding party. However, the raid was doomed to failure. Baum's men were exhausted; they hadn't slept for nearly 48 hours. Baum decided to wait until morning before leaving. This fateful decision allowed time for several hastily formed SS men to get into position. These SS soldiers were young trainees at one of the Waffen-SS NCO Schools that littered Germany. Now mobilized for action, they were determined to win.

When Baum started off the next morning, the Germans blocked his task force and forced them onto a small hill west of Hammelburg. The attacking SS soldiers forced the GIs to burn their remaining vehicles. Baum's men assembled into small groups and attempted a breakout to the west. Bouck and Reid, both armed with M3 grease guns, participated in the brief battle, but to no avail. Bouck was hit in the left knee and both men were recaptured.

Bouck was held in a riding stable and received two pieces of sausage and a chunk of bread before being put on train headed east. East of Nuremberg, he detrained and walked through the devastated city. He endured friendly B-17 strikes along the way. He and Reid attempted another escape just before reaching the Danube. Recaptured, Bouck ended up in Moosburg with thousands of other prisoners. On 29 April, members of the 14th Armored Division liberated him. Nearby, elements of the 99th liberated LT Rose and SGT Rausch of Company K.

A few days after returning to the 99th, LT Bouck felt ill. He began throwing up his food and, after a medical examination, a surgeon diagnosed hepatitis. Bouck spent the rest of his time in Europe in a Paris hospital. After returning to the United States, Bouck still could not shake the aches and pains of acute hepatitis contracted while in German captivity. He remembered that, as a boy, an aunt who was a masseuse helped heal a back injury for him. Bouck and several other men at his new post decided to see a chiropractor and, after six weeks of treatment, felt better.[11]

Reassigned to recruiting duty at Cape Girardeau, Bouck decided to stay in the Army. He applied for the permanent rank of lieutenant. Now married and living in a small, one-room apartment, Bouck had high hopes for a promising career in the Army. He soon received notification of acceptance into the Regular Army. However, another event quickly overshadowed this good news. Bouck had also applied for back pay due him while a prisoner in Germany. The money arrived that same day, but it was much less than expected. When he called the responsible agency, he discovered that anyone with any amount of enlisted time would receive back compensation at that pay scale. Angered and disillusioned, Bouck tore up his commission. Soon thereafter he met a graduate of a chiropractic school, who espoused the merits of the field. Bouck, remembering the positive effects it had for him, soon decided to follow that path. He eventually established a successful chiropractic practice in St. Louis.

With his new future ahead of him, Bouck put the war behind him. In December 1965, however, Hugh M. Cole published the official U.S. Army history of the battle, *The Ardennes: Battle of the Bulge*. William Tsakanikas, Bouck's runner and foxhole-mate from the I&R Platoon, read the book and was outraged to find that it failed to mention the participation of the I&R Platoon. This omission struck Tsak to the core. Because of his serious face wound, Tsak endured 20 years of painful operations. He was married and, after attending the University of Pennsylvania's Wharton School of Business, became active in local politics in Port Chester, New York. He also changed his name to William James. Still smarting over the perceived slight in Cole's book, he decided to do something about it and wrote a letter to his former platoon leader, Lyle Bouck. Portions of the letter read as follows:

> Bouck—We were responsible for blunting the main spearhead of the whole German offensive for that whole first 24 hour period. However, you would never know it without having been there and then reading the account from the American position and the German position.

Listen, Bouck, I would like to see our unit cited, but more importantly, I want the world to know, but for your calm determination, it could have been another story. Remember when you used to say Fuck the torpedos [sic], straight ahead. What are your orders this time?

The letter ended by chiding Bouck to contact members of the U.S. Senate about the slight. But Bouck was reluctant to do so, for he saw no reason to dig up old memories from the war. At that time, he felt that he and his men had done nothing more than anyone else. Reliving old pains and anguish would solve nothing.

But the obsessed Tsak called Bouck and then flew out to see him in St. Louis, continually exhorting the former platoon leader to do something. At this time, John S.D. Eisenhower, the son of General of the Army and President Dwight D. Eisenhower, began research on a book about the Ardennes Offensive. Eisenhower was the first to begin serious inquiries into the actions of the I&R Platoon at Lanzerath. This new interest seemed to satisfy Tsak, and both he and Bouck offered assistance to the author. Bouck sent for a copy of his official records to help refresh his memory. By requesting these records, the true significance of his actions at Lanzerath was about to come into focus.

Prompted by the request for his records, a letter arrived in June 1966 indicating that MG Walter Lauer, his former division commander, had awarded him the Silver Star 20 years earlier. Bouck now became concerned about accuracy. If Eisenhower was going to tell the story of his men, then it had to be accurate and the truth. It would perhaps ease some of the pain Bouck felt about the action. He believed that the capture of his platoon had been a dereliction of duty. This notion haunted him for many years. Perhaps an opportunity to put things into perspective might solve his unanswered questions.

John Eisenhower asked Bouck to return to Lanzerath and describe the battle to him. But Bouck, busy with his practice, declined. Eisenhower then asked Tsak, but Tsak couldn't afford to pay his way. Bouck decided to foot the bill. The amazed John Eisenhower watched in awe as Tsak ran up and down his former positions on the hill overlooking Lanzerath, emotionally describing the action that led to his severe wound. Eisenhower thought he would have to carry the man's dead body off the hill that day.

Eisenhower again turned to Bouck for assistance. The author had had problems getting a response from the former commander of Kampfgruppe Peiper, Joachim Peiper. Aware that the Eisenhower name might have put the former SS officer off, Eisenhower asked Bouck to write Peiper on his behalf. Perhaps, he said, a letter from Bouck might lend more credibility to the request for information. Bouck agreed and prefaced his letter to the man convicted of the Malmedy Massacre as follows:

I know you faced charges of having your men shoot prisoners of war at Honsfeld, Bullingen and Malmedy. Because we were not molested after a day of severe battle with the best German troops, I have always thought you had been accused of something for which you had no control. It is well known that in the heat of battle tempers flare and men will do things they normally would not do. Many situations like this happened with our troops.

The letter struck the right chord with Peiper, whose notoriety had brought him a lifetime of frustration. Sentenced to life in prison at the Dachau Trials for the massacre, he served only 11 years at Landsberg Prison. His reputation cost him many good jobs and prominent positions, something Bouck was not aware of at the time. Peiper promptly replied and offered his perspective on the events in the "Bulge." He described his "disgusted impression" that the whole paratrooper regiment at Lanzerath "had gone to bed instead of waging war." Peiper offered these observations and much more, providing tremendous insights for Eisenhower's book.

Bouck then asked Peiper if he would be willing to take part in a meeting of both German and American veterans in Belgium. Bouck was still unaware of how the past had plagued the former SS officer's life; probably for this very reason Peiper begged off. Peiper wrote that "many people still live on the unsettled past and prosper on wounds artificially kept open."

Lyle Bouck continued to assist Eisenhower with the book project. He and Tsak, together with their wives, met the author at Gettysburg. Bouck openly stated that if he were in the same situation today, he would have pulled out with the tank destroyer unit. But that was the key: youth. It was Bouck's and his men's own sense of youthful invulnerability that made them stand and fight. An older, more mature person might have left.

Eisenhower published *The Bitter Woods* in 1969; it is perhaps one of the finest and most groundbreaking accounts of the battle ever written. He dedicated almost nine pages of text to the actions of the I&R Platoon at Lanzerath. Finally everything was in perspective, and Bouck was able to see the true significance of his men's bravery. They had genuine reason to be proud.

In that same year, Eisenhower, now U.S. ambassador to Belgium, invited Bouck and other veterans to meet in Belgium with nearly 70 former German paratroopers who fought at Lanzerath. They spent three days together, toured old battlefields, and relived memories of past escapades. During the course of the visit, one German veteran approached Bouck and placed his arm around the man's shoulder.

"Lyle," he began, "we haven't talked since that day. Do you remember someone who asked, 'Who is the commandant?' It was me."

Bouck's entire body tingled with the realization of who this man was. He was the former feldwebel, Vince Kuhlbach, the veteran paratrooper who so vehemently contested the idiotic assault tactics of his inexperienced officers. Kuhlbach was now an accountant in Germany, and the reunion of the two men was powerful and emotional.

In 1977, after 36 painful operations on his face, William James, formerly Tsakanikas, died of his wounds. A campaign began to honor him with the Congressional Medal of Honor. In 1979, a *Parade* magazine article dated 25 March carried Tsak's story with a headline that read "Why This Dead Hero

Should Get the Medal of Honor." Next to the headline was a photo of the youthful William Tsakanikas with a picture of the Congressional Medal of Honor superimposed below. Journalist Jack Anderson authored the piece. It caught the eye of many people. Tsak's congressman, Richard Ottinger, took the case to higher levels. The story so impressed George Steinbrenner, owner of baseball's New York Yankees, that he invited Tsak's widow to throw out the first ball for his team that season. Steinbrenner subsequently brought Bouck and 12 other members of the I&R Platoon to New York for the game as well. He wined and dined them and their wives in luxury at his expense.

That same year, the House of Representatives heard the testimony given by Bouck, his former regimental S-2 and later commander of the 2nd Battalion, Robert Kriz, and others. They recommended that the secretary of defense award Tsak the Medal of Honor and other decorations for valor to the men of the platoon. Bouck quietly refused any award for himself.

In 1981, everything came to a close at an awards ceremony where Tsak was posthumously awarded the Distinguished Service Cross. Platoon sergeant Bill Slape, who spent 30 years as a career soldier in the Army, and Risto Milosevich, the machine gunner turned civilian contractor, received the same decoration. Lou Kalil, Aubrey McGehee, "Pop" Robinson, James Silvola, and John Creger all received the Silver Star, and Bronze Stars for Valor went to everyone else. Lyle Bouck, the young platoon leader who thought he had let his men down, received the Distinguished Service Cross as well. Including the four Silver Stars won by LT Springer's FO party, the I&R Platoon became one of the most decorated units of its size in the entire Second World War.[12]

On 17 December 1944, the 12th Volksgrenadier Division finally made it to Murringen. They ultimately dislodged the 394th Infantry and the 1st Battalion, 23rd Infantry, sometime before midnight. Oberstleutnant Wilhelm Osterhold led a column of 10 sturmgeschutzen into the small town, and he guided the column forward with his captured American jeep. With him was the commander of the assault gun battalion, Major Gunther Holz.[13] North of the 12th Volksgrenadier, the 277th Volksgrenadier worked their way through the Schwarzenbruch and Weisser Stein Trails. They cleared a path for the panzers of the 12th SS Panzer Division "Hitlerjugend" to exploit. In the south, the 3rd Fallschirmjaeger Division followed Kampfgruppe Peiper. The kampfgruppe cleared away any remaining American resistance as they went. One battalion of paratroopers temporarily remained with the battle group as they pressed forward to the west. Kampfgruppe Peiper made one of the deepest penetrations of any German unit in the offensive.

During their drive west, Kampfgruppe Peiper took part in the notorious prisoner massacre at the Baugnez Crossroads, otherwise referred to as the Malmedy Massacre. At the end of the war, Joachim Peiper was tried by a War Crimes Commission at Dachau, the infamous concentration camp just north of Munich. As prisoner number 42, Peiper testified that he never gave orders to his men to shoot prisoners, but he accepted responsibility for their actions. An

American officer he captured and questioned near La Gleize, Belgium, during the battle testified on Peiper's behalf. MAJ Hal McCown insisted that neither Peiper nor his men ever mistreated him and other prisoners.

Despite McCown's striking testimony, the Commission found Peiper and other former SS officers in his chain of command, such as Sepp Dietrich, guilty of these crimes and sentenced them to harsh prison terms or death penalties. Peiper drew a death sentence but, as noted earlier, served only 11 years before a review board released him from Landsberg Prison in 1956. He found work with Porsche in Stuttgart, but his notorious reputation dogged him and cost him his position. He then went to work for Volkswagen, but Italian authorities raised the issue of a past atrocity. Peiper had shelled the Italian village of Boves in 1943 as retribution for the capture of two of his NCOs by Italian soldiers. Over 30 civilians died in that incident. As a result, Peiper again found himself jobless. After determining that German society was "bankrupt," Peiper moved to the small town of Traves-sur-Saône, France, 80 miles from the German border. On two acres of land, he built a home for himself, his wife, and their three children. He earned a living translating military history tomes for a publisher in Stuttgart. While in Traves-sur-Saône, he managed to find relative peace for a short while.

Three years later, in the mid-1970s, a local newspaper, which had learned about Peiper's past from some French Communists, featured a story about their infamous German resident. When approached, Peiper acerbically scolded them, saying that he thought France was a democracy and a place where people could be free. Hostility toward him built through routine threats until he felt compelled to send his wife back to Germany. As Bastille Day 1976 arrived, a mob of angry, vengeful villagers armed with torches and rifles allegedly descended upon Peiper's land. But Peiper was waiting for them with his two dogs. Armed with a rifle, Peiper supposedly exchanged gunfire with the mob. Peiper's house was torched and burned to the ground. The next day, as investigators sifted through the smoking rubble, they found the remains of Peiper's two dogs, both shot to death, and a charred human torso. They had difficulty positively identifying the body as Peiper's. Naturally, rumors abounded that Peiper had managed to escape the onslaught and that the charred remains were those of a villager planted there by the former SS officer. These rumors have yet been proven true.[14]

The end of the war was not as unpleasant for other Germans as it was for Peiper. Despite internment by either the Russians or Americans (it was far worse with the Russians), many former German soldiers began new lives after their release from captivity in the late 1940s to mid-1950s. However, some had unpleasant duties to perform for the Wehrmacht before the war actually ended.

Oberstleutnant Horst Freiherr von Wangenheim, chief of staff of the 277th Volksgrenadier Division, and his commander, Oberst (later Generalmajor) Viebig, had to write a report of justification explaining why their division had such a poor success rate during the offensive. Besides the obvious reasons—poor recruits and lack of equipment—the division's leadership had to formally accept responsibility, in writing, for the division's failures. Von Wangenheim assured me in a letter after the war that I should try to avoid being placed in a similar position in my own army. Things can get very "unpleasant."[15]

Things were more positive for the officers of the 12th Volksgrenadier Division, however. Despite initial problems in and around the Losheimergraben Crossroads, the division quickly recovered and moved forward to its subsequent objectives. The German High Command recognized much of the excellent German leadership in this particular division. Awards for valor and leadership proved this belief. Oberstleutnant Lemm's 1st Battalion commander in the 27th Fusilier Regiment, Hauptmann Claus Breger, killed while leading his troops against the American positions on the first day, received the coveted Oakleaves to his Knights Cross of the Iron Cross.[16] Lemm himself later ended the war as one of the most decorated infantry officers in the Wehrmacht. Sometime in March 1945, two months before VE (Victory in Europe) day, Heinz-Georg Lemm received the Oakleaves and Swords to his Knight's Cross.

Lemm's fellow regimental commander and long-time friend was decorated as well. Oberstleutnant Wilhelm Osterhold, commander of the 48th Grenadier Regiment, received the Oakleaves in February 1945.[17] His 7th Company commander, Oberleutnant Kurt Steinhofel, received the Iron Cross, 1st Class, in Murringen on 17 December for his part in finding a gap between the American positions. Since awards of this sort were difficult to come across in the field at this time of the war, the regimental adjutant gave Steinhofel his own personal decoration. Steinhofel kept it despite nine months in American captivity and a short stay in the Soviet sector. Today, he lives near Hamburg, Germany. He still has his Iron Cross.[18]

Major Moldenhauer was evacuated after wounds received on 16 December from his own artillery. Today, he is alive and well and living in western Germany. On 5 January 1945, while the Allies fought to reduce the "bulge," Major Kruse, the 2nd Battalion commander, was wounded and evacuated by plane to Germany. During the flight, his plane was shot down, and everyone aboard was killed. Two hours after Kruse received his wounds, Oberstleutnant Osterhold rushed to a location north of Lierneux, Belgium. He had received word that a battalion of engineers, placed under his command to act as infantry, were faltering under the pressure of an American tank attack. When Osterhold arrived, he saw several tanks firing directly at his engineers. Grabbing a panzerfaust, a disposable anti-tank weapon, Osterhold stalked one of the tanks. He fully intended to add another single-handed panzer kill to his credit. His right sleeve already had three badges for the single-handed destruction of a tank, so Osterhold was no stranger to this type of action. However, before he could fire the panzerfaust, fate caught up with him. The tank's gunner spied Osterhold running forward and fired the main gun directly at him. The round exploded in front of Osterhold. The impact knocked him backward and sent shards of hot shrapnel into his throat. He bled profusely. Osterhold's trusty driver managed to get the officer into his jeep and to an aid station in the rear. The war was finally over for Wilhelm Osterhold; Major Holz took over his regiment temporarily while Osterhold recovered in a hospital in Germany. While in hospital Osterhold received notification from Hitler that he was the 732nd officer of the German Wehrmacht to receive the Oakleaves to the Knight's Cross of the Iron Cross.[19]

Osterhold escaped Allied captivity because of his wounds, and after the war worked as a truck driver. When the German Army reformed in the late 1950s, Osterhold joined as an Oberstleutnant. He held a series of positions, including work on developing new hand-held anti-tank weapons. He retired in the early 1970s as an Oberst and now lives near Hamburg. He occasionally visits his former 7th Company commander, Kurt Steinhofel, who lives right down the road.

Oberst Osterhold hosted me in his home for a weekend in October 1987. I listened in amazement to a modest retelling of his exploits in the Second World War. As a veteran of both the Eastern and Western fronts, he had seen and participated in battles barely imaginable to a young infantry officer. I was awestruck by his tales. I felt that he must have considered it a privilege to have participated in so many historical battles. When I made this comment to him, he just looked at me and smiled. After a brief pause, he spoke in a very low and deliberate tone.

"I'm just happy to be alive."

APPENDIX A

Table of Comparative Ranks

The following table presents a comparison between the rank structure of the U.S. Army, the German Army, and the Waffen-SS. This book uses the specific rank of the individual when available. However, when referring to a German Army or Waffen-SS soldier, the rank appears in German to avoid confusion. These ranks are not in English translation because some have no American Army equivalent. Several of these ranks are only approximations to their counterparts.[1]

U.S. ARMY	GERMAN ARMY	WAFFEN-SS
General of the Army	Generalfeldmarschall	Reichsfuehrer
General (4)* (GEN)	Generaloberst	Oberstgruppenfuehrer
Lt. General (3) (LTG)	General der Infanterie, Artillerie, etc.	Obergruppenfuehrer
Maj. General (2) (MG)	Generalleutnant	Gruppenfuehrer
Brig. General (1) (BG)	Generalmajor	Brigadefuehrer
No equivalent	No equivalent	Oberfuehrer
Colonel (COL)	Oberst	Standartenfuehrer
Lt. Colonel (LTC)	Oberstleutnant	Obersturmbannfuehrer
Major (MAJ)	Major	Sturmbannfuehrer
Captain (CPT)	Hauptmann	Hauptsturmfuehrer
1st Lieutenant (1LT)	Oberleutnant	Obersturmfuehrer
2nd Lieutenant (2LT)	Leutnant	Untersturmfuehrer
Master SGT (1st grade) (MSG)	Stabsfeldwebel	Sturmscharfuehrer
1st SGT (1st grade) (1SG)	No equivalent	No equivalent
Tech. SGT (2nd grade) (T/SGT)	Oberfeldwebel	Hauptscharfuehrer
Staff SGT (3rd grade)** (SSG)	Feldwebel	Oberscharfuehrer
Sergeant (4th grade)** (SGT)	Unterfeldwebel	Scharfuehrer

Corporal (5th grade)** (CPL)	Unteroffizier	Unterscharfuehrer
Private First Class (PFC)	Gefreiter / Obergefreiter***	Rottenfuehrer
Private (PVT)	Schuetze / Oberschuetze	Oberschuetze / Sturmmann

* Indicates number of stars.

** These three ranks have equivalent technician grades indicated by a "T" beneath the chevrons. These ranks have no German equivalents.

*** The Germans have varying grades of privates and corporals. The grades indicated are the most common, but there are also different grades based on time in service. In addition, the basic private grade depends on the soldier's branch of service. The example shown is for a basic infantry private, a *schuetze*. Other possibilities include *grenadier* for a panzergrenadier (mechanized infantry), *kanonier* for an artilleryman, and so on.

APPENDIX B

Awards and Decorations

The following compilation of awards is not all inclusive and pertains predominantly to individuals featured in the book. The list is incomplete, with much of the information in the hands of the men themselves or their families. The sources for much of this information were the 394th Infantry Regiment's After-Action Reports, Jean-Paul Pallud's *Battle of the Bulge Then and Now*, and individual and personal accounts otherwise unavailable to the general public. Many more awards than those listed here were rendered to the men, both German and American, who fought in the battle from 16 to 17 December 1944. Where possible, a complete citation for the award is presented. However, in many cases only a standard name line, rank, and date are available. Many of the grades held by the recipients indicate their rank at the time of the award. Occasionally, this rank is different from the grade actually held during the battle.

Only the highest awards for valor, both American and German, are listed. For the Germans, the Knights Cross of the Iron Cross with subsequent grades (Oakleaves, Oakleaves and Swords) represents the highest award in the German Wehrmacht for bravery or leadership in battle. To earn this award, the individual not only risked himself personally in one or more acts of valor but also significantly influenced the course of a battle. Lesser grades of this award are the Iron Cross First and Second Classes.

American awards for valor cover a much larger spectrum. The decorations listed here are the Distinguished Service Cross, the Silver Star, and the Bronze Star. The first two are for significant acts of gallantry in action, whereas the Bronze Star may be awarded for either meritorious service or valor (later indicated by a metal "V" device on the medal). The Distinguished Service Cross is second only to the Congressional Medal of Honor. All infantry personnel received the Combat Infantryman's Badge (CIB), and all forward medical personnel received the Combat Field Medical Badge (CFMB). All battle-wounded soldiers received the Purple Heart Medal. In addition, citations for the Presidential Unit Citation, an award given to entire units for conspicuous gallantry in action, are listed.

AMERICAN AWARDS

Distinguished Service Cross

T/Sgt. Eddie Dolenc, D, Dec. 16, 1944...saw left flank of his platoon cut off, secured machine gun, mounted it in plain view of enemy. Using free traverse, Dolenc killed or wounded 30 Jerries, forced remainder of large force to withdraw. Soon the Germans struck back, this time in even larger numbers. Correctly estimating the gravity of the situation, he ordered his men to make their way to safety. Dolenc stayed alone at his post. When last seen, he was pouring a hail of bullets into the Germans. Missing in action. PW, liberated in May.[1]

Award of the Silver Star Medal

LT. Colonel ROBERT H. DOUGLAS, 0129212, Commanding Officer, 1st Battalion, 394th Infantry, was awarded the Silver Star Medal for gallantry in action during the period 16–17 December 44. Colonel DOUGLAS fought his battalion in a commendable manner during the above period of time. He exposed himself to enemy fire on numerous occasions to lead his battalion. He personally contacted commanders of isolated units to insure their withdrawal to prevent annihilation. (Authority, General Orders #23, Headquarters 99th Infantry Division)

2nd Lieut HARVEY E. WILLIAMSON, 01319697, Platoon Leader, Company "D" 394th Infantry, was awarded the Silver Star Medal for gallantry in action against the enemy on 16 December 44, in Germany. During the intense enemy artillery barrage, Lt. WILLIAMSON left his foxhole to give aid to an injured man from Company "B," 394th Infantry, when all others refused. His clothes were torn by flying shrapnel and his helmet knocked off, but he succeded [sic] in carrying the man back to cover. Lt. WILLIAMSON is missing in action. Authority, Section I, General Orders #25, Headquarters 99th Infantry Division, dated 31 December 44 as amended by Section 5, General Orders #3, Headquarters 99th Infantry Division, dated 8 January 45.[2]

First Lieutenant Warren P. Springer, 01173092, 371st Field Artillery Battalion, United States Army, for gallantry in action against the enemy on 16 December 1944, in Germany. Lieutenant Springer was a forward observer. During a German counter-attack, he and his party were cut off from their infantry unit. They continued to call for artillery fire on wave after wave of attacking enemy, until their radio was knocked out. Realizing the desperate situation, Lieutenant Springer manned a machine gun and fired it at the attacking enemy until one of his men became a casualty and his ammunition was expended. Lieutenant Springer was taken prisoner. The gallant action of Lieutenant Springer reflect [sic] high credit upon himself and the finest traditions of the armed forces of the United States. Entered military service from Massachusetts.

Sergeant Peter A. Gacki, 35349748, 371st Field Artillery Battalion, United States Army, for gallantry in acting against the enemy on 16 December 1944, in Germany. Sargeant [sic] Gacki was a member of a forward observer party. During a German counter-attack, he and his party were cut off from their infantry unit. They continued to call for fire on wave after wave of attacking enemy until their radio was knocked out. Realizing the desperate situation, Sergeant Gacki remained with the party until one of the party was killed and the ammunition all expended. Sergeant Gacki was taken prisoner. The gallant and courageous action of Sergeant Gacki reflect [sic] high credit upon himself and the finest traditions of the armed forces of the United States. Entered military service from South Bend, Indiana. Inducted in Ohio.

Appendix B 165

Technician Fourth Grade Willard J. Wibben, 35719032, 371st Field Artillery Battalion, United States Army, for gallantry in action against the enemy on 16 December 1944, in Germany. Sergeant Wibben was a member of a forward observer party. During a German counter-attack, he and his party were cut off from their infantry unit. They continued to call for artillery fire on wave after wave of attacking enemy, until their radio was knocked out. Realizing the desperate situation, Sergeant Wibben manned a machine gun and fired it at the attacking enemy until one of the men became a casualty and the ammunition was expended. Sergeant Wibben was taken prisoner. The gallant actions of Sergeant Wibben reflect high credit upon himself and the finest traditions of the armed forces of the United States. Entered military service from Indiana.

Technician Fifth Grade Billy S. Queen (POSTHUMOUS AWARD),356-42420, 371st Field Artillery Battalion, United States Army, for gallantry in action against the enemy on 16 December 1944, in Germany. Technician Fifth Grade Queen was a member of a forward observer party when cut off from their infantry unit by a heavy enemy counter-attack. They continued to call for artillery fire on wave after wave of attacking enemy until their radio was knocked out. The situation becoming more desperate, Technician Fifth Grade Queen manned a nearby machine gun position and fired at the attacking enemy until killed by the enemy fire. The courage and gallant actions displayed by Technician Fifth Grade Queen reflect high credit upon himself and the finest traditions of the armed forces of the United States. Entered military service from West Virginia. Residence: General Delivery, Crum, West Virginia.[3]

T/SGT Savino Travalini, AT, 3rd Battalion, Dec. 16, 1944...silenced MG nest that was pinning down buddies, then kayoed another in blockhouse with 5 rounds, firing rifle at fleeing Jerries after each round.[4]

1/Lt. John W. Vaughan, D, Dec. 16, 1944...prevented a penetration by 100 Germans 25 feet from his positions by calling for 89-degree mortar fire. Rounds fell 10 feet from his foxholes.

1/Lt. Griffith E. Benson, AT, Dec. 16-17, 1944...organized his AT platoon as riflemen after all guns had been knocked out, held off fanatical Nazis at Losheimergraben for over 24 hours.

2/Lt. Lyle O. Frank, A, Dec. 16-17, 1944...surprised 100-man German patrol that was attacking company CP by hitting them with marching fire from flank with two other men, repulsed enemy, later exposed self rescuing pinned-down buddies.

1/Sgt. Wesley Kibler, B, Dec. 16-17, 1944...as T/Sgt., skillfully organized men into defensive positions, exposed self to direct fire on enemy tank.

1/Lt. Dewey A. Plankers, C, Dec. 16-17, 1944...helped delay enemy over 24 hours at Losheimergraben.

T/Sgt. Fred A. Wallace, E, Dec. 16-18, 1944...prevented breach in lines by calling for artillery and mortar fire close to, and even on, his own isolated position.

Pfc. James A. Cotter, B, Dec. 17, 1944...with only 4 rounds of Bazooka ammo, demolished 1 tank, stopped another while under fire of a third. Missing in action.

Col. Don Riley, Regt. Hq., Dec. 17, 1944...successfully withdrew regiment, short on ammo, to Murringen after it was virtually surrounded by enemy.

Award of the Bronze Star Medal

Technical Sergeant Arthur C. Piar, 15018474, Platoon Sergeant, Anti-Tank Company, 394th Infantry, was awarded the Bronze Star Medal for heroic achievement in connection with military operations against the enemy during the period 16–18 December 44 in Germany. Technical Sergeant Piar greatly assisted his platoon leader and another officer in organizing the defense of Losheimergraben, Germany which successfully delayed the German advance in that sector for more than twenty four hours. (Authority, Section II, General Orders #25, Headquarters 99th Infantry Division, dated 31 December 44).[5]

S/Sgt. Delbert J. Stumpff, D[6]
1/Sgt. Elmer P. Klug, L
Capt. Robert R. McGee Jr., 2d Bn.
T/Sgt. Robert R. Ferguson, K

UNIT BATTLE HONORS

Presidential Unit Citation "...for outstanding performance of duty..."

1st Battalion, 394th Infantry
Company K, 394th Infantry

The First Battalion, Three Ninety Fourth Infantry Regiment, is cited for outstanding performance of duty in action against the enemy during period 16 to 28 December, 1944, near Losheimergraben, Germany, and near Murringen and Elsenborn, Belgium. The German's Ardennes Offensive was spearheaded directly at the First Battalion, Three Ninety Fourth Infantry Regiment, which was defending a front of thirty-five hundred yards and protecting the right flank of the Ninety Ninth Infantry Division, which was holding the vital Northern shoulder of the Ardennes bulge. The enemy launched his initial attack on the position held by the First Battalion, Three Ninety Fourth Infantry Regiment, with an unprecedented artillery concentration lasting one and three-quarters hours, followed by an attack of six battalions of infantry, supported by tanks, dive bombers, flame throwers, and rockets. For two days and nights they were under intense small arms fire and continuous artillery concentrations. They had little food and water, and no hope of replenishing their rapidly dwindling supply of ammunition. Knowing that no reserves were available, the men of this Battalion, with indomitable spirit and confidence in their cause, beat back the superior numbers of the enemy forces coming at them from the front, flanks, and rear. Many times the men rose out of their foxholes to meet the enemy in fierce hand-to-hand combat. Outnumbered six to one they inflicted casualties in the ratio of four to one. Finally ordered to withdraw to more secure positions the First Battalion, Three Ninety Fourth Infantry Regiment, moved through enemy infested areas, and from their new positions successfully defended against determined enemy attacks for the next nine days. By their tenacious stand the First Battalion, Three Ninety Fourth Infantry Regiment, destroyed over fifty percent of two German Infantry Regiments, and prevented the enemy from expanding the base of his bulge. The courage and devotion to duty displayed by members of the First Battalion, Three Ninety Fourth Infantry Regiment, in the face of overwhelming odds was in keeping with the highest traditions of the Military Service.[7]

Intelligence and Reconnaissance Platoon (awarded 16 September 1981)

By virtue of the authority vested in me as President of the United States and as Commander in Chief of the Armed Forces of the United States, I have today awarded THE PRESIDENTIAL UNIT CITATION (ARMY) FOR EXTRAORDINARY HEROISM TO THE INTELLIGENCE AND RECONNAISSANCE PLATOON, 394TH INFANTRY REGIMENT, 99th INFANTRY DIVISION. The Intelligence and Reconnaissance Platoon, 394th Regiment, 99th Infantry Division, distinguished itself by ex-

Appendix B

traordinary heroism in action against enemy forces on 16 December 1944 near Lanzerath, Belgium. The German Ardennes Offensive which began the Battle of the Bulge was directed initially against a small sector defended by the Intelligence and Reconnaissance Platoon. Following a two-hour artillery barrage, enemy forces of at least battalion strength launched three separate frontal attacks against the small Intelligence and Reconnaissance Platoon of 18 men. Each attack was successfully repelled by the platoon. The platoon position was becoming untenable as casualties mounted and ammunition was nearly exhausted. Plans were made to break contact with the enemy and withdraw under cover of darkness. Before this could be accomplished, a fourth enemy attack finally overran the position and the platoon was captured at bayonet point. Although greatly outnumbered, through numerous feats of valor and an aggressive and deceptive defense of their position, the platoon inflicted heavy casualties on the enemy forces and successfully delayed for nearly 24 hours a major spearhead of the attacking German forces. Their valorous actions provided crucial time for other American forces to prepare to defend against the massive German offensive. The extraordinary gallantry, determination and esprit de corps of the Intelligence and Reconnaissance Platoon in close combat against a numerically superior enemy force are in keeping with the highest traditions of the United States Army and reflect great credit upon the Unit and the Armed Forces of the United States.[8]

signed
//Jimmy Carter//

The following is a press release dated 16 September, 1981 chronicling the I&R Platoon's unit and individual awards (IMMEDIATE RELEASE No. 429-81, OXford 73189 (Copies), OXford 75131 (Info), 16 September 1981).

ARMY HONORS WORLD WAR II SOLDIERS

Secretary of the Army John O. Marsh, Jr., announced today that 18 World War II soldiers will be honored with medals for Valor for their courageous and almost forgotten last ditch stand at Lanzerath, Belgium, December 16, 1944, during the initial phases of the Battle of the Bulge.

Valor awards for members of the Intelligence and Reconnaissance Platoon, 394th Infantry Regiment, 99th Infantry Division include the Presidential Unit Citation, four (4) Distinguished Service Crosses (Army's second highest award for valor next to the Medal of Honor), five (5) Silver Stars, and nine (9) Bronze Stars with Valor Device. This recognition makes the unit one of the most highly decorated combat units in World War II history.

Official accounts credit the platoon, outnumbered 15 to 1, with repelling three major enemy frontal attacks while inflicting severe casualties on the enemy over an 18 hour period. Completely surrounded, out of ammunition, with several platoon members severely wounded, the platoon was captured at gun point and held captive for the remainder of the war.

Official recognition of this heroic defence follows a lengthy effort on the part of the former platoon leader, Lyle J. Bouck, Jr., St. Louis, MO, and others to recognize the bravery of these men.

Secretary Marsh will host an awards ceremony in Washington, October 26, to recognize these men and their survivors. Platoon members will be presented medals for bravery at that time. The names of platoon members, rank at time of discharge, medals awarded and hometowns are:

CPT Lyle J. Bouck, Jr.—Distinguished Service Cross—St. Louis, MO.
SGM William L. Slape—Distinguished Service Cross—Shreveport, LA.
SGT Risto Milosevich—Distinguished Service Cross—El Toro, CA.
CPL William James Tsakanikas (deceased)—Distinguished Service Cross—Port Chester, NY.
CPL Aubrey P. McGehee, Jr.—Silver Star—McComb, MS.
CPL Jordan H. Robinson—Silver Star—Blaine, TN.
PFC James R. Silvola—Silver Star—Ocala, FL.
PFC Louis J. Kalil—Silver Star—Mishawaka, IN.
PFC John B. Creger—Silver Star—Richmond, VA.
SFC James Fort—Bronze Star with Valor Device
SSG George H. Redmond—Bronze Star with Valor Device—Greensboro, NC.
SSG William R. Dustman (deceased)—Bronze Star with Valor Device—Albany, OR.
SGT Samuel L. Jenkins—Bronze Star with Valor Device—El Paso, TX.
CPL Robert H. Preston—Bronze Star with Valor Device—Silver Springs, MD.
PFC Clifford R. Fansher—Bronze Star with Valor Device—Enid, OK.
PVT Robert J. Baasch (deceased)—Bronze Star with Valor Device—Clarksburg, WV.
PVT Robert D. Adams (deceased)—Bronze Star with Valor Device—Akron, OH.
PVT Joseph A. McConnell—Bronze Star with Valor Device—Tempe, AZ.
*SGT Robert L. Lambert—Irvine, CA.
*PFC Elmer J. Nowacki (deceased)—Cleveland, OH.
*PFC Carlos A. Fernandez—El Paso, TX.
*PFC John P. Frankovitch—Cleveland, OH.
*PVT Samuel J. Oakley—Danville, VA.
*PVT Vernon G. Leopold—Huntington Woods, MI.

*Indicates other members of the I&R Platoon at time of action but not directly involved in the actual battle—all platoon members share the Presidential Unit Citation.[9]

GERMAN AWARDS[10]

Knight's Cross of the Iron Cross with Oakleaves and Swords

SS-Obersturmbannfuehrer Joachim Peiper

Knight's Cross of the Iron Cross with Oakleaves

Oberstleutnant Wilhelm Osterhold (732nd recipient, February 1945)
Hauptmann Claus Breger (December 1944, posthumously)

Knight's Cross of the Iron Cross

Oberstleutnant Gerhard Lemcke

Iron Cross, First Class

Oberleutnant Kurt Steinhofel (17 December 1944)

APPENDIX C

Select Order of Battle

The following is a select order of battle based solely on German and American units that participated in the fighting. Major commands, such as army and corps headquarters, are included to add perspective to each organization. Where known, names of commanders and special platoon leaders follow that particular unit's designation. In addition, authorized and actual strengths, if known, follow specific unit designations. Sources for these data are Mitcham (1985); Parker (1991); MacDonald (1985); 394th After-Action Reports; Pallud (1986); *War Department Handbook on German Military Forces TM-E 30-451*; and Stanton (1991).

AMERICAN

1st United States Army—LTG Courtney H. Hodges

V US Corps—MG Leonard T. Gerow
    2nd Infantry Division
    8th Infantry Division
    78th Infantry Division
    102d Cavalry Group, Mechanized
    99th Infantry Division

99th Infantry Division—MG Walter Lauer
    393rd Infantry Regiment
    *394th Infantry Regiment
    395th Infantry Regiment
    370th Field Artillery Battalion
    371st Field Artillery Battalion
    372nd Field Artillery Battalion
    924th Field Artillery Battalion
    196th Field Artillery Battalion
    776th Field Artillery Battalion
    99th Reconnaissance Troop (Mechanized)

324th Engineer Combat Battalion
535th AAA Auto-Wpns Battalion (attached 11 December 44–9 May 45)
801st Tank Destroyer Battalion (towed)

*394th Infantry Regiment—COL Don Riley (authorized strength 3257; actual strength as of 1 December 1944: 3087)
    Regimental S-2—MAJ Robert L. Kriz
    Headquarters Company—CPT Joseph H. Mills
    Service Company—CPT George M. Leuty
    Anti-Tank Company—CPT Harold Z. Moore
    Medical Detachment—CPT Stephen M. Gillespie
    Intelligence and Reconnaissance Platoon—1LT Lyle Bouck, Jr.

1st Battalion—LTC Robert Douglas (authorized strength 836)
    Company A—1LT Willard W. Clark
    Company B—CPT Sidney A. Gooch
    Company C—CPT James A. Graham, Jr.
    Company D—CPT John S. Sandiland
    Ammunition and Pioneer Platoon
    Anti-Tank Platoon
    Mine Platoon
    Heavy Weapons Platoon—2LT Charles E. Butler

2nd Battalion—MAJ Ben Legare (acting commander) (authorized strength 836)
    Battalion Executive Officer—MAJ Ben Legare
    Battalion S-3—CPT Robert McGee
    Company E—CPT William G. Patterson
    Company F—1LT John A. Goodner
    Company G—CPT John N. Haymaker
    Company H—CPT Robert E. Mannheimer
    Ammunition and Pioneer Platoon
    Anti-Tank Platoon
    Mine Platoon
    Heavy Weapons Platoon

3rd Battalion—MAJ Norman Moore (authorized strength 836)
    Battalion Executive Officer—MAJ George Clayton
    Battalion S-3—CPT Charles P. Roland
    Company I—CPT James J. Morris, Jr. (detached to 393rd Infantry Regiment 13 December 1944)
    Company K—CPT Wesley Simmons
    Company L—1LT Neil Brown
    Company M—CPT Joseph M. Shank (2nd Platoon detached to 393rd Infantry Regiment 13 December 1944)
    Ammunition and Pioneer Platoon
    Anti-Tank Platoon
    Mine Platoon
    Heavy Weapons Platoon

Appendix C 171

1st Battalion, 23rd Infantry, 2nd Infantry Division—LTC John Hightower (attached to 394th from 17–18 December 1944)

GERMAN
6th SS Panzer Army—SS-Oberstgruppenfuehrer Sepp Dietrich
Chief of Staff—SS-Brigadefuehrer Fritz Kraemer
I SS Panzer Corps—SS-Gruppenfuehrer Hermann Priess
1st SS Panzer Division "Leibstandarte-SS Adolf Hitler"—SS-Oberfuehrer Wilhelm Mohnke
12th SS Panzer Division "Hitlerjugend"—SS-Standartenfuehrer Hugo Kraas
277th Volksgrenadier Division—Oberst Wilhelm Viebig
12th Volksgrenadier Division—Generalmajor Gerhard Engel
3rd Fallschirmjaeger Division—Generalmajor Walther Wadehn

1st SS Panzer Division "Leibstandarte-SS Adolf Hitler"—SS-Oberfuehrer Wilhelm Mohnke
    1st SS Panzer Regiment (+) (*Kampfgruppe Peiper*)—SS- Obersturmbannfuehrer Joachim Peiper

277th Volksgrenadier Division—Oberst Wilhelm Viebig (authorized strength: 10,072; listed at 80 percent strength on the eve of the battle)
    Chief of Staff—Oberstleutnant Horst Freiherr von Wangenheim
    989th Grenadier Regiment
    990th Grenadier Regiment—Oberstleutnant Josef Bremm
    991st Grenadier Regiment
    Sturmgeschutze Kompanie 1277 (6 Jagdpanzer 38(t))
    277th Artillery Regiment
    277th Fusilier Battalion
    277th Anti-Tank Battalion
    277th Engineer Battalion

12th Volksgrenadier Division—Generalmajor Gerhard Engel (authorized strength: 10,072; strength in autumn, 1944: 14,800; listed at 80 percent strength on the eve of the battle.)
    27th Fusilier Regiment—Oberstleutnant Heinz-Georg Lemm
    48th Grenadier Regiment—Oberstleutnant Wilhelm Osterhold
    89th Grenadier Regiment—Oberstleutnant Gerhard Lemcke
    Sturmgeschutze Kompanie 1012—(6 StuGs) Major Gunther Holz (overall assault gun commander)
    12th Artillery Regiment
    12th Fusilier Battalion
    12th Reconnaissance Battalion
    12th Anti-Tank Battalion
    12th Engineer Battalion

3rd Fallschirmjaeger Division—Generalmajor Walther Wadehn (authorized strength: 15,976; listed at 75 percent strength on the eve of the battle)

5th Fallschirmjaeger Regiment
8th Fallschirmjaeger Regiment
9th Fallschirmjaeger Regiment—Oberst Helmut von Hofmann
3rd FJ Artillery Regiment
3rd FJ Anti-Tank Battalion
3rd FJ Engineer Battalion
3rd Heavy Mortar Unit (FJ)

APPENDIX D

Glossary of Terms and Equipment

The following is a basic list of terms and equipment, both American and German, intended to supplement the text. Where possible, detailed information is given on all terms or weapons systems mentioned. Only relevant data are listed and are not all inclusive. The primary sources for this information are Angolia and Schlicht (1987) and Hogg and Weeks (1985).

Bazooka—U.S. hand-held, 2.36 inch anti-tank weapon. Reusable and effective, the bazooka saw significant service throughout the war.

CP—Command Post.

FO—Artillery Forward Observer.

Fusilier—Like grenadier, a term that renamed a standard infantryman based on German military tradition. Each Volksgrenadier division had one fusilier regiment; therefore, the appropriate term for a member of the regiment was fusilier. The same concept applied to members of the grenadier regiment.

GI—Standard term for a U.S. soldier in World War II. GI technically stands for "government issue," but many soldiers interpreted the term as meaning "government instrument."

Grenadier—Like fusilier, a name that is only an honorific title and short for Volksgrenadier. By renaming his infantrymen Volksgrenadiers, Hitler planned to invoke past German traditions to create an air of elitism among the ranks.

Kriegsgefangener—German word for a prisoner of war. The American term was *kriegie*.

Kriegsmarine—German Navy.

Luftwaffe—German Air Force.

M1—Standard U.S.-issue .30 caliber, the "Garand" was a self-loading service rifle used throughout the war.

M1 Carbine—A smaller version of the M1 Garand. This .30 caliber light rifle used a magazine and could fire in the semiautomatic mode. The M1 carbine was a favorite with junior leaders.

M1918 (Browning) (BAR)—Browning Automatic Rifle. Intended as a light assault machine gun, the BAR never really lived up to its expectations. Too heavy to be a rifle, the BAR fell between the two. On an average, the BAR could fire 500 rounds per minute (RPM).

M1919 .30 Caliber Machine Gun—Belt-fed, light machine gun often found in infantry company weapons platoons. This machine gun fired 500 RPM and used a 250-round fabric belt.

M34 8cm German Mortar—Standard German heavy mortar found at the infantry battalion level. The mortar's maximum range was 2,400 meters; the Germans could rapidly employ this mortar with great accuracy.

M42 12cm Heavy Mortars—German heavy mortar normally found in the late-war infantry regiment's Infantry Howitzer Company. This mortar moved on a two-wheeled, towed carriage.

MG42—German belt-fed 7.92mm light machine gun. The "Spandau," named for the weapons works where it was produced, had a cyclic rate of 1,200 RPM and was effective and reliable in the field. The MG42's forerunner was the MG34, which also saw service until the end of the war.

MP40—German 9mm sub-machine gun that could fire only on automatic. Produced early in the war, the "Schmeisser" was a favorite weapon among the German ranks, significantly enhancing the firepower of the German infantryman prior to the advent of the StG 44.

OP—Observation Post.

RTO—Radio-Telephone Operator.

Panzerfaust—A German hand-held disposable anti-tank weapon developed in the middle stages of the war.

PW (or POW)—Prisoner of War.

SCR-300—Standard U.S. Army wireless field radio of limited range and capability. SCR stands for Set, Complete, Radio.

SdKfz 251/3 Ausf. D—German variation of a half-track. There were many different varieties of this vehicle. They tended to be larger than the typical U.S. half-track.

Siegfried Line—Nickname given the fortifications and "dragon's teeth" that lined the German border in the west.

Stalag—German prisoner of war camp; short for Stammlager.

StG 44—German Sturmgewehr 44. A late-war, stamped-metal, semi- and fully automatic assault rifle intended to improve the firepower of the average German infantryman. With a 7.92mm round, the StG 44 was the forerunner of many modern-day assault rifles, including the Soviet AK-47. The StG 44 could fire 500 RPM and had a maximum effective range of 600 meters for single shots and 300 meters on automatic.

Sturmgeschutze(n)—German armored assault gun. Not a tank but a self-propelled, direct-fire artillery piece. Assault guns had no turrets; therefore, they had to pivot left or right to acquire a target. Weapon calibers varied; however, the vehicles mentioned in this battle are predominantly StuG IIIs that employed a 75mm main gun and an MG34 7.92mm coaxial machine gun. The 75mm gun's maximum effective range was approximately 1,000 meters.

Wehrmacht—German Armed Forces.

7.5cm PAK Light Infantry Guns—Two-wheeled, towed German infantry support gun. Late-war infantry regiments usually had one or two platoons of these guns, often detached for direct support to one of the two battalions.

Appendix D

- **15cm Heavy Infantry Gun**—German two-wheel, towed infantry support gun normally found in the Infantry Howitzer Company of a late-war infantry regiment. This gun had a maximum effective range of 4,700 meters.
- **.50 Caliber Machine Gun**—The M2, or "ma deuce," a heavy, belt-fed machine gun used either in the ground mode or mounted on tanks or jeeps. The M2 required the headspace and timing to be set before firing and was often used in the antiaircraft role. The M2 had a maximum effective range of approximately 1,000 to 1,200 meters and could fire from 500 to 800 RPM.
- **57mm Anti-Tank Gun**—Towed, two-wheeled, crew-served anti-tank gun that fired a 57mm round from a breech block in the rear.
- **60mm Mortar**—Standard U.S. infantry company light mortar.
- **81mm Mortar**—Standard U.S. crew-served mortar commonly found in the Heavy Weapons Company of an infantry battalion.
- **98K Mauser**—Standard German 7.92mm, bolt-action service rifle used throughout the war. The 98k's maximum effective range was approximately 800 meters.

Notes

The following is a list of source notes and other specific references that form the basis for the information presented in the book. Documenting all of these sources has been a difficult task. I began researching this battle in 1986, and much of the information I pieced together seems almost second nature to me. In many cases, I heard about a particular action or detail from several people, forming a picture in my mind based on a mixture of these accounts. Because of this mixture of details, it becomes difficult to identify in all cases every specific source. The following is my best attempt, and I believe these notes are quite thorough.

Chapter 1
The Great Gamble

1. Much of the information in this chapter is a synopsis of the battle's general origins found in numerous published accounts. Among the best are Cole (1965), Eisenhower (1969), MacDonald (1985), Parker (1991), and Arnold (1990). Other works certainly figure in but are too numerous to specify.

2. William C.C. Cavanagh, *Krinkelt-Rocherath: The Battle for the Twin Villages* (Mass.: Christopher Publishing House, 1986), 1.

3. The best account of the Allied intelligence problems is in Charles B. MacDonald, *A Time for Trumpets: The Untold Story of the Battle of the Bulge* (New York: Bantam Books, 1985), Chapters 2 and 3.

Chapter 2
The "Checkerboard" Men

1. *First United States Army Report of Operations, 1 August 1944–22 February 1945*.

2. Shelby L. Stanton, *World War II Order of Battle* (New York: Galahad Books, 1991), 175.

3. Ibid.

4. 1/LT Walton T. Farrar, *The Combat History of the 394th Infantry Regiment*, PFC James L. Haseltine, ed. (Privately Published), 2.

5. Wesley J. Simmons, "The Operations of Company K, 394th Infantry, (99th Infantry Division) in Defensive Action near Elsenborn, Belgium, 16-21 December 1944 (Ardennes-Alsace Campaign)" (Personal Experience of a Company Commander). Unpublished Monograph (Advanced Infantry Officers Course, 1949-1950) U.S. Army Infantry School, Fort Benning, Georgia, 5.

6. Personal letter to the author from Howard Bowers, dated 17 January 1989.

7. Dick Byers, "Fight for Losheimergraben," *The Checkerboard,* March 1990, 6.

8. Farrar, 3.

9. Simmons, 7.

10. Dick Byers, "Buzz Bomb Alley Part II," *The Checkerboard,* February 1993, 7.

11. Charles B. MacDonald, *A Time for Trumpets: The Untold Story of the Battle of the Bulge* (New York: Bantam Books, 1985), 629.

Chapter 3
Germany's Last Warriors

1. Jean-Paul Pallud, *Battle of the Bulge Then and Now* (London: Battle of Britain International Limited, 1986), 40.

2. Ibid., 41; Samuel W. Mitcham, *Hitler's Legions: The German Army Order of Battle, World War II* (New York: Stein and Day, 1985), 202-203.

3. Personal letter to the author from Horst Freiherr von Wangenheim, dated 13 August 1987.

4. Ibid.

5. Ibid.

6. Pallud, *Battle of the Bulge Then and Now,* 41.

7. Ibid.

8. Peter Elstob, *Hitler's Last Offensive: The Full Story of the Battle of the Ardennes* (New York: Macmillan Co., 1971), 70.

9. Mitcham, 49-51.

10. Personal letter to the author from Kurt Steinhofel, dated 5 November 1990.

11. Pallud, *Battle of the Bulge Then and Now,* 41.

12. Personal letter to the author from Oberst a. D. Wilhelm Osterhold, dated 19 June 1987. I received additional information from Oberst Osterhold during a later personal interview.

13. Letter to Richard Byers from Walter Wittlinger, dated 2 December 1985.

14. Pallud, *Battle of the Bulge Then and Now,* 41; Mitcham, 418-419.

15. Letter to Byers from Wittlinger.

16. Pallud, *Battle of the Bulge Then and Now,* 41.

17. Ibid.

18. Letter to the author from Wilhelm Osterhold.

19. Telephone conversation with Wilhelm Osterhold on 7 October 1990.

20. Personal letters to the author from Wilhelm Osterhold (19 June 1987) and Kurt Steinhofel (5 November 1990). The information provided is a mixture of the experiences of both men in the planning and preparation phase of the battle. However, the predominant information came from Osterhold.

Chapter 4
Seize the Crossroads!

1. Both Cole and MacDonald give excellent accounts of the planning and purpose of the preparatory artillery bombardment. Dick Byers, "Fight for Losheimergraben," *The*

Notes 179

Checkerboard, March 1990, highlights the effect the artillery had on many of the men in the 394th Infantry Regiment.

2. The following account of the 48th Grenadier Regiment's initial assault comes from a personal letter to the author from Wilhelm Osterhold dated 19 June 1987. Subsequent phone conversations and interviews provided additional details and insight into the action. Osterhold is the primary source except where otherwise noted.

3. Both Wilhelm Osterhold and Kurt Steinhofel agree on this specific compass heading.

4. This specific conversation is from a letter to the author by Kurt Steinhofel, dated 5 November 1990.

5. Dick Byers, "Fight for Losheimergraben," *The Checkerboard,* March 1990, 6; copy of a letter to Charles Kent from Danny Dalyai, dated 17 February 1991.

6. 1/LT Walton T. Farrar, *The Combat History of the 394th Infantry Regiment,* PFC James L. Haseltine, ed. (Privately Published), 46.

7. Byers, "Fight for Losheimergraben," 5–6; copy of a letter to Charles Kent from Kermit M. Ball, dated January 1992.

8. Byers, "Fight for Losheimergraben," 7.

9. Ibid., 6; William C.C. Cavanagh, *Krinkelt-Rocherath: The Battle for the Twin Villages* (Mass.: Christopher Publishing House, 1986), 24.

10. The primary source for the actions by the 2nd Battalion, 48th Grenadier Regiment, comes from a personal letter to the author from Kurt Steinhofel, dated 5 November 1990.

11. Byers, "Fight for Losheimergraben," 7.

12. Ibid., 8.

13. Charles B. MacDonald, *A Time for Trumpets: The Untold Story of the Battle of the Bulge* (New York: Bantam Books, 1985), 172; Farrar, 44.

14. Byers, "Fight for Losheimergraben," 6.

15. Ibid., 7.

16. This account is a mixture of information from Byers, "Fight for Losheimergraben," and phone conversations with William Sears (12 April 1993) and Charles Kent (20 April 1993). Sears and Kent provided a detailed and intimate account of their actions during this engagement.

17. Mudcat remains an unknown feature of this action. Neither Sears nor Kent know who he was or where he was from. They assume Mudcat came from their own company, Company B. T/SGT Wesley Kibler moved Mudcat to their position around noon that day, and the man remained until the Germans came from behind Sears and Kent's foxhole. Bill Sears remembers him as a "comical figure" who seemed a bit "odd." Perhaps that's how he got the nickname.

Chapter 5
Fusiliers in the Flank

1. Written account by Robert Newbrough, dated July 1980.

2. William C.C. Cavanagh, *Krinkelt-Rocherath: The Battle for the Twin Villages* (Mass.: Christopher Publishing House, 1986), 23.

3. Personal letter to the author from Heinz-Georg Lemm, dated 24 March 1988. The account of the 27th Fusilier Regiment relies on various details from this letter.

4. Conversation with Wilhelm Osterhold in October 1987.

5. Dick Byers, "Fight for Losheimergraben," *The Checkerboard,* March 1990, 8.

6. Ibid., 7; Kirkbride's account is strictly from his perspective.

7. Written account by Bob Newbrough, dated July 1980. This and subsequent information about his experiences come from the same account. MacDonald and Cavanagh used this same information for their books as well.

8. Cavanagh, 24–25.

9. Ibid., 25; Newbrough.

10. 1/LT Walton T. Farrar, *The Combat History of the 394th Infantry Regiment*, PFC James L. Haseltine, ed. (Privately Published), 9.

11. Ibid., 7, 46.

12. Byers, "Fight for Losheimergraben," 7.

13. Ibid.

14. Personal letter to the author from Gerhard Lemcke, dated 1 September 1989.

15. Byers, "Fight for Losheimergraben," 8.

16. Cavanagh, 25.

17. Byers, "Fight for Losheimergraben," 8.

18. Ibid.

Chapter 6
Buchholz Station

1. The information in this chapter, from the American perspective, relies strongly on unpublished monographs written by Simmons and Clayton. Wesley Simmons further added to this information with several personal letters to the author.

2. Wesley J. Simmons, "The Operations of Company K, 394th Infantry, (99th Infantry Division) in Defensive Action near Elsenborn, Belgium, 16–21 December 1944 (Ardennes-Alsace Campaign)" (Personal Experience of a Company Commander). Unpublished Monograph (Advanced Infantry Officers Course, 1949–1950), U.S. Army Infantry School, Fort Benning, Georgia, 11; open letter from Ralph Hill to Danny Parker (*The Checkerboard*, Vol. 48, Number 3, 1995).

3. Simmons, 11.

4. William C.C. Cavanagh, *Krinkelt-Rocherath: The Battle for the Twin Villages* (Mass.: Christopher Publishing House, 1986), 26–27.

5. Ibid., 27; telephone conversation with George Bodnar on 6 April 1993.

6. Cavanagh, 27.

7. Hugh M. Cole, *The Ardennes: Battle of the Bulge* (Washington, D.C.: Dept. of the Army, Chief of Military History, 1965), 84.

8. Personal letter to the author from Heinz-Georg Lemm, dated 24 March 1988.

9. Cavanagh, 28; 1/LT Walton T. Farrar, *The Combat History of the 394th Infantry Regiment*, PFC James L. Haseltine, ed. (Privately Published), 46; Travalini's account also appears in Charles B. MacDonald, *A Time for Trumpets: The Untold Story of the Battle of the Bulge* (New York: Bantam Books, 1985), 174.

10. George A. Clayton, "The Operations of the 3rd Battalion, 394th Infantry (99th Infantry Division) in the German Ardennes Counter-Offensive, 16 December–1 January 1945" (Personal Experience of a Battalion Executive Officer). Unpublished Monograph (Advanced Infantry Officers Course, 1947–1948). U.S. Army Infantry School, Fort Benning, Georgia, 3.

Chapter 7
Defense of the Weisser Stein

1. The 2nd Battalion's account comes almost entirely from Legare's unpublished monograph, except for specific details otherwise noted.

Notes

2. Ben W. Legare, "The Operations of the 2nd Battalion, 394th Infantry (99th Infantry Division) in the German Counteroffensive, vicinity of Losheimergraben, Germany, 16–19 December 1944" (Personal Experience of a Battalion Executive Officer) (Ardennes Campaign). Unpublished Monograph (Advanced Infantry Officers Course, 1949–1950). U.S. Army Infantry School, Fort Benning, Georgia, 6.

3. Personal letter to the author from Horst Freiherr von Wangenheim, dated 13 August 1987.

4. Legare, 8; 1/LT Walton T. Farrar, *The Combat History of the 394th Infantry Regiment*, PFC James L. Haseltine, ed. (Privately Published), 47.

5. I have consciously chosen not to mention the battalion commander's name in the interest of good taste and in an effort not to expose his family name to prejudice or embarrassment.

Chapter 8
Lanzerath: "Hold At All Costs!"

1. The actions of the I&R Platoon at Lanzerath are well known to "bulge" historians. Considering the significance of the action, the event has received detailed treatment from Cavanagh (1986), MacDonald (1985), Eisenhower (1969), and Astor (1992). Eisenhower dedicates almost nine full pages to the engagement. I have filled in many of the blanks about this action, relying on the above texts as well as letters and phone conversations with Dr. Lyle J. Bouck, Jr. My intent is to form a more cohesive narrative that shows significant details, both known and unknown, of the battle at Lanzerath.

2. Background on Lyle Bouck comes from Al Hemingway, "Ghost Front Attack," *Military History Magazine*, August 1992, 52–53 and Gerald Astor, *A Blood-Dimmed Tide: The Battle of the Bulge by the Men Who Fought It* (New York: Donald I. Fine, 1992), 33–37.

3. John S.D. Eisenhower, *The Bitter Woods* (New York: G.P. Putnam's Sons, 1969), 225–226.

4. Letter from Ralph G. Hill, Jr. to Raphael d'Amico-Gerard, dated 28 September 1988, 2.

5. William C.C. Cavanagh, *Krinkelt-Rocherath: The Battle for the Twin Villages* (Mass.: Christopher Publishing House, 1986), 18–19; Charles B. MacDonald, *A Time for Trumpets: The Untold Story of the Battle of the Bulge* (New York: Bantam Books, 1985), 106–107.

6. Eisenhower, 229.

7. MacDonald, 176.

8. Warren Springer, "Action at Lanzerath," *The Checkerboard*, March 1990, 14.

9. Letter to the author from Warren P. Springer, dated 18 April 1993.

10. It is doubtful whether the Germans, at this early time, were capable of bringing rear firing batteries under small-arms fire. However, panic and confusion because of the artillery barrage and subsequent attacks on the forward positions may account for this discrepancy. The batteries were finally able to fire the artillery mission sometime after Springer and his party left Lanzerath. The rounds actually landed about 200 meters farther south than intended. Cavalrymen from the 14th Cavalry Group observed them impact near one of their own positions.

11. Hemingway, 55.

12. Ibid.

13. Telephone conversation with Risto Milosevich on 23 April 1993.

14. Astor, 107.

15. Ibid., 107–108.
16. Personal letter to the author from Louis Kalil, dated 20 April 1993.
17. Astor, 108.
18. Jack Anderson, "Why This Dead Hero Should Get The Medal Of Honor," *Parade Magazine*, 25 March 1979, 7.
19. Astor, 109.
20. Ibid.
21. Personal letter to the author from Peter Gacki, dated 22 April 1993.
22. Telephone conversation with Dr. Lyle Bouck, Jr., on 1 June 1993. Cliff Fansher, the man in the foxhole with Billy Queen, later told Bouck why the man had died.
23. MacDonald, 178.
24. Eisenhower, 236.
25. Astor, 113–115; MacDonald, 178–179.

Chapter 9
Desperate Stand

1. George A. Clayton, "The Operations of the 3rd Battalion, 394th Infantry (99th Infantry Division) in the German Ardennes Counter-Offensive, 16 December–1 January 1945" (Personal Experience of a Battalion Executive Officer). Unpublished Monograph (Advanced Infantry Officers Course, 1947–1948). U.S. Army Infantry School, Fort Benning, Georgia, 17.
2. Wesley J. Simmons, "The Operations of Company K, 394th Infantry, (99th Infantry Division) in Defensive Action near Elsenborn, Belgium, 16–21 December 1944 (Ardennes-Alsace Campaign)" (Personal Experience of a Company Commander). Unpublished Monograph (Advanced Infantry Officers Course, 1949–1950) U.S. Army Infantry School, Fort Benning, Georgia, 15.
3. Clayton, 17.
4. Personal letter to the author from COL (ret.) Wesley Simmons, dated 17 April 1989.
5. Simmons, 16.
6. Gerald Astor, *A Blood-Dimmed Tide: The Battle of the Bulge by the Men Who Fought It* (New York: Donald I. Fine, 1992), 111.
7. Ibid; Astor, 270–271; Charles B. MacDonald, *A Time for Trumpets: The Untold Story of the Battle of the Bulge* (New York: Bantam Books, 1985), 182–183; Al Hemingway, "Ghost Front Attack," *Military History Magazine*, (August 1992), 57. There are many varying accounts of the incident in Lanzerath with Peiper and von Hofmann. Bouck was an eyewitness to the feud but couldn't understand what the two men were saying. Some accounts state that von Hofmann meekly acquiesced to Peiper's ridicule of him; Pallud, *Battle of the Bulge Then and Now,* 132, believes that von Hofmann wasn't impressed by Peiper and gave the SS officer just as much grief in return. I believe it was a mixture of the two versions.
8. Hemingway, 56.
9. Astor, 115–118; William C.C. Cavanagh, *Krinkelt-Rocherath: The Battle for the Twin Villages* (Mass.: Christopher Publishing House, 1986), 41–42.
10. This vehicle is roughly the German equivalent of an American half-track but much larger.
11. Jean-Paul Pallud, *Ardennes 1944: Peiper and Skorzeny,* Osprey Elite Series, No. 11 (London: Osprey Publishing, Ltd., 1987), 23.
12. Astor, 81–82.

Notes

13. John S.D. Eisenhower, *The Bitter Woods* (New York: G. P. Putnam's Sons, 1969), 271.
14. Personal letter to the author from Alvin Rausch, dated 5 May 1989; Simmons, 16.
15. Simmons, 16.

Chapter 10
The Final Push

1. Dick Byers, "Fight for Losheimergraben," *The Checkerboard*, March 1990, 7, 9; telephone conversations with Mel Weidner (7 April 1993) and John Hilliard (13 April 1993).
2. Wesley J. Simmons, "The Operations of Company K, 394th Infantry, (99th Infantry Division) in Defensive Action near Elsenborn, Belgium, 16–21 December 1944 (Ardennes-Alsace Campaign)" (Personal Experience of a Company Commander). Unpublished Monograph (Advanced Infantry Officers Course, 1949–1950) U.S. Army Infantry School, Fort Benning, Georgia, 16–17.
3. Charles B. MacDonald, *A Time for Trumpets: The Untold Story of the Battle of the Bulge* (New York: Bantam Books, 1985), 182; conversations with Wilhelm Osterhold.
4. Simmons, 16; William C.C. Cavanagh, *Krinkelt-Rocherath: The Battle for the Twin Villages* (Mass.: Christopher Publishing House, 1986), 52.
5. Hugh M. Cole, *The Ardennes: Battle of the Bulge* (Washington, D.C.: Dept. of the Army, Chief of Military History, 1965), 93; Byers, "Fight for Losheimergraben," 9.
6. Personal letter to the author from Carl Combs, dated 23 April 1993.
7. Cavanagh, 52–53.
8. Byers, "Fight for Losheimergraben," 9.
9. Ibid.; copy of a letter to Charles Kent from Kermit M. Ball, dated January 1992.
10. Byers, "Fight for Losheimergraben," 9.
11. Ibid., 12.
12. Cavanagh, 53; Simmons, 17; There seems to be a discrepancy between the actual withdrawal time. Simmons says he saw the 1st Battalion move past him at about 1030. The 394th's After-Action Report indicates that the *entire* regiment withdrew at 1530, which is true, but it is more likely that the 1st Battalion began to leave earlier as witnessed by Simmons. However, many 1st Battalion men waited until dark to withdraw, such as LTC Douglas and his command group. This group included PFC Combs and PVT Cotter.
13. Ben W. Legare, "The Operations of the 2nd Battalion, 394th Infantry (99th Infantry Division) in the German Counteroffensive, vicinity of Losheimergraben, Germany, 16–19 December 1944" (Personal Experience of a Battalion Executive Officer) (Ardennes Campaign). Unpublished Monograph (Advanced Infantry Officers Course, 1949–1950). U.S. Army Infantry School, Fort Benning, Georgia, 10.
14. Ibid., 11–12.
15. Byers, "Fight for Losheimergraben," 9; personal letter to the author from Carl Combs, dated 23 April 1993.
16. Cavanagh, 53.
17. Simmons, 17.
18. Legare, 12–13.
19. Byers, "Fight for Losheimergraben," 9.
20. Ibid.

21. Ibid.; 1/LT Walton T. Farrar, *The Combat History of the 394th Infantry Regiment*, PFC James L. Haseltine, ed. (Privately Published), 46; telephone conversation with Mel Weidner (7 April 1993).

Chapter 11
The Customs Houses

1. Most of the information in this chapter comes from a long personal letter to the author by Wilhelm Osterhold dated 19 June 1987. Conversations, both on the phone and in person, as well as dozens of personal documents, supplement Osterhold's account of the battle and his personal history. Strangely enough, Osterhold seems to remember this incident as taking place the day before. However, I actually believe that the incident occurred on 17 December, respectfully taking into consideration Oberst Osterhold's superb memory.

2. Charles B. MacDonald, *A Time for Trumpets: The Untold Story of the Battle of the Bulge* (New York: Bantam Books, 1985), 171.

3. Dick Byers, "Fight for Losheimergraben," *The Checkerboard*, March 1990, 9.

4. Ibid.

5. Ibid., 12.

Chapter 12
Completing the Record

1. Personal letter to the author from William Sears, dated 15 April 1993.

2. Personal letter to the author from Warren Springer, dated 18 April 1993.

3. Hugh M. Cole, *The Ardennes: Battle of the Bulge* (Washington, D.C.: Dept. of the Army, Chief of Military History, 1965), 93.

4. Walter Niedermayer, *Into the Deep Misty Woods of the Ardennes* (Pa.: A. G. Halldin Publishing Co., 1990), 140.

5. Gerald Astor, *A Blood-Dimmed Tide: The Battle of the Bulge by the Men Who Fought It* (New York: Donald I. Fine, 1992), 508–509; J. P. Speder, "Now It Can Be Told," *The Checkerboard* March 1991, 17.

6. Ben W. Legare, "The Operations of the 2nd Battalion, 394th Infantry (99th Infantry Division) in the German Counteroffensive, vicinity of Losheimergraben, Germany, 16–19 December 1944" (Personal Experience of a Battalion Executive Officer) (Ardennes Campaign). Unpublished Monograph (Advanced Infantry Officers Course, 1949–1950). U.S. Army Infantry School, Fort Benning, Georgia, 15; William C.C. Cavanagh, *Krinkelt-Rocherath: The Battle for the Twin Villages* (Mass.: Christopher Publishing House, 1986), 118.

7. Personal letters to the author from COL (ret.) Wesley Simmons, dated 17 April 1989, 5 June 1989, and 8 April 1993.

8. Personal letter to the author from Richard Byers, dated 28 February 1989.

9. Astor, 410–411.

10. Charles Whiting, *48 Hours to Hammelburg* (New York: Jove Books, 1984).

11. Astor, 435–440.

12. Ibid., 480–486.

13. Conversation with Wilhelm Osterhold.

14. Astor, 485; Jean-Paul Pallud, *Battle of the Bulge Then and Now* (London: Battle of Britain International Limited, 1986), 189–192; Charles Whiting, *Massacre at Malmedy* (New York: Stein and Day, 1984), 190–198.

15. Personal letter to the author from Horst Freiherr von Wangenheim, dated 13 August 1987.
16. Pallud, *Battle of the Bulge Then and Now*.
17. Conversation with Wilhelm Osterhold.
18. Personal letter to the author from Kurt Steinhofel, dated 5 November 1990.
19. Personal letter to the author from Wilhelm Osterhold, dated 19 June 1987.

Appendix A
Table of Comparative Ranks
1. Andrew Mollo, *The Armed Forces of World War II* (New York: Military Press, 1987), 239; Danny S. Parker, *Battle of the Bulge: Hitler's Ardennes Offensive, 1944–1945* (Philadelphia: Combined Books, 1991), 315.

Appendix B
Awards and Decorations
1. 1/LT Walton T. Farrar, *The Combat History of the 394th Infantry Regiment*, PFC James L. Haseltine, ed. (Privately Published), 44.
2. *394th Infantry Regiment Unit History* (1–31 December 1944), 46 (both Douglas and Williamson).
3. Dick Byers provided copies of the citations for Springer, Gacki, Wibben, and Queen. The award for Queen is still controversial and unjustified in the eyes of Lyle Bouck and many of his men.
4. The following Silver Star citations are from Farrar, 46–47.
5. *394th Infantry Regiment Unit History*, 47.
6. The following Bronze Star roster is from Farrar, 50–51.
7. Walter Niedermayer, *Into the Deep Misty Woods of the Ardennes* (Pennsylvania: A. G. Halldin Publishing Co., 1990), 140.
8. Ibid., 143–144.
9. Ibid., 145–146.
10. Jean-Paul Pallud, *Battle of the Bulge Then and Now* (London: Battle of Britain International Limited, 1986), 516.

Selected Bibliography

BOOKS

Angolia, John R., and Adolf Schlicht. *Uniforms and Traditions of the German Army 1933–1945.* Volume 3. Calif.: R. James Bender Publishing, 1987.

Arnold, James R. *Ardennes 1944: Hitler's Last Gamble in the West.* Osprey Campaign Series, Number 5. London: Osprey Publishing Ltd., 1990.

Astor, Gerald. *A Blood-Dimmed Tide: The Battle of the Bulge by the Men Who Fought It.* New York: Donald I. Fine, 1992.

Cavanagh, William C.C. *Krinkelt-Rocherath: The Battle for the Twin Villages.* Mass.: Christopher Publishing House, 1986.

Clayton, George A. "The Operations of the 3rd Battalion, 394th Infantry (99th Infantry Division) in the German Ardennes Counter-Offensive, 16 December–1 January 1945" (Personal Experience of a Battalion Executive Officer). Unpublished Monograph (Advanced Infantry Officers Course, 1947–1948). U.S. Army Infantry School, Fort Benning, Georgia.

Cole, Hugh M. *The Ardennes: Battle of the Bulge.* Washington, D.C.: Dept. of the Army, Chief of Military History, 1965.

Eisenhower, John S.D. *The Bitter Woods.* New York: G. P. Putnam's Sons, 1969.

Elstob, Peter. *Hitler's Last Offensive: The Full Story of the Battle of the Ardennes.* New York: Macmillan Co., 1971.

Farrar, Walton T. 1/LT. *The Combat History of the 394th Infantry Regiment.* Ed. PFC James L. Haseltine. (Privately Published), 1945.

Giles, Janice Holt. *The Damned Engineers.* (Reprinted by Office of the Chief of Engineers, U.S. Army, Washington D.C., 1987.) Boston: Houghton Mifflin Co., 1970.

Hogg, Ian V., and John Weeks. *Military Small Arms of the 20th Century.* Illinois: DBI Books, Inc., 1985.

Lauer, Walter. *Battle Babies: The Story of the 99th Infantry Division in World War II.* Baton Rouge, La.: Military Press of Louisiana, 1951.

Legare, Ben W. "The Operations of the 2nd Battalion, 394th Infantry (99th Infantry Division) in the German Counteroffensive, vicinity of Losheimergraben, Germany, 16–19 December 1944" (Personal Experience of a Battalion Executive Officer) (Ardennes Campaign). Unpublished Monograph (Advanced Infantry Officers Course, 1949–1950). U.S. Army Infantry School, Fort Benning, Georgia.

MacDonald, Charles B. *A Time For Trumpets: The Untold Story of the Battle of the Bulge.* New York: Bantam Books, 1985.

Merriam, Robert E. *The Battle of the Bulge* (Abridged Version of *Dark December*). New York: Ballantine Books, 1966.

Meyer, Hubert. *Kriegsgeschichte der 12. SS-Panzerdivision "Hitlerjugend" II.* Osnabruck, Germany: Munin Verlag GmbH, 1982.

Mitcham, Samuel W., Jr. *Hitler's Legions: The German Army Order of Battle, World War II.* New York: Stein and Day, 1985.

Mollo, Andrew. *The Armed Forces of World War II.* New York: Military Press, 1987.

Niedermayer, Walter. *Into the Deep Misty Woods of the Ardennes.* Pa.: A. G. Halldin Publishing Company, 1990.

Pallud, Jean-Paul. *Ardennes 1944: Peiper and Skorzeny.* Osprey Elite Series, No. 11. London: Osprey Publishing, Ltd., 1987.

———. *Battle of the Bulge Then and Now.* London: Battle of Britain Prints International Limited, 1986.

Parker, Danny S. *Battle of the Bulge: Hitler's Ardennes Offensive, 1944-1945.* Philadelphia: Combined Books, 1991.

Simmons, Wesley J. "The Operations of Company K, 394th Infantry, (99th Infantry Division) in Defensive Action near Elsenborn, Belgium, 16–21 December 1944 (Ardennes-Alsace Campaign)" (Personal Experience of a Company Commander). Unpublished Monograph (Advanced Infantry Officers Course, 1949–1950). U.S. Army Infantry School, Fort Benning, Georgia.

Stanton, Shelby L. *World War II Order of Battle.* New York: Galahad Books, 1991.

Toland, John. *Battle: The Story of the Bulge.* New York: Random House, 1959.

Whiting, Charles. *48 Hours to Hammelburg.* New York: Jove Books, 1984.

———. *Massacre at Malmedy.* New York: Stein and Day, 1984.

MAGAZINES AND PUBLICATIONS

Anderson, Jack. "Why This Dead Hero Should Get the Medal Of Honor." *Parade Magazine,* 25 March 1979, 6–8.

Byers, Dick. "Fight for Losheimergraben." *The Checkerboard,* March 1990, 6–12, 19.

———. "Losheimergraben." *The Checkerboard,* April 1991, 8–9.

———. "The Battle at Lanzerath." *The Checkerboard,* March 1990, 10–15.

———. "Buzz Bomb Alley Part II." *The Checkerboard,* February 1993, 7.

Hemingway, Al. "Ghost Front Attack." *Military History Magazine,* August 1992, 50–57.

Speder, J. P. "Now It Can Be Told." *The Checkerboard,* March 1991, 17.

Springer, Warren. "Action at Lanzerath." *The Checkerboard,* March 1990, 14.

Whitehead, Rex. "Withdrawal Through Murringen." *The Checkerboard,* March 1991, 13, 16.

Various open letters to *The Checkerboard* (99th Division Association Publication) from 1988 to 1993 by participants of the battle.

AFTER-ACTION AND OFFICIAL REPORTS

First United States Army Report of Operations 1 August 1944–22 February 1945.
Handbook on German Military Forces, War Department TM-E 30-451 dated 15 March 1945. Reprinted by Baton Rouge: Louisiana State University Press, 1990.
3rd Battalion, 394th Infantry Post-Combat Interview with LTC Norman A. Moore and members of the battalion dated 29 January 1945.
394th Infantry Regiment Unit History, 1–31 December 1944, 20–53.
394th Infantry Regiment After / Action Report dated 1 January 1945 for the period 1–31 December 1944.

CORRESPONDENCE

Copies of Correspondence between Dr. Lyle J. Bouck, Jr., and Warren Springer (18 December 1989; 1 January 1990; 8 January 1990; 2 February 1990; 20 August 1990; 22 August 1990).
Copies of Correspondence between Ralph G. Hill, Jr. and Raphael d'Amico-Gerard (28 September 1988); Dr. Lyle J. Bouck, Jr. (5 January 1989); Colonel Charles Biggio, Jr. (17 October 1989); Danny Parker (Open Letter to Danny Parker in *The Checkerboard*, 48, No. 3, 1995).
Copy of Correspondence between Richard Byers and Walter Wittlinger (2 December 1985).
Copies of Correspondence to Charles Kent from William Sears (22 December 1945); Danny Dalyai (17 February 1991); Kermit Ball (January 1992); Mel Weidner (20 December 1990); Carl Combs (10 December 1990, 15 January 1991).
Personal Letters to the author from Oberstleutnant a. D. (ret.) Horst Freiherr von Wangenheim, Oberst a. D. Wilhelm Osterhold, Generalmajor a. D. Heinz-Georg Lemm, Kurt Steinhofel, Oberstleutnant a. D. Gerhard Lemcke, Colonel (ret.) Wesley Simmons, Richard Byers, Dr. Lyle Bouck, Jr., Alvin Rausch, Robert Newbrough, Howard Bowers, Melvin Weidner, Charles Kent, Warren P. Springer, John Hilliard, William Sears, Louis Kalil, Peter Gacki, Arthur Mings, Carl Combs, John S. D. Eisenhower, and George Bodnar.

INTERVIEWS

Personal interviews and / or telephone conversations with Oberst a. D. Wilhelm Osterhold, Melvin Weidner, George Bodnar, William Sears, Warren Springer, John Hilliard, Charles Kent, Dr. Lyle Bouck, Jr., Risto Milosevich, and Richard Byers.

FILM

The Battle for Elsenborn Ridge: The Story of the 99th Infantry Division in the Battle of the Bulge. Bill Stokes Associates, 1991.
This Time in Peace. (99th Division Veterans Return to the Battlefield.) Privately produced, 1991.

Index

I SS Panzer Corps, 14, 21, 62, 113, 123
1st SS Panzer Division Leibstandarte-SS "Adolf Hitler," 13–14, 20, 22, 112
1st SS Panzer Regiment (Kampfgruppe Peiper), 112, 145
First U.S. Army, 7
2nd Infantry Division, 11, 17, 64, 147, 150
II SS Panzer Corps, 14
Third Army, 7
3rd Fallschirmjaeger Division, 14, 20–21, 84, 91, 104, 156
9th Fallschirmjaeger Regiment, 21–22, 84, 91, 100, 111
V Corps, 7, 86
6th SS Panzer Army, 4, 13–14, 24, 147
VII Corps, 7
VIII Corps, 7–8, 64, 73, 86
9th Infantry Division, 7–9, 63, 85
60th Infantry Regiment, 9, 63
9th SS Panzer Division, 14
12th SS Panzer Division "Hitlerjugend," 14, 17, 77, 145, 156
12th Volksgrenadier Division, 14, 18–20, 23, 112, 123, 128, 141, 156, 158
14th Cavalry Group: Task Force X, 8, 64, 73, 86

15th Army, 20
23rd Infantry: 1st Battalion, 147, 156
27th Fusilier Regiment, 19–20, 23, 56, 65–66, 68, 72, 97, 126, 158; 1st Battalion, 49–50, 52, 56–58, 68–70, 72, 97, 125, 158
3rd Battalion, 49–50, 59, 68–69, 72, 98
48th Grenadier Regiment, 19–20, 23, 25, 28, 31, 121, 132, 137, 141, 145, 158
1st Battalion, 22–23, 26, 29, 31–32, 34, 43, 124, 132
2nd Battalion, 22, 26, 28, 32, 34–35, 37, 40, 43, 61, 122–124, 132, 135, 139, 158; 5th Company, 35, 40–41, 62, 132, 135, 139, 142–143; 7th Company, 34–35, 38–39, 41, 61, 158–159; 8th Company, 35, 38
LXVII Corps, 14
89th Grenadier Regiment, 19–20
99th Infantry Division, xiv, 7–8, 10–11, 17, 45, 64, 73, 85, 147, 150–151
106th Infantry Division, 11
277th Volksgrenadier Division, 14, 16–19, 61, 77, 79, 129, 147, 156–157
989th Grenadier Regiment, 16–17

990th Fusilier Regiment, 16–17, 77, 79, 82, 129
991st Grenadier Regiment, 16–17
371st Field Artillery: Battery C, 89, 113
374th Volksgrenadier Division, 16
393rd Infantry Regiment, 8, 11, 81, 107, 149, 150
394th Infantry Regiment, 8–11, 26, 32, 38, 45, 49, 63–64, 69, 77, 82, 85, 107, 124, 132–133, 139, 147–149, 152, 156
  1st Battalion, 9, 26, 32, 45, 51, 59, 62–63, 65, 68–69, 73, 76, 82, 85, 88, 94, 97, 107–111, 121–122, 124, 127–134, 137, 139, 141, 149; Company A, 8, 28, 45–46, 50–51, 53, 56, 59, 60–61, 64, 68, 73, 86–87, 108, 121, 125, 128; Company B, 9, 26, 28–30, 32–33, 35, 36–37, 40–43, 59–61, 121, 124–128, 131, 136–137, 149; Company C, 10, 28, 33, 42, 60–61, 76, 79, 85, 121, 128, 130, 134, 141, 152; Company D, 9, 30, 36, 41, 45–46, 53, 59, 61, 65, 149
  2nd Battalion, 9, 58, 61, 75, 77, 79, 81, 128–130, 149–150; Company E, 76–79, 81, 129; Company F, 76; Company G, 61, 76, 79; Company H, 76–77
  3rd Battalion, 10–11, 45, 61, 63–64, 67, 70, 73, 89, 102, 107, 109–110, 114, 119, 122, 134, 150; Company K, 65, 68–70, 72, 108–111, 114, 116–118, 120, 133, 135, 150, 153; Company L, 64–70, 73, 108–111, 119, 122; Company M, 64, 67–68; Ammunition and Pioneer (A&P) Platoon, 67–68
  Cannon Company, 45, 49
  I&R Platoon, xiv, 83–86, 96, 98, 100, 102, 114, 148, 151, 153–156
  Service Company, 10
395th Infantry Regiment, 8, 11, 64
612th Tank Destroyer Battalion, 86
820th Tank Destroyer Battalion: Company A, 8, 64, 86–87, 89
1012th Sturmgeschutze Company, 20
1277th Sturmgeschutze Company, 17

Aachen, 7, 19, 34, 141
Anderson, Jack, 156
Anti-Tank Company, 10, 45, 67, 126
Antwerp, xiii, 2, 4, 10, 13
Ardennes forest, 2–3, 25
Ardennes Offensive, xiii–xiv, 19, 21, 152, 154
Army Group Center, 18–19, 140
Army Specialized Training Program (ASTP), 8, 86

Bail, SGT, 126, 137
Ball, SGT Kermit, 7, 30, 41, 126
Ballinger, SSG George, 9, 29–30, 35–38, 149
Bamber, Generalleutnant Rudolf, 18
Bastogne, xiii, 4
Baum, CPT Abe, 152
Benson, LT Gifford, 51, 57, 60, 126
Bero, CPL George, 48, 53
"Big Moose," 30, 126
Bittrich, SS-Obergruppenfuehrer Willi, 14
Blankenheim, 19
Bodnar, T/5 George, 66–67
Boggs, PVT George, 35–36
Bouck, 1LT Lyle, Jr., xv, 10, 83–88, 90–94, 96, 98–100, 102–105, 111, 113, 148, 151–156
Bowers, PFC Howard, 9
Brandenberger, General der Panzertruppen Erich, 4
Breger, Hauptmann Claus, 23, 49–50, 59, 69, 73, 158
Bremm, Oberstleutnant Josef, 16–18, 79
Brown, 1LT Neil, 65–66, 108, 110
Buchholz Station, xii, 9–11, 61, 63–64, 66, 68–70, 72, 89, 97–98, 102, 107–115, 118–121, 123, 133, 148, 150–151
Buenger, 1LT Edward, 83
Bullingen, 40, 62, 107, 111, 121, 154
Butler, LT Charles E., 30
Buzz Bomb Alley, 10
Byers, SGT Dick, xv, 113–119, 151

Caen, 14
Cafe Scholzen, 94, 105, 111, 113, 115
Camp Van Dorn, 7

Index

Cavender, COL Charles, 151
Clark, LT Willard W., 45, 48, 50, 57–58, 60–61
Clarkson, PVT, 35–36
Claypool, PVT John, 66–67
Clayton, MAJ George A., 73, 107–108
Collins, MG J. Lawton, 7
Combs, PFC Carl, 33–34, 124, 131
Cotter, PVT Jim, 131
Creepy Corner, 9, 38
Creger, PVT John, 88, 91–94, 156

Dalyai, PFC Danny, 30
Dean, 2LT Charles N., 122, 141
Demjansk, 18
Diefenthal, SS-Sturmbannfuehrer Josef, 115
Dietrich, SS-Oberstgruppenfuehrer Sepp, 2, 4, 13–14, 18–19, 24, 46, 157
Dolenc, T/SGT Edward, 41
Douglas, LTC Robert, 9, 32–33, 59, 60–62, 108, 111, 121–122, 124, 128–132, 149
Dueren, 19, 141

Eisenhower, John S.D., 154–155
Elsenborn Ridge, 147, 149–150
Engel, Generalmajor Gerhard, 18–19, 24, 123–124, 140–141
Epstein, 2LT Bernard, 49
Esultante, PFC Angelo, 52, 57–58

Falaise Pocket, 14, 21
Fletcher, SGT Curtis, 113–117
Frank, 1SG Lyle O., 56–57
Frauenkron, 19, 23–24, 49, 141

Gacki, SGT Peter, 89, 98, 102
Gamber, PFC Ralph, 30, 41, 126, 136–137, 142
Genovino, PVT Joe, 67
Gerow, MG Leonard T., 7
Gooch, CPT Sidney A., 28, 125–127
Goode, COL Paul R., 152
Goodner, 1LT John A., 76
Graham, CPT Jim, 33, 121, 130
Grimm, SGT George, 35–37
Guderian, General Heinz, 140

Hammelburg, 148, 151–152

Haymaker, CPT John, 76
Hightower, LTC John, 147
Hilliard, SSG John, 122, 136
Hitler, Adolf, xiii, 1–5, 13, 21, 29, 140, 145, 159
Hitzfeld, Generalleutnant Maximilian Otto, 14
Hodges, LTG Courtney, 7–8, 11
Hollerath, 14, 17
Holz, Major Gunther, 20, 32, 123–124, 132, 156, 158
Hunningen, 10, 20, 23, 76, 102, 117, 119, 147, 149

International Highway, 10, 38

Jenkins, CPL Sam, 102
Juelich, 19

Kalil, PVT Lou, 99–100, 105, 156
Kent, PFC Charles, 41–43, 137
Kibler, T/SGT Wesley, 42, 121, 131
Kirkbride, PFC William, 51–53, 57–60, 126–128, 132, 135–137, 142, 143–144, 148
Klug, 1SG Elmer, 65–66
Knight, CPT Joseph, 77–78, 80, 119
Kraas, SS-Standartenfuehrer Hugo, 14
Kraemer, SS-Brigadefuehrer Fritz, 13, 17, 22
Krinkelt-Rocherath, 17, 147
Kriz, MAJ Robert L., 85–86, 88, 156
Kruse, Major Gerhard, 22–24, 28–29, 32, 34–36, 39–41, 43, 61–62, 122, 132, 139, 158
Kuhlbach, Feldwebel Vince, 103, 155

La Gleize, 145, 148, 157
Landsberg Prison, 155, 157
Lanzerath, xi, xv, 8, 10, 14, 20, 22, 45, 51–52, 63–64, 83–84, 86–93, 97–98, 103, 108–109, 111–112, 114–115, 117, 121, 126, 148, 151, 154–155
Lauer, MG Walter, 7–9, 11, 64–65, 76, 109–110, 154
Legare, CPT Ben W., 10, 75–77, 79, 81–82, 129–130, 134
Lemcke, Oberstleutnant Gerhard, 19–20, 58, 141

Lemm, Oberstleutnant Heinz-Georg, 19, 23, 26, 49, 50, 58–59, 68–69, 70, 72, 123–125, 126, 132, 140–141, 158
Lilly, SGT, 30, 41, 126, 136–137
Losheim, 2–4, 8–10, 16, 20, 22–23, 26, 30, 33, 35, 45, 49, 51, 64, 73, 86, 89, 112, 124, 127, 135, 136
Losheim Gap, xiii, 2–4, 8, 64, 73, 86
Losheimergraben, xiv–xv, 7–9, 14, 19–20, 23, 26, 28–29, 32–35, 40, 45–46, 49, 51–52, 61–64, 73, 77, 86–87, 91, 97–98, 107, 109, 111–112, 120–121, 124, 135, 138–139, 141, 148–150, 152, 158
Losheimergraben Crossroads, 10, 49

Malmedy Massacre, xiv, 113, 154, 156
Mannheimer, CPT Robert, 78
Mathena, SGT Guy, 35–37
Mayer, 1LT Harold, 113–119
McConnell, PVT Joe, 102, 105
McCown, MAJ Hal, 157
McGee, CPT Bob, 76, 81, 134, 149–150
McGehee, CPL Aubrey, 93–94, 96–98, 156
McQuarry, LT Marion, 53–54
Meuse River, 2–3
Middleton, MG Troy, 7
Milosevich, CPL Risto, 93–94, 96, 100–103, 156
Mings, PFC Arthur, 50–51, 73
Model, Generalfeldmarschall Walter, 2, 13
Mohnke, SS-Oberfuehrer Wilhelm, 14, 112
Moldenhauer, Major Siegfried, 22–24, 26, 29, 31–32, 158
Monschau, 4, 8, 11, 14
Moore, CPT Harold Z., 45, 57–58
Moore, MAJ Norman, 10, 61, 63–66, 68–69, 72–73, 107–111, 115, 119–120, 122, 150
Moosburg, 150, 153
Mudcat, 42–43, 137
Murray, SSG James F., Jr., 41
Murringen, 10, 20, 23, 76, 128, 131, 133–134, 141, 147, 149–150, 156, 158

Newbrough, PFC Bob, 46, 53–57, 149

Osterhold, Oberstleutnant Wilhelm, xiv–xv, 19–20, 22–26, 28–29, 31–32, 34, 43, 49–50, 122–124, 132, 139, 140–145, 156, 158–159

"Pap," 30, 126, 136–137
Patterson, CPT William G., 76–81, 129
Patton, LTG George S., Jr., 152
Peiper, SS-Obersturmbannfuehrer Joachim, 112–115, 117, 119–121, 145, 147–148, 151, 154–157
Piar, T/SGT Arthur C., 51, 60, 126
Plankers, LT Dewey A., 122, 127, 137, 141
Praum, Generalleutnant Albert, 16
Preston, PFC Robert, 102
Priess, SS-Gruppenfuehrer Hermann, 14, 62, 123

Queen, T/5 Billy S., 89, 98, 102, 151

Ralston, LT Richard A., 65–66, 130, 133
Rausch, SGT Alvin, 110, 114–115, 117–119, 150–151, 153
Red Ball Express, 7
Redmond, SGT George, 99–100, 105
Reid, LT Matthew, 122, 136, 152–153
Riley, COL Don, 9–10, 61, 64, 76, 79, 81, 109–110, 120, 122, 128
Robertson, SGT Fred, 33–34
Robinson, PVT Jordan "Pop," 85, 93–94, 97–98, 156
Rodman, PVT Dan, 128, 144
Roer River Dams, 11, 17, 33, 64–65, 77, 107
Roland, CPT Charles P., 107, 111
rollbahnen (Routes A–E), 14
Rose, 1LT Joseph P., 66, 68, 110–111, 114–118, 120, 150–151, 153
Ryan, PVT Joe, 67

Schimpf, Generalmajor Richard, 20–21
Schlemmer, LT Norman C., 68, 70, 108, 133
Schnee Eifel, 152

Index

Scholzen, Tine, 94
Schur, Adolf, 87–88, 90, 103, 105
Schur, Suzanne (Sany), 87–88,
Schwarzenbruch Trail, 17
Sears, SSG Bill, 41–42, 148
Seel Jean-Louis, 149
Siegfried Line, 1, 7–8, 10, 16, 25, 59, 97, 112, 148
Silvola, PVT James, 93–94, 97–98, 156
Simmons, CPT Wesley, xv, 65–66, 68–70, 72, 108–111, 120, 122–123, 130, 131–135, 150–151
Sito, PFC Alphonse, 35–36, 149
Slape, T/SGT Bill, 83–84, 86–88, 91–94, 99–103, 105, 156
Speder, Jean-Philippe, 149
Speer, Albert, 141
Spencer, LT Charles, 65, 72, 115, 150
Springer, LT Warren, 89–90, 92, 96, 100, 102, 114, 148, 151
St. Lô, 21, 104
Steinhofel, Oberleutnant Kurt, 34–35, 38–40, 61, 123, 158–159
Stumpff, SGT Delbert, 55–57

Thibadeaux, LT Ray, 68, 72, 115
Travalini, SGT Savino, 70, 72
Traves-sur-Saône, 157
Trent, T/SGT John, 122
Tsakanikas, PVT William, 84, 87–88, 90–91, 94, 96, 99, 103–105, 111, 153, 155, 156

Udenbreth, 9, 17, 129

V-1 Rocket, 10
Vacha, LT William, 46, 48, 53–54
Vaughan, 1LT, 45–46, 48, 53–55
Viebig, Oberst Wilhelm, 16–17, 18, 77, 79, 82, 157
von Hofmann, Oberst Helmut, 22, 91–92, 111–113
von Manteuffel, General der Panzertruppen Hasso, 4
von Rundstedt, Generalfeldmarschall Gerd, 2, 13, 51, 73, 109
von Stauffenberg, Oberst Graf, 140
von Wangenheim, Oberstleutnant Horst Freiherr, 16–18, 79, 157

"Wacht am Rhein," xiii, 4, 11, 13
Wadehn, Generalmajor Walther, 20–21
Wallace, T/SGT Fred, 79–81
Waters, LTC John, 152
Weidner, SSG Mel, 122, 127, 135–137, 141–142, 144, 148
Weisser Stein Trail, 10, 17–18, 76–77, 79, 81, 129
Wibben, T/4 Willard, 89, 98
Williams, PFC Nolan, 118–119
Williamson, LT Harvey F., 30
Wirtzfeld, 8
Wittlinger, Gefreiter Walter, 21
Wolfschanze, 1, 140

Stackpole Military History Series

Real battles. Real soldiers. Real stories.

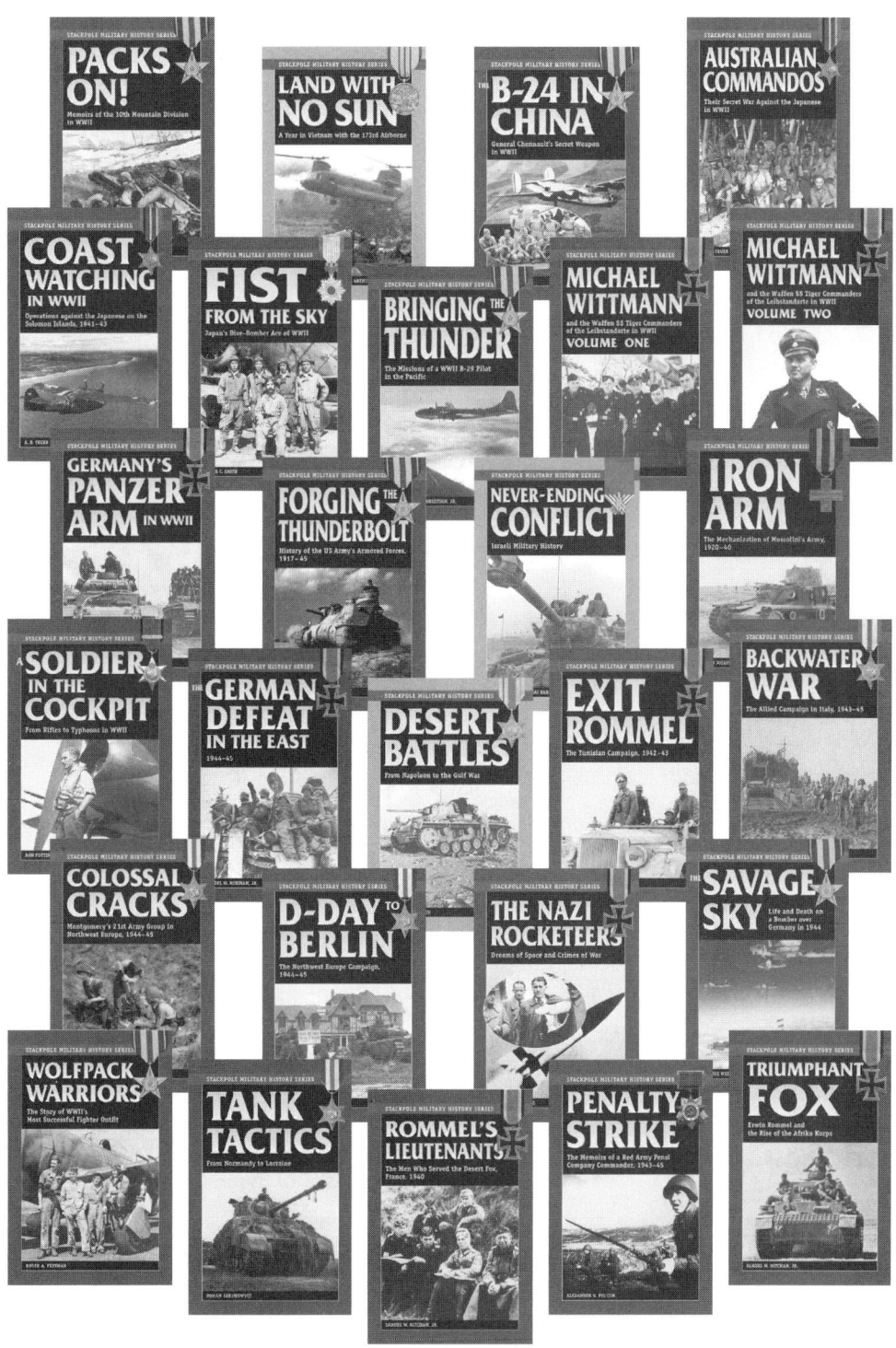

Stackpole Military History Series

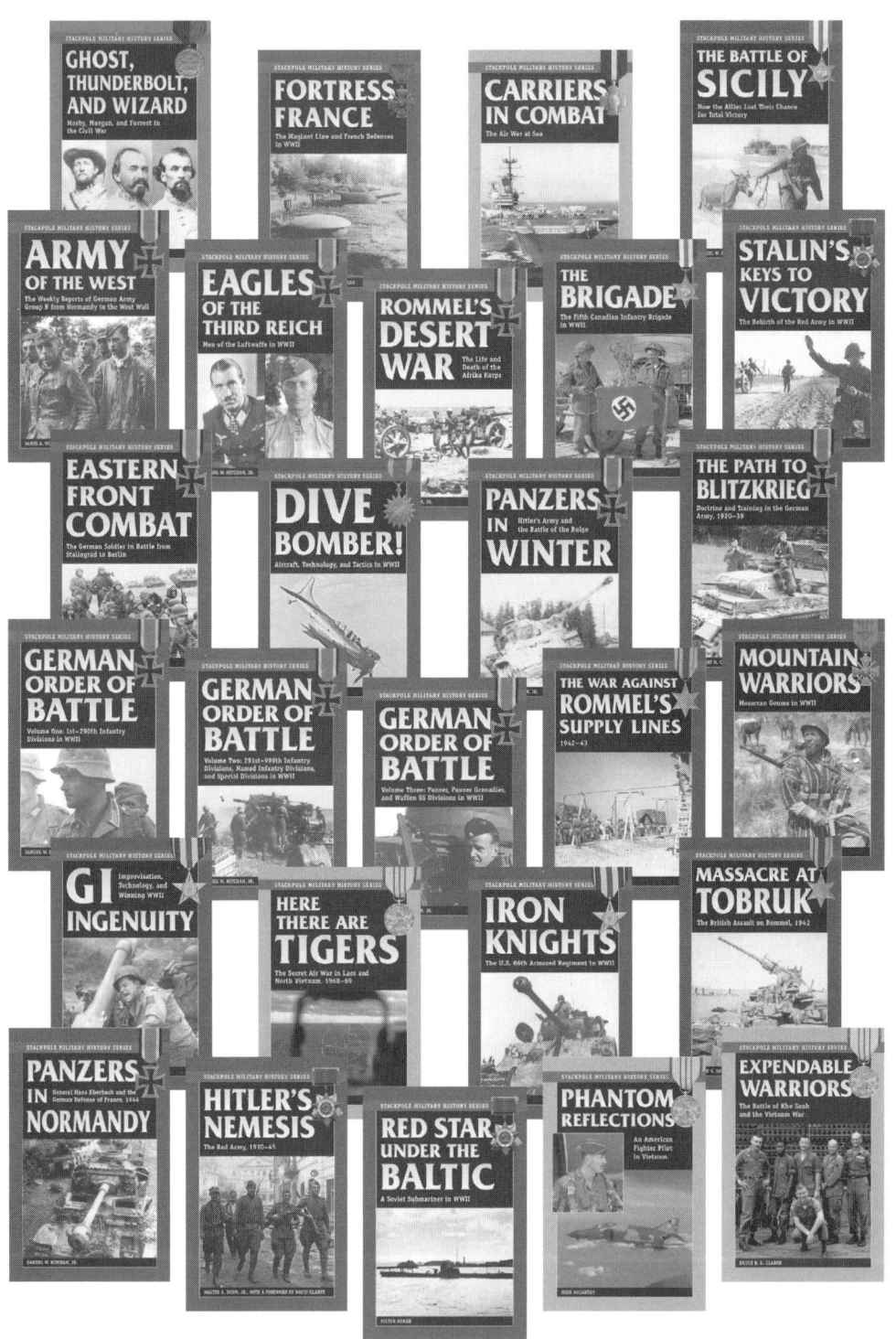

Real battles. Real soldiers. Real stories.

Stackpole Military History Series

Real battles. Real soldiers. Real stories.

Stackpole Military History Series

PANZERS IN WINTER
HITLER'S ARMY AND THE BATTLE OF THE BULGE
Samuel W. Mitcham, Jr.

Before dawn on December 16, 1944, German forces rolled through the frozen Ardennes in their last major offensive in the west, thus starting the Battle of the Bulge, which would become the U.S. Army's bloodiest engagement of World War II. Catching the Allies by surprise, the Germans made early gains, demolished the inexperienced U.S. 106th Infantry Division, and fought hard, but American counterattacks—and tenacious resistance in towns like Bastogne—combined with mounting German casualties and fuel shortages to force the German Army into a retreat from which it never recovered.

$16.95 • Paperback • 6 x 9 • 240 pages • 27 b/w photos • 14 maps

WWW.STACKPOLEBOOKS.COM
1-800-732-3669

Stackpole Military History Series

KAMPFGRUPPE PEIPER AT THE BATTLE OF THE BULGE

David Cooke and Wayne Evans

In December 1944, the Tiger tanks of Kampfgruppe Peiper, Germany's most formidable battle group, roared through the snowy Ardennes as the spearhead of Hitler's last-ditch offensive that aimed to seize Allied supply ports and started the Battle of the Bulge. In one of World War II's most notorious actions, the unit—commanded by the seasoned SS officer Jochen Peiper—massacred American prisoners near Malmedy during its drive to the Meuse River. Fuel shortages and stiffening U.S. resistance later forced the group to retreat back to German lines on foot.

$16.95 • Paperback • 6 x 9 • 208 pages • 99 b/w photos, 24 maps

**WWW.STACKPOLEBOOKS.COM
1-800-732-3669**

Stackpole Military History Series

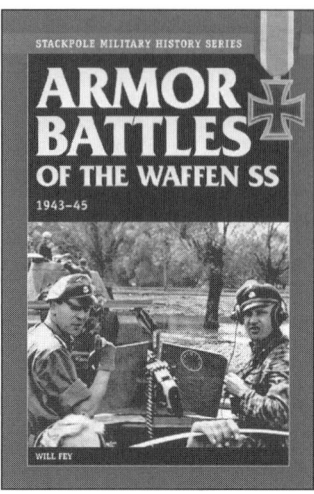

ARMOR BATTLES OF THE WAFFEN-SS
1943–45
Will Fey, translated by Henri Henschler

The Waffen-SS were considered the elite of the German armed forces in the Second World War and were involved in almost continuous combat. From the sweeping tank battle of Kursk on the Russian front to the bitter fighting among the hedgerows of Normandy and the offensive in the Ardennes, these men and their tanks made history.

$19.95 • Paperback • 6 x 9 • 384 pages
32 photos • 15 drawings • 4 maps

WWW.STACKPOLEBOOKS.COM
1-800-732-3669

Stackpole Military History Series

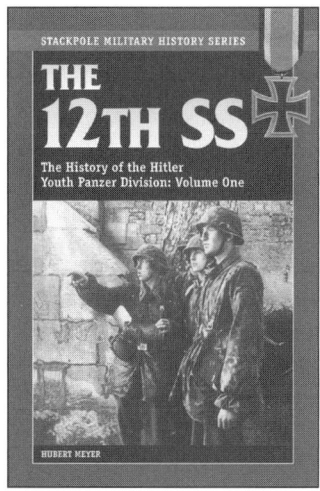 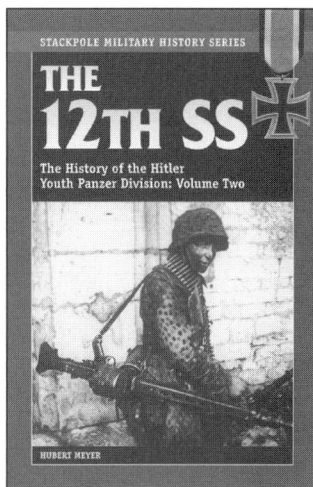

THE 12TH SS
THE HISTORY OF THE HITLER YOUTH PANZER DIVISION
Hubert Meyer

Recruited from the ranks of the Hitler Youth, the elite 12th SS Panzer Division consisted largely of teenage boys who were fanatically devoted to the German cause. Volume One covers the division's baptism of fire in Normandy, including its bloody battles for the city of Caen. Volume Two picks up with the conclusion of the Normandy campaign, recounts the Battle of the Bulge, and follows the 12th SS into Hungary for its final stand.

Volume One: $19.95 • Paperback • 6 x 9 • 592 pages
113 photos, 5 illustrations, 13 maps

Volume Two: $19.95 • Paperback • 6 x 9 • 608 pages
60 b/w photos, 4 maps

WWW.STACKPOLEBOOKS.COM
1-800-732-3669

Stackpole Military History Series

PANZER ACES
GERMAN TANK COMMANDERS OF WORLD WAR II
Franz Kurowski

With the order "Panzers forward!" German tanks rolled into battle, smashing into the enemy with engines roaring and muzzles flashing. From Poland and the Eastern Front to the Ardennes, Italy, and northern Africa, panzers stunned their opponents—and the world—with their lightning speed and raw power, and the soldiers, like Michael, who manned these lethal machines were among the boldest and most feared of World War II.

$19.95 • Paperback • 6 x 9 • 480 pages • 60 b/w photos

**WWW.STACKPOLEBOOKS.COM
1-800-732-3669**

Stackpole Military History Series

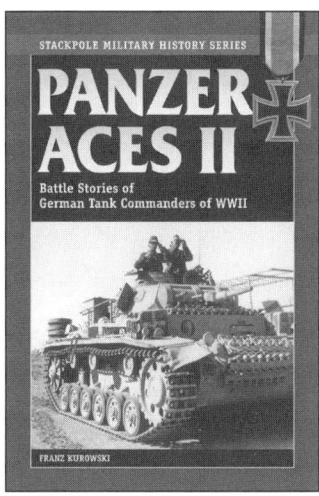

PANZER ACES II
BATTLE STORIES OF GERMAN TANK COMMANDERS OF WORLD WAR II

Franz Kurowski,
translated by David Johnston

With the same drama and excitement of the first book, Franz Kurowski relates the combat careers of six more tank officers. These gripping accounts follow Panzer crews into some of World War II's bloodiest engagements—with Rommel in North Africa, up and down the Eastern Front, and in the hedgerows of the West. Master tacticians and gutsy leaders, these soldiers changed the face of war forever.

$19.95 • Paperback • 6 x 9 • 496 pages • 71 b/w photos

WWW.STACKPOLEBOOKS.COM
1-800-732-3669

Stackpole Military History Series

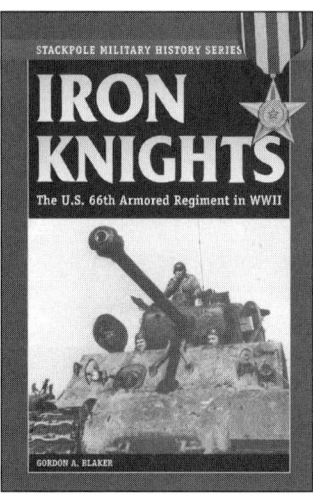

IRON KNIGHTS
THE U.S. 66TH ARMORED REGIMENT IN WORLD WAR II
Gordon A. Blaker

This is the combat history of the U.S. Army's oldest armored regiment, a legendary unit whose story began in the mud of the Western Front in 1918. But it was during World War II that the 66th Armored Regiment came into its own as one of the U.S.'s premier tank formations. As part of the 2nd Armored Division—the famed "Hell on Wheels"—the 66th battled German panzers in North Africa, Sicily, Normandy, and the Battle of the Bulge and defeated fanatical last-ditch resistance in Germany itself in 1945.

$19.95 • Paperback • 6 x 9 • 448 pages • 157 b/w photos, 26 maps

WWW.STACKPOLEBOOKS.COM
1-800-732-3669

Stackpole Military History Series

D-DAY TO BERLIN
THE NORTHWEST EUROPE CAMPAIGN, 1944–45
Alan J. Levine

The liberation of Western Europe in World War II required eleven months of hard fighting, from the beaches of Normandy to Berlin and the Baltic Sea. In this crisp, comprehensive account, Alan J. Levine describes the Allied campaign to defeat Nazi Germany in the West: D-Day, the hedgerow battles in France during the summer of 1944, the combined airborne-ground assault of Operation Market-Garden in September, Hitler's winter offensive at the Battle of the Bulge, and the final drive across the Rhine that culminated in Germany's surrender in May 1945.

$16.95 • Paperback • 6 x 9 • 240 pages

WWW.STACKPOLEBOOKS.COM
1-800-732-3669

Stackpole Military History Series

BEYOND THE BEACHHEAD
THE 29TH INFANTRY DIVISION IN NORMANDY
Joseph Balkoski

Previously untested in battle, the American 29th Infantry Division stormed Omaha Beach on D-Day and began a summer of bloody combat in the hedgerows of Normandy. Against a tenacious German foe, the division fought fiercely for every inch of ground and, at great cost, liberated the town of St. Lô. This new and expanded edition of Joseph Balkoski's classic follows the 29th through the final stages of the campaign and the brutal struggle for the town of Vire.

*$19.95 • Paperback • 6 x 9 • 352 pages
36 b/w photos, 30 maps*

WWW.STACKPOLEBOOKS.COM
1-800-732-3669

Stackpole Military History Series

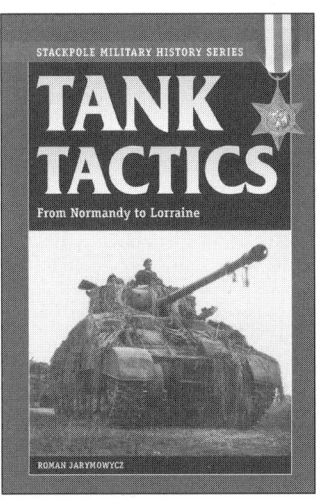

TANK TACTICS
FROM NORMANDY TO LORRAINE
Roman Jarymowycz

Roman Jarymowycz draws on after-action reports, war diaries, and other primary sources to examine the tactical ideas underpinning World War II tank warfare as conducted by Allied commanders in France from July to September 1944. His study focuses on Operation Goodwood, Montgomery's attack near Caen; Operations Cobra and Spring, the Normandy breakout by Bradley's U.S. First Army and the Canadians' simultaneous assault to the east; Operation Totalize, the effort to break through German defenses south of Caen; Operation Tractable, the Canadian and Polish attempt to capture Falaise; and Patton's September battles in Lorraine.

*$21.95 • Paperback • 6 x 9 • 384 pages
10 b/w photos, 14 maps, 19 diagrams*

**WWW.STACKPOLEBOOKS.COM
1-800-732-3669**

Also available from Stackpole Books

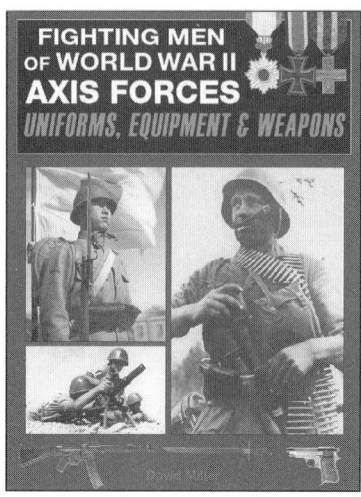
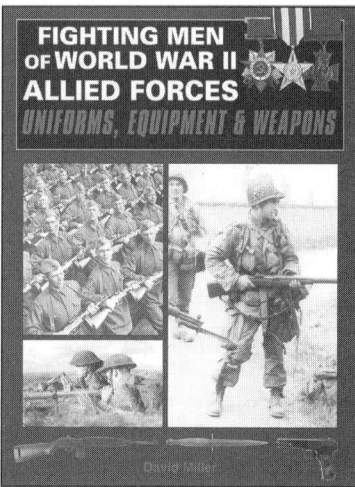

FIGHTING MEN OF WORLD WAR II
VOLUME 1: AXIS FORCES
VOLUME 2: ALLIED FORCES
David Miller

These comprehensive volumes present a full-color look at Axis and Allied soldiers in World War II, covering their weapons, equipment, clothing, rations, and more. The Axis volume includes Germany, Italy, and Japan while the Allied volume presents troops from the United States, Great Britain, and the Soviet Union. These books create a vivid picture of the daily life and battle conditions of the fighting men of the Second World War.

$49.95 • Hardcover • 9 x 12 • 384 pages • 600 color illustrations

WWW.STACKPOLEBOOKS.COM
1-800-732-3669